Reed Richards has ever been a man ahead of his time. And when he saw the think tanks of the wor...
found a solution: to save the future, put it in the hands of those who will live it. These are the sma...
Their curriculum starts with survival and ends with the edge of an eternal tomorrow. Their vi...

Jeremy Whitley
WRITER

Will Robson (#1-3), **Paco Diaz** (#2-3) & **Alti Firmansyah** (#4-5)
PENCILERS

Will Robson (#1-3), **Daniele Orlandini** (#1-2), **Paco Diaz** (#2-3) & **Alti Firmansyah** (#4-5)
INKERS

Greg Menzie (#1-3) & **Tríona Farrell** (#3-5) with **Chris O'Halloran** (#2)
COLORISTS

──────────── "SPEED OF LIGHT" ────────────

Will Robson
PENCILER

Daniele Orlandini with **Will Robson**
INKS & FINISHES

Greg Menzie
COLORIST

VC's Joe Caramagna
LETTERER

Carlos Pacheco, Rafael Fonteriz & **Matt Yackey**
COVER ART

Sarah Brunstad
EDITOR

Tom Brevoort
EXECUTIVE EDITOR

Mark D. Beazley COLLECTION EDITOR
Maia Loy ASSISTANT MANAGING EDITOR
Caitlin O'Connell ASSISTANT EDITOR
Jennifer Grünwald SENIOR EDITOR, SPECIAL PROJECTS

Jeff Youngquist VP PRODUCTION & SPECIAL PROJECTS
Adam Del Re BOOK DESIGNER
David Gabriel SVP PRINT, SALES & MARKETING
C.B. Cebulski EDITOR IN CHIEF

FUTURE FOUNDATION. Contains material originally published in magazine form as FUTURE FOUNDATION (2019) #1-5 and FANTASTIC FOUR (2018) #12. First printing 2020. ISBN 978-1-302-92098-2. Published by MARVEL WORLDWIDE, INC., a subsidiary of MARVEL ENTERTAINMENT, LLC. OFFICE OF PUBLICATION: 1290 Avenue of the Americas, New York, NY 10104. © 2020 MARVEL No similarity between any of the names, characters, persons, and/or institutions in this magazine with those of any living or dead person or institution is intended, and any such similarity which may exist is purely coincidental. **Printed in Canada.** KEVIN FEIGE, Chief Creative Officer; DAN BUCKLEY, President, Marvel Entertainment; JOHN NEE, Publisher; JOE QUESADA, EVP & Creative Director; TOM BREVOORT, SVP of Publishing; DAVID BOGART, Associate Publisher & SVP of Talent Affairs; Publishing & Partnership; DAVID GABRIEL, VP of Print & Digital Publishing; JEFF YOUNGQUIST, VP of Production & Special Projects; DAN CARR, Executive Director of Publishing Technology; ALEX MORALES, Director of Publishing Operations; DAN EDINGTON, Managing Editor; SUSAN CRESPI, Production Manager; STAN LEE, Chairman Emeritus. For information regarding advertising in Marvel Comics or on Marvel.com, please contact Vit DeBellis, Custom Solutions & Integrated Advertising Manager, at vdebellis@marvel.com. For Marvel subscription inquiries, please call 888-511-5480. **Manufactured between 1/3/2020 and 2/4/2020 by SOLISCO PRINTERS, SCOTT, QC, CANADA.**

10 9 8 7 6 5 4 3 2 1

"SPEED OF LIGHT"

MY NAME IS **ALEX POWER**. I AM THE LEADER OF THE **FUTURE FOUNDATION**, AND I AM HOPELESSLY **LOST**.

WE STARTED AS A THINK TANK OF YOUNG GENIUSES FOUNDED BY **REED RICHARDS**, BUT WE'VE BEEN ON A MISSION TO RECOVER THE PIECES OF OUR FRIEND THE MOLECULE MAN IN AN EFFORT TO REASSEMBLE HIM. IT'S GOING...

CONGRATULATIONS, POWER! YOU FINALLY GOT US ALL KILLED!

*

...NOT GREAT.

ASTEROID 1984-JA.

SHUT UP, BENTLEY!

TONG, ONOME, IDEAS WOULD BE WELCOME!

SCARY MONSTERS ARE **PHOTOPHOBIC**! WE MUST BE DEVISING A PLAN OF EGRESS BEFORE THE LIGHTS ARE LOSING POWER.

IF I CAN GET ENOUGH TIME TO SET UP MY STATIONARY WORK LIGHT, I CAN PROVIDE US A FEW HOURS OF LIGHT TO WORK OUT A SOLUTION.

PROFESSOR POWER, WE CAN'T LOSE OUR FIRST PIECE OF OWEN! I WILL DISTRACT THEM--THE REST OF YOU, **RUN**!

BROTHER KORR'S LIGHT IS DIMINISHING! WE MUST BE PROTECTING THE MOLECULE MAN!

DOCTOR RICHARDS SHOULD HAVE NEVER LEFT ME IN CHARGE. I'M GOING TO GET US ALL KILLED.

I'M NOT LEAVING YOU BEHIND, DRAGON MAN. AND SEALING OFF A TUNNEL IS **ONE** THING I **CAN** DO.

THE ONLY THING!

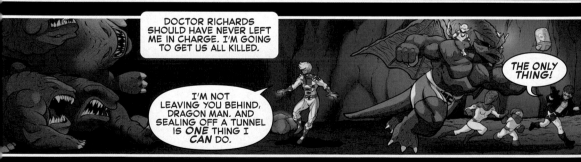

I DON'T KNOW IF I'LL SURVIVE THIS, BUT IF I DON'T, I HOPE SOMEONE TELLS MY FAMILY.

JULIE WILL TAKE CARE OF THEM. SHE'S ALWAYS BEEN THE BEST OF US. IF SHE WERE HERE, SHE'D KNOW WHAT TO DO.

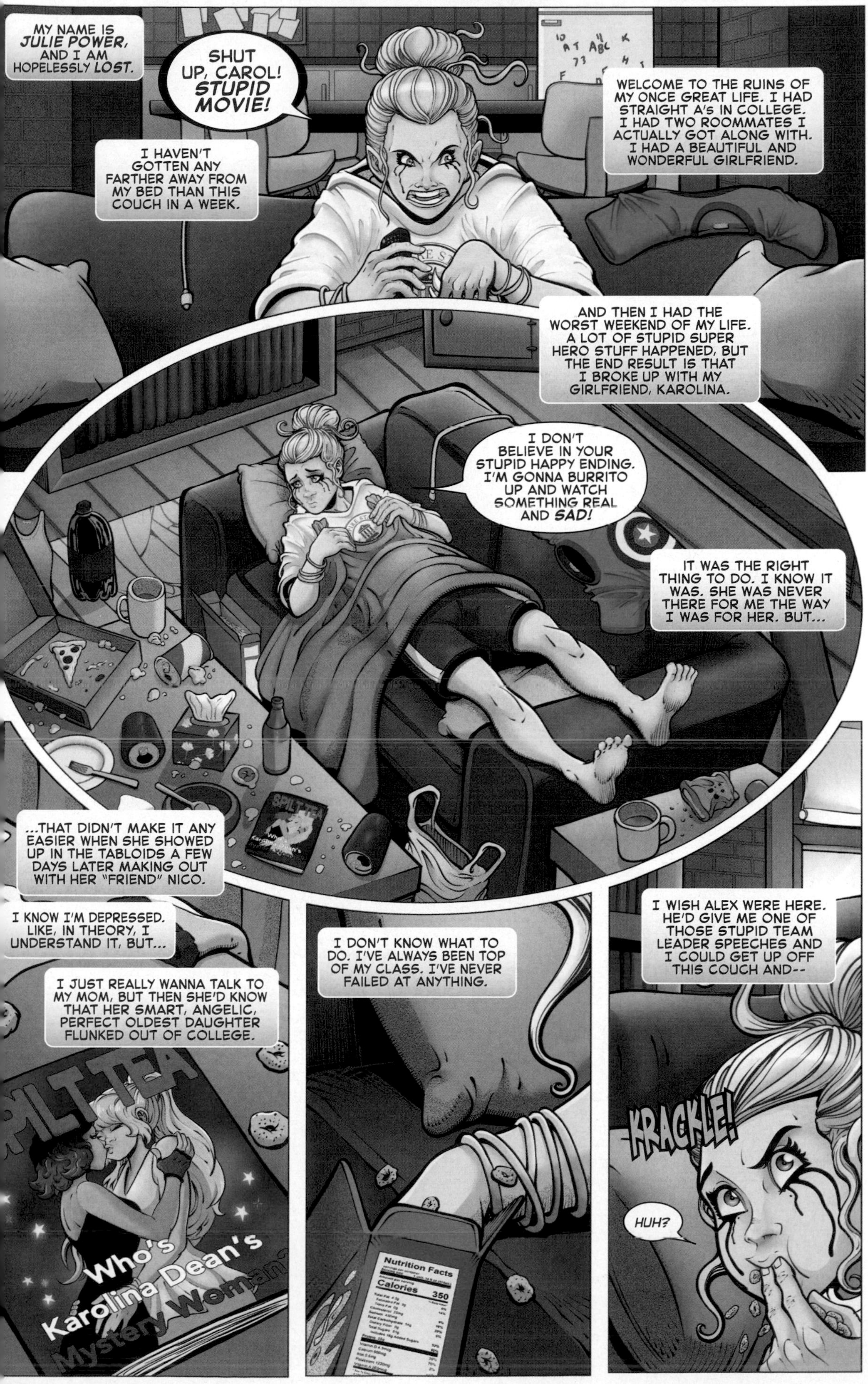
MY NAME IS JULIE POWER, AND I AM HOPELESSLY LOST.
SHUT UP, CAROL! STUPID MOVIE!
I HAVEN'T GOTTEN ANY FARTHER AWAY FROM MY BED THAN THIS COUCH IN A WEEK.
WELCOME TO THE RUINS OF MY ONCE GREAT LIFE. I HAD STRAIGHT A's IN COLLEGE. I HAD TWO ROOMMATES I ACTUALLY GOT ALONG WITH. I HAD A BEAUTIFUL AND WONDERFUL GIRLFRIEND.
AND THEN I HAD THE WORST WEEKEND OF MY LIFE. A LOT OF STUPID SUPER HERO STUFF HAPPENED, BUT THE END RESULT IS THAT I BROKE UP WITH MY GIRLFRIEND, KAROLINA.
I DON'T BELIEVE IN YOUR STUPID HAPPY ENDING. I'M GONNA BURRITO UP AND WATCH SOMETHING REAL AND SAD!
IT WAS THE RIGHT THING TO DO. I KNOW IT WAS. SHE WAS NEVER THERE FOR ME THE WAY I WAS FOR HER. BUT...
...THAT DIDN'T MAKE IT ANY EASIER WHEN SHE SHOWED UP IN THE TABLOIDS A FEW DAYS LATER MAKING OUT WITH HER "FRIEND" NICO.
I KNOW I'M DEPRESSED. LIKE, IN THEORY, I UNDERSTAND IT, BUT...
I JUST REALLY WANNA TALK TO MY MOM, BUT THEN SHE'D KNOW THAT HER SMART, ANGELIC, PERFECT OLDEST DAUGHTER FLUNKED OUT OF COLLEGE.
SPILT TEA
Who's Karolina Dean's Mystery Woman?
I DON'T KNOW WHAT TO DO. I'VE ALWAYS BEEN TOP OF MY CLASS. I'VE NEVER FAILED AT ANYTHING.
Nutrition Facts
Calories 350
I WISH ALEX WERE HERE. HE'D GIVE ME ONE OF THOSE STUPID TEAM LEADER SPEECHES AND I COULD GET UP OFF THIS COUCH AND--
KRACKLE!
HUH?

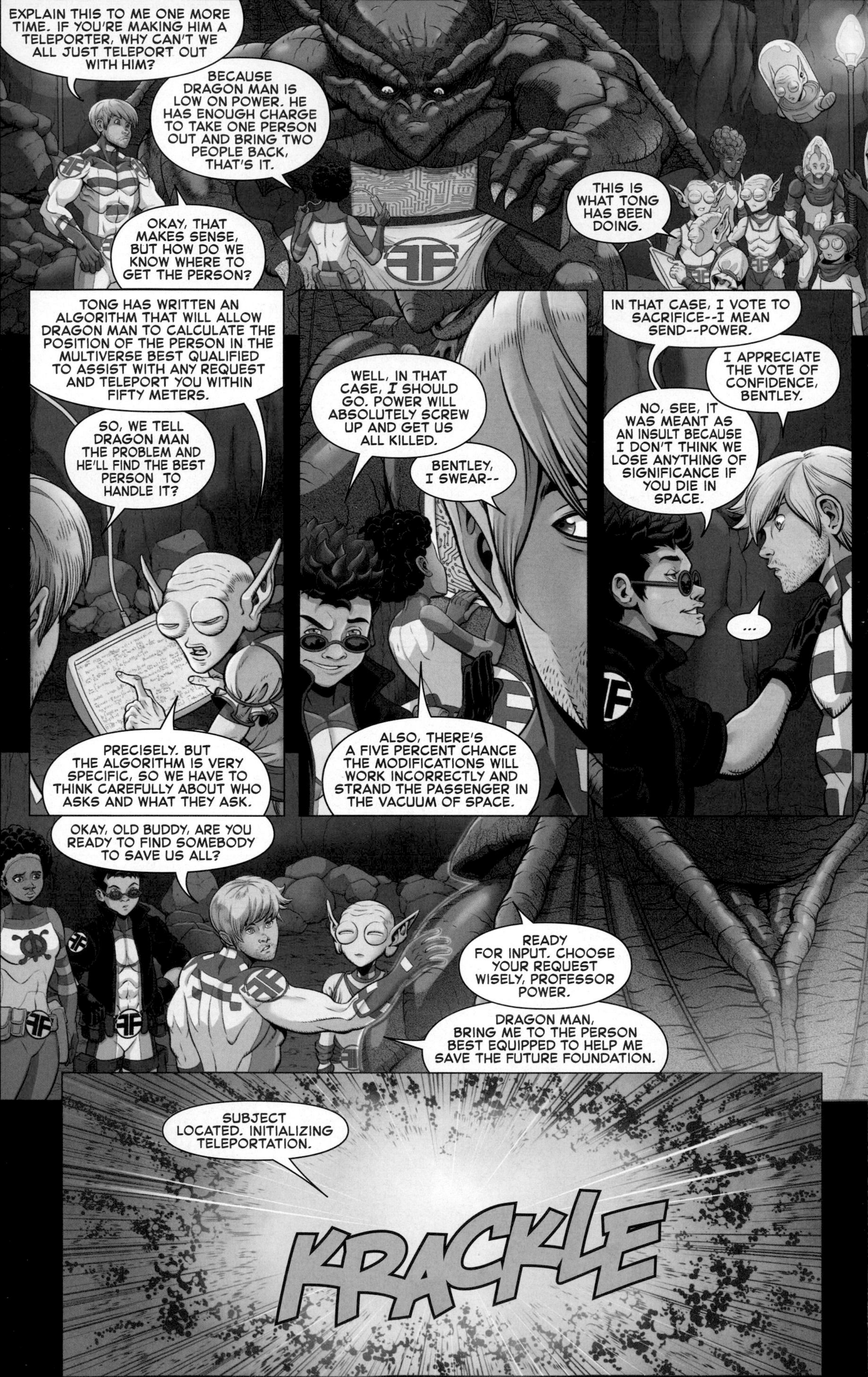

EXPLAIN THIS TO ME ONE MORE TIME. IF YOU'RE MAKING HIM A TELEPORTER, WHY CAN'T WE ALL JUST TELEPORT OUT WITH HIM?
BECAUSE DRAGON MAN IS LOW ON POWER. HE HAS ENOUGH CHARGE TO TAKE ONE PERSON OUT AND BRING TWO PEOPLE BACK, THAT'S IT.
OKAY, THAT MAKES SENSE, BUT HOW DO WE KNOW WHERE TO GET THE PERSON?
THIS IS WHAT TONG HAS BEEN DOING.
TONG HAS WRITTEN AN ALGORITHM THAT WILL ALLOW DRAGON MAN TO CALCULATE THE POSITION OF THE PERSON IN THE MULTIVERSE BEST QUALIFIED TO ASSIST WITH ANY REQUEST AND TELEPORT YOU WITHIN FIFTY METERS.
SO, WE TELL DRAGON MAN THE PROBLEM AND HE'LL FIND THE BEST PERSON TO HANDLE IT?
PRECISELY. BUT THE ALGORITHM IS VERY SPECIFIC, SO WE HAVE TO THINK CAREFULLY ABOUT WHO ASKS AND WHAT THEY ASK.
WELL, IN THAT CASE, *I* SHOULD GO. POWER WILL ABSOLUTELY SCREW UP AND GET US ALL KILLED.
BENTLEY, I SWEAR--
ALSO, THERE'S A FIVE PERCENT CHANCE THE MODIFICATIONS WILL WORK INCORRECTLY AND STRAND THE PASSENGER IN THE VACUUM OF SPACE.
IN THAT CASE, I VOTE TO SACRIFICE--I MEAN SEND--POWER.
I APPRECIATE THE VOTE OF CONFIDENCE, BENTLEY.
NO, SEE, IT WAS MEANT AS AN INSULT BECAUSE I DON'T THINK WE LOSE ANYTHING OF SIGNIFICANCE IF YOU DIE IN SPACE.
...
OKAY, OLD BUDDY, ARE YOU READY TO FIND SOMEBODY TO SAVE US ALL?
READY FOR INPUT. CHOOSE YOUR REQUEST WISELY, PROFESSOR POWER.
DRAGON MAN, BRING ME TO THE PERSON BEST EQUIPPED TO HELP ME SAVE THE FUTURE FOUNDATION.
SUBJECT LOCATED. INITIALIZING TELEPORTATION.
KRACKLE

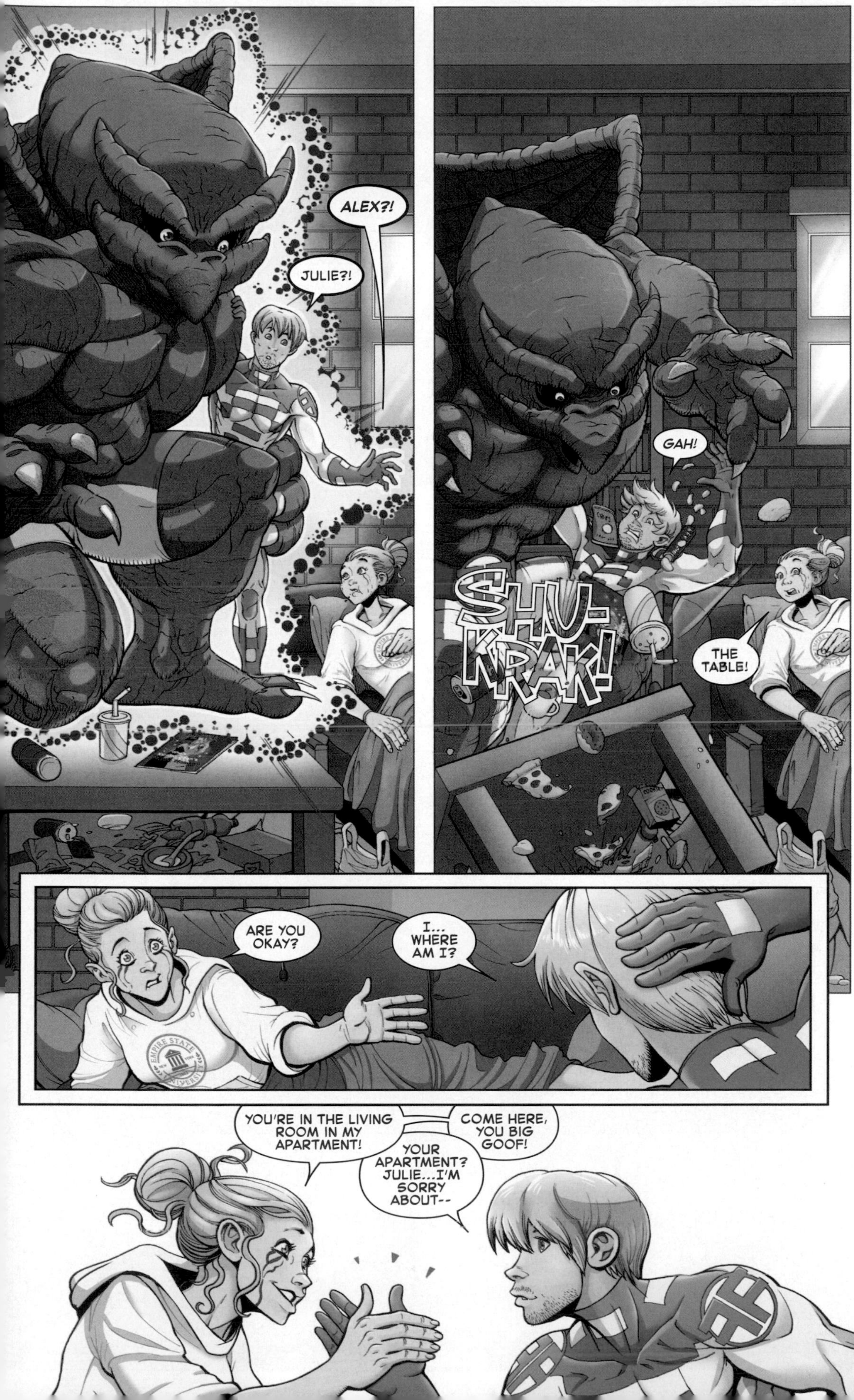
ALEX?!
JULIE?!
GAH!
SHU-KRAK!
THE TABLE!
ARE YOU OKAY?
I... WHERE AM I?
YOU'RE IN THE LIVING ROOM IN MY APARTMENT!
YOUR APARTMENT? JULIE...I'M SORRY ABOUT--
COME HERE, YOU BIG GOOF!

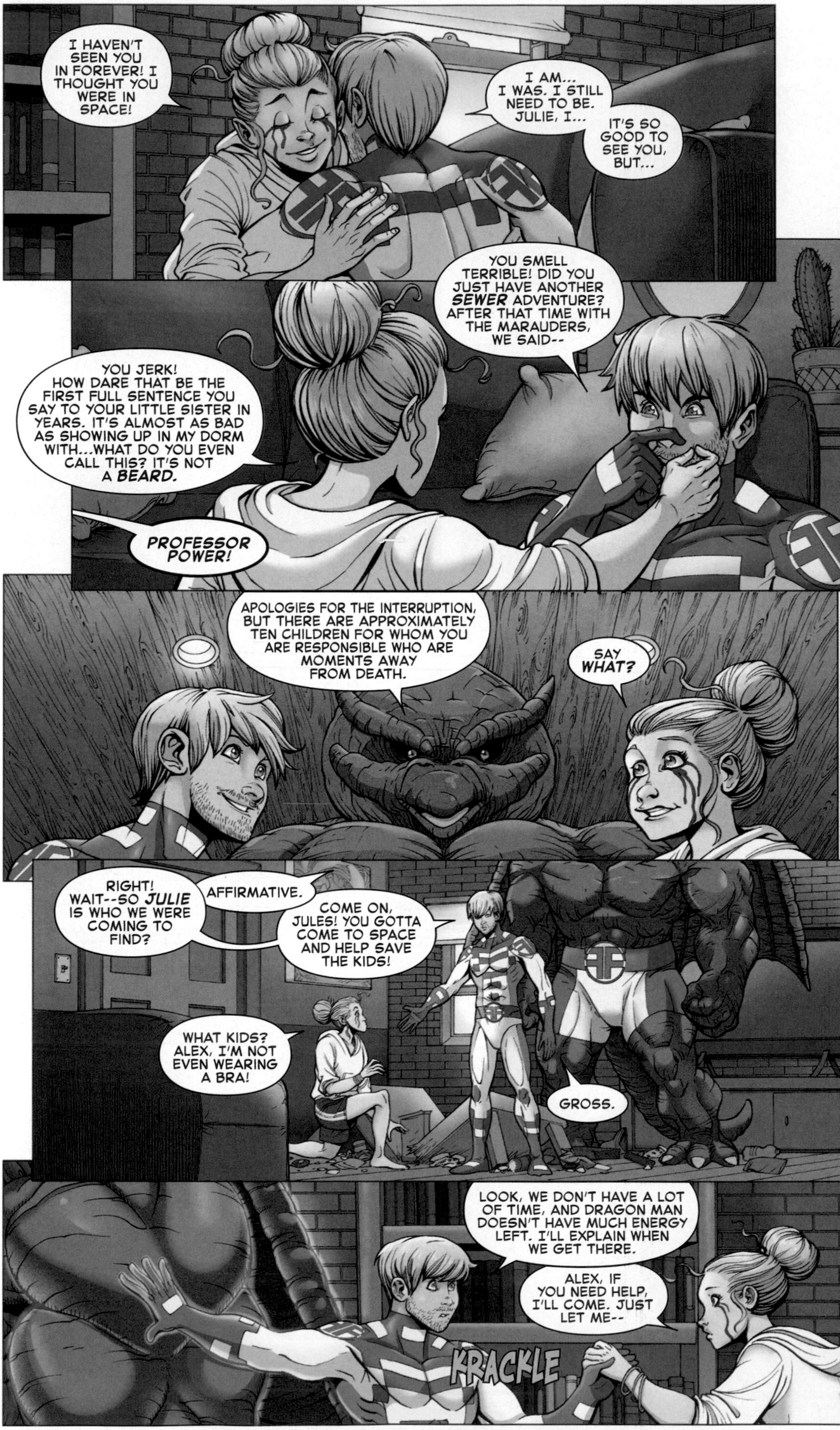
I HAVEN'T SEEN YOU IN FOREVER! I THOUGHT YOU WERE IN SPACE!
I AM... I WAS. I STILL NEED TO BE. JULIE, I...
IT'S SO GOOD TO SEE YOU, BUT...
YOU SMELL TERRIBLE! DID YOU JUST HAVE ANOTHER **SEWER** ADVENTURE? AFTER THAT TIME WITH THE MARAUDERS, WE SAID--
YOU JERK! HOW DARE THAT BE THE FIRST FULL SENTENCE YOU SAY TO YOUR LITTLE SISTER IN YEARS. IT'S ALMOST AS BAD AS SHOWING UP IN MY DORM WITH...WHAT DO YOU EVEN CALL THIS? IT'S NOT A **BEARD.**
PROFESSOR POWER!
APOLOGIES FOR THE INTERRUPTION, BUT THERE ARE APPROXIMATELY TEN CHILDREN FOR WHOM YOU ARE RESPONSIBLE WHO ARE MOMENTS AWAY FROM DEATH.
SAY **WHAT?**
RIGHT! WAIT--SO **JULIE** IS WHO WE WERE COMING TO FIND?
AFFIRMATIVE.
COME ON, JULES! YOU GOTTA COME TO SPACE AND HELP SAVE THE KIDS!
WHAT KIDS? ALEX, I'M NOT EVEN WEARING A BRA!
GROSS.
LOOK, WE DON'T HAVE A LOT OF TIME, AND DRAGON MAN DOESN'T HAVE MUCH ENERGY LEFT. I'LL EXPLAIN WHEN WE GET THERE.
ALEX, IF YOU NEED HELP, I'LL COME. JUST LET ME--
KRACKLE

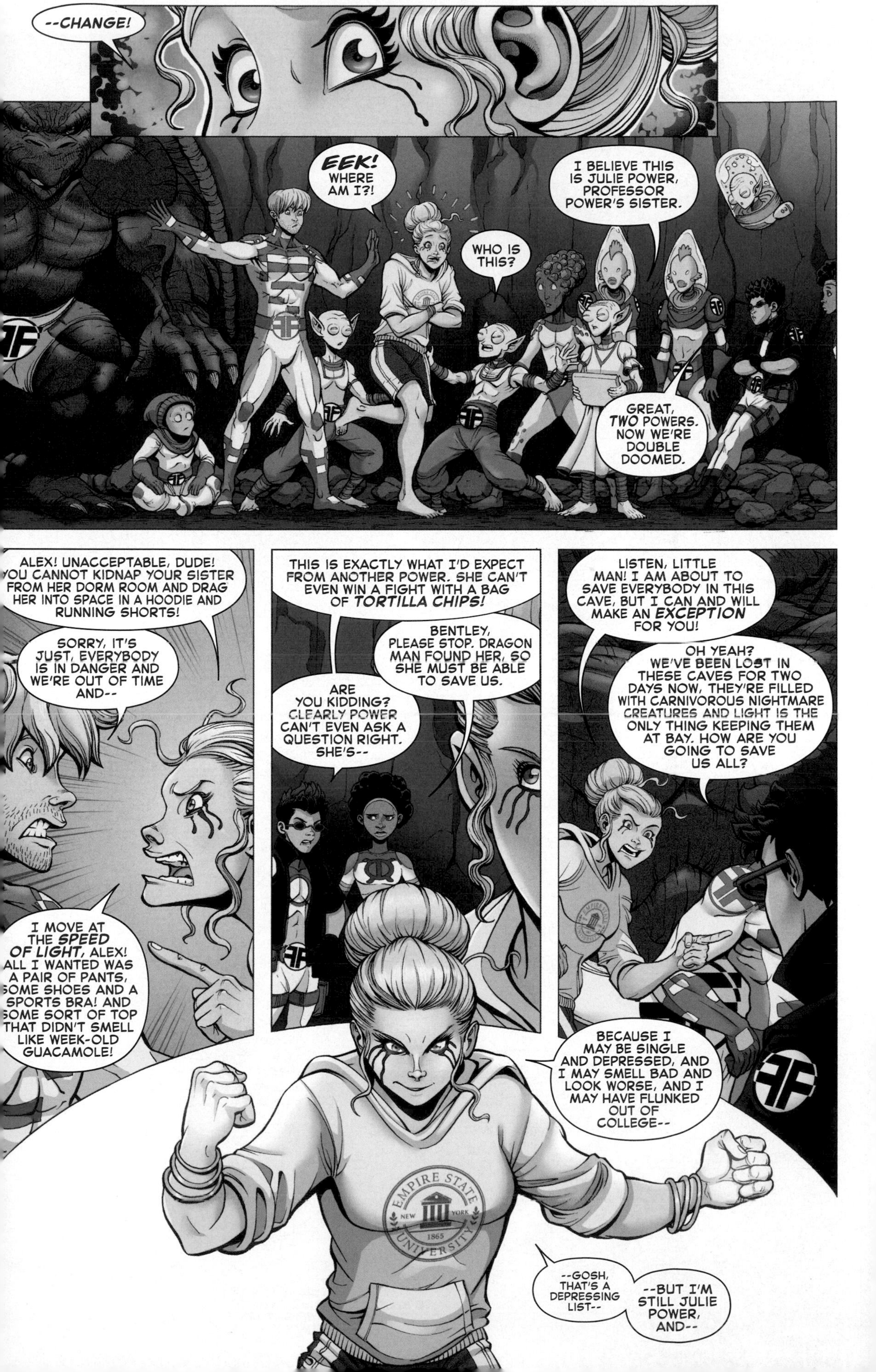
--CHANGE!
EEK! WHERE AM I?!
WHO IS THIS?
I BELIEVE THIS IS JULIE POWER, PROFESSOR POWER'S SISTER.
GREAT, TWO POWERS. NOW WE'RE DOUBLE DOOMED.
ALEX! UNACCEPTABLE, DUDE! YOU CANNOT KIDNAP YOUR SISTER FROM HER DORM ROOM AND DRAG HER INTO SPACE IN A HOODIE AND RUNNING SHORTS!
SORRY, IT'S JUST, EVERYBODY IS IN DANGER AND WE'RE OUT OF TIME AND--
I MOVE AT THE SPEED OF LIGHT, ALEX! ALL I WANTED WAS A PAIR OF PANTS, SOME SHOES AND A SPORTS BRA! AND SOME SORT OF TOP THAT DIDN'T SMELL LIKE WEEK-OLD GUACAMOLE!
THIS IS EXACTLY WHAT I'D EXPECT FROM ANOTHER POWER. SHE CAN'T EVEN WIN A FIGHT WITH A BAG OF TORTILLA CHIPS!
BENTLEY, PLEASE STOP. DRAGON MAN FOUND HER, SO SHE MUST BE ABLE TO SAVE US.
ARE YOU KIDDING? CLEARLY POWER CAN'T EVEN ASK A QUESTION RIGHT. SHE'S--
LISTEN, LITTLE MAN! I AM ABOUT TO SAVE EVERYBODY IN THIS CAVE, BUT I CAN AND WILL MAKE AN EXCEPTION FOR YOU!
OH YEAH? WE'VE BEEN LOST IN THESE CAVES FOR TWO DAYS NOW, THEY'RE FILLED WITH CARNIVOROUS NIGHTMARE CREATURES AND LIGHT IS THE ONLY THING KEEPING THEM AT BAY. HOW ARE YOU GOING TO SAVE US ALL?
BECAUSE I MAY BE SINGLE AND DEPRESSED, AND I MAY SMELL BAD AND LOOK WORSE, AND I MAY HAVE FLUNKED OUT OF COLLEGE--
--GOSH, THAT'S A DEPRESSING LIST--
--BUT I'M STILL JULIE POWER, AND--
EMPIRE STATE UNIVERSITY NEW YORK 1865

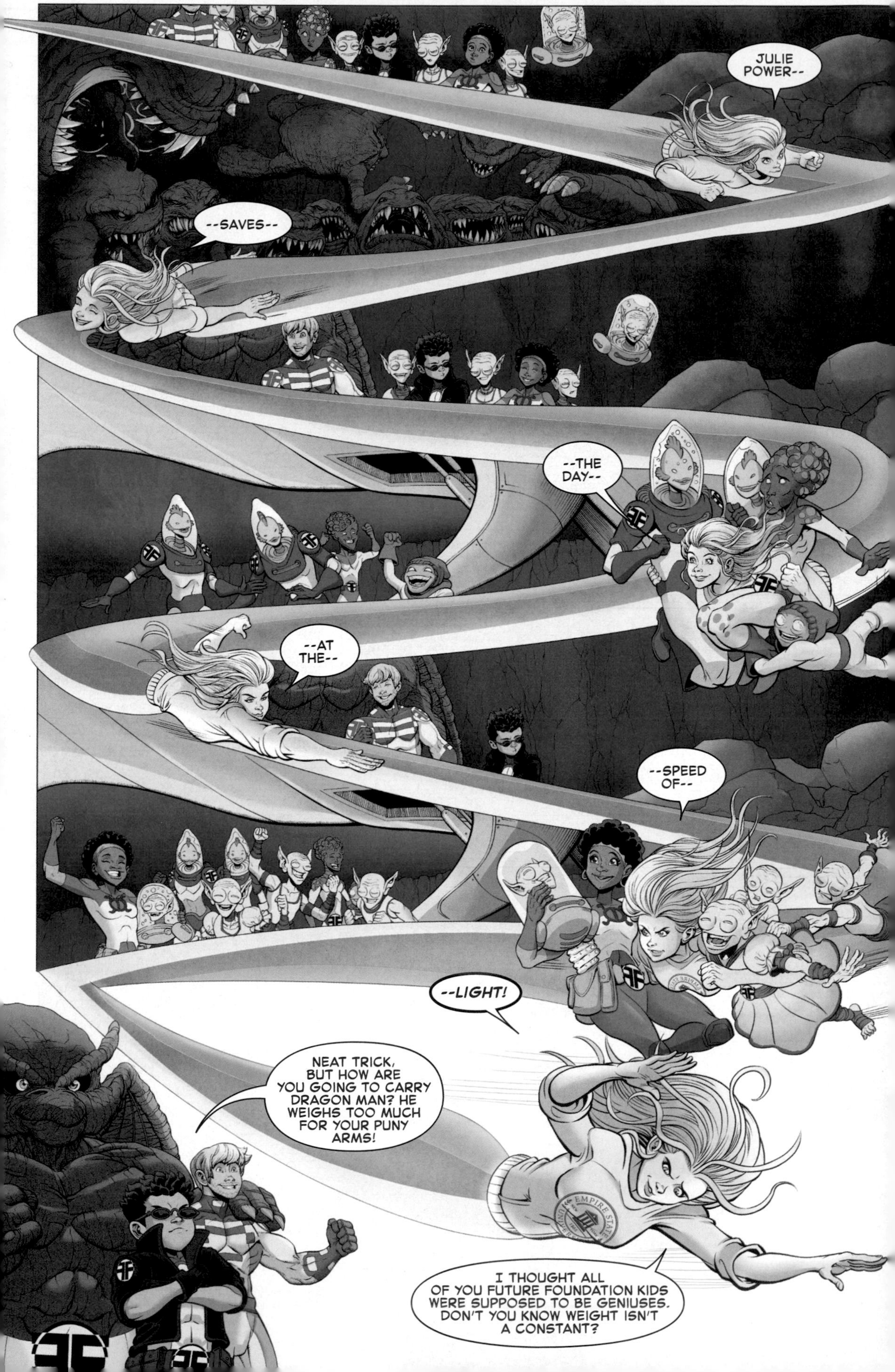
JULIE POWER--
--SAVES--
--THE DAY--
--AT THE--
--SPEED OF--
--LIGHT!
NEAT TRICK, BUT HOW ARE YOU GOING TO CARRY DRAGON MAN? HE WEIGHS TOO MUCH FOR YOUR PUNY ARMS!
I THOUGHT ALL OF YOU FUTURE FOUNDATION KIDS WERE SUPPOSED TO BE GENIUSES. DON'T YOU KNOW WEIGHT ISN'T A CONSTANT?

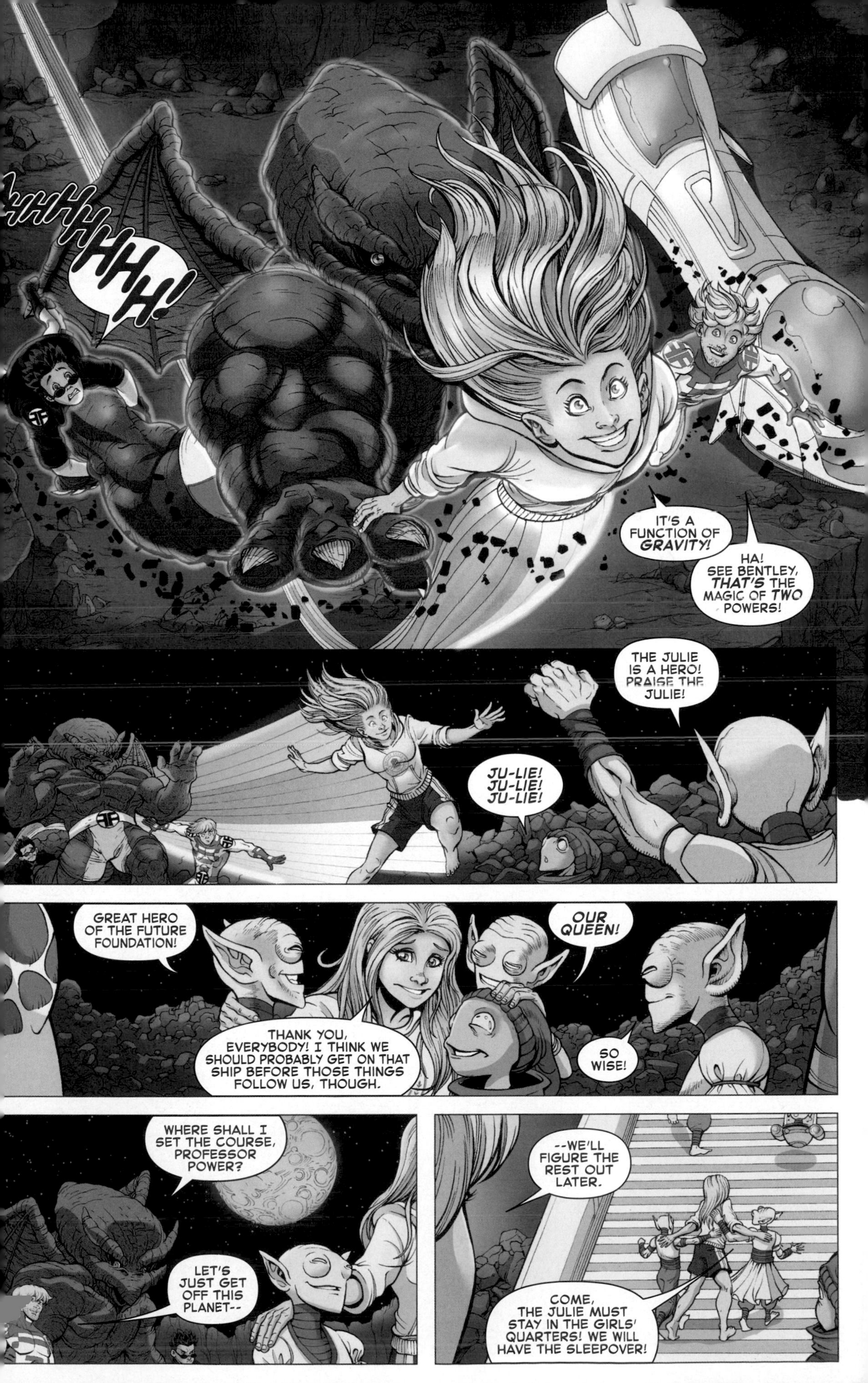
AHHHHHHHHH!
IT'S A FUNCTION OF GRAVITY!
HA! SEE BENTLEY, THAT'S THE MAGIC OF TWO POWERS!
THE JULIE IS A HERO! PRAISE THE JULIE!
JU-LIE! JU-LIE! JU-LIE!
GREAT HERO OF THE FUTURE FOUNDATION!
OUR QUEEN!
THANK YOU, EVERYBODY! I THINK WE SHOULD PROBABLY GET ON THAT SHIP BEFORE THOSE THINGS FOLLOW US, THOUGH.
SO WISE!
WHERE SHALL I SET THE COURSE, PROFESSOR POWER?
LET'S JUST GET OFF THIS PLANET--
--WE'LL FIGURE THE REST OUT LATER.
COME, THE JULIE MUST STAY IN THE GIRLS' QUARTERS! WE WILL HAVE THE SLEEPOVER!

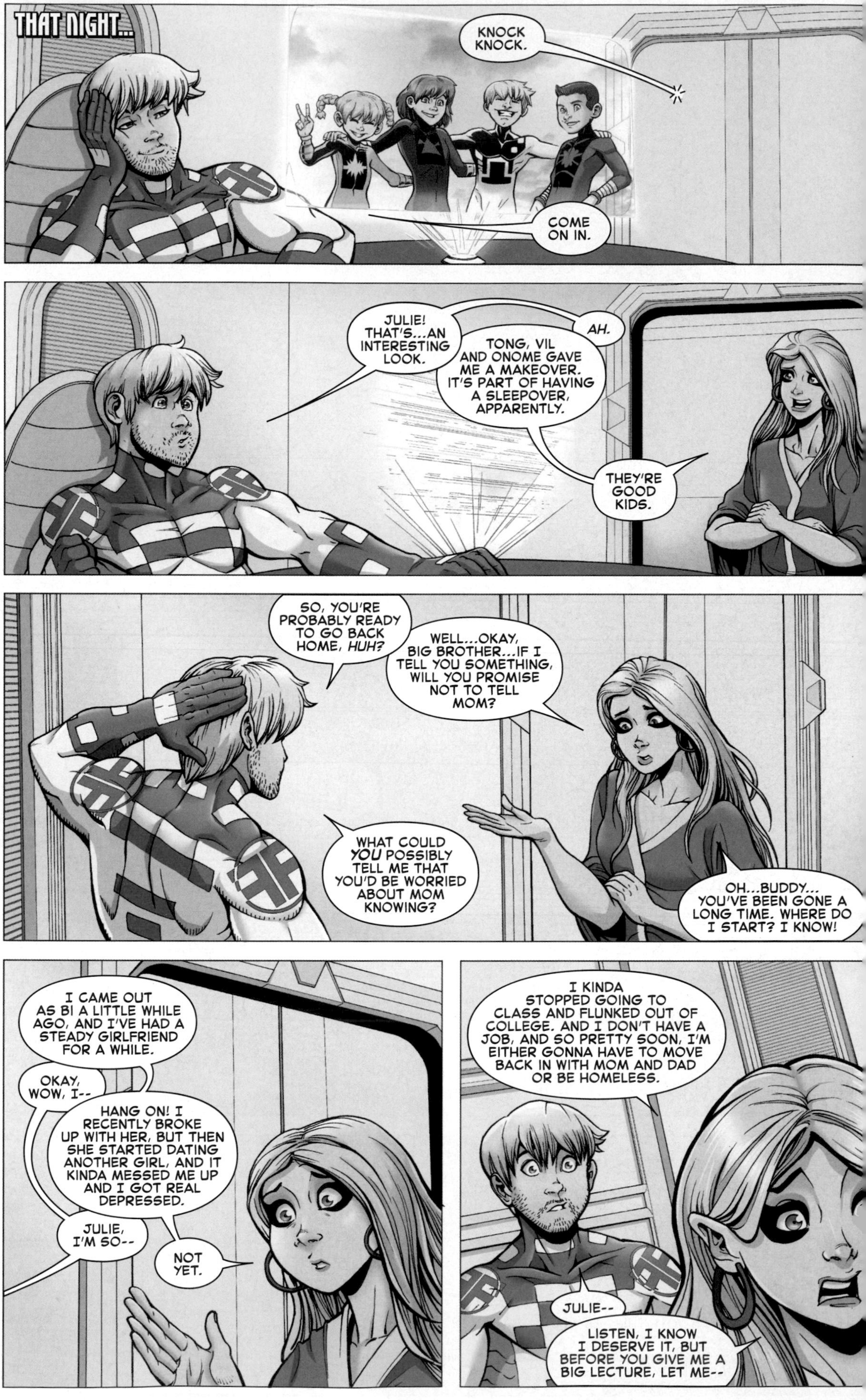
THAT NIGHT...
KNOCK KNOCK.
COME ON IN.
JULIE! THAT'S...AN INTERESTING LOOK.
AH.
TONG, VIL AND ONOME GAVE ME A MAKEOVER. IT'S PART OF HAVING A SLEEPOVER, APPARENTLY.
THEY'RE GOOD KIDS.
SO, YOU'RE PROBABLY READY TO GO BACK HOME, HUH?
WELL...OKAY, BIG BROTHER...IF I TELL YOU SOMETHING, WILL YOU PROMISE NOT TO TELL MOM?
WHAT COULD YOU POSSIBLY TELL ME THAT YOU'D BE WORRIED ABOUT MOM KNOWING?
OH...BUDDY... YOU'VE BEEN GONE A LONG TIME. WHERE DO I START? I KNOW!
I CAME OUT AS BI A LITTLE WHILE AGO, AND I'VE HAD A STEADY GIRLFRIEND FOR A WHILE.
OKAY, WOW, I--
HANG ON! I RECENTLY BROKE UP WITH HER, BUT THEN SHE STARTED DATING ANOTHER GIRL, AND IT KINDA MESSED ME UP AND I GOT REAL DEPRESSED.
JULIE, I'M SO--
NOT YET.
I KINDA STOPPED GOING TO CLASS AND FLUNKED OUT OF COLLEGE. AND I DON'T HAVE A JOB, AND SO PRETTY SOON, I'M EITHER GONNA HAVE TO MOVE BACK IN WITH MOM AND DAD OR BE HOMELESS.
JULIE--
LISTEN, I KNOW I DESERVE IT, BUT BEFORE YOU GIVE ME A BIG LECTURE, LET ME--

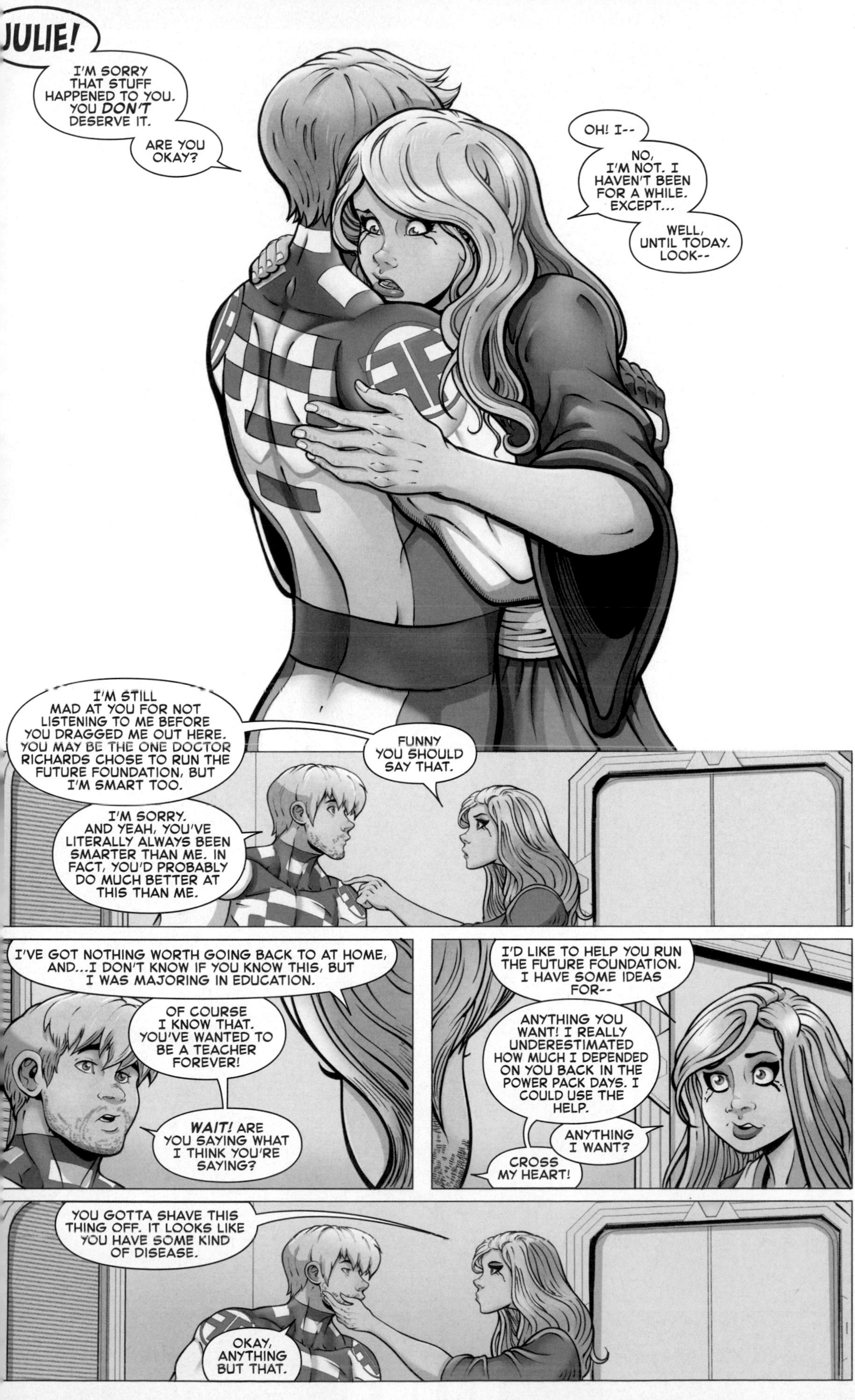
JULIE!
I'M SORRY THAT STUFF HAPPENED TO YOU. YOU DON'T DESERVE IT.
ARE YOU OKAY?
OH! I--
NO, I'M NOT. I HAVEN'T BEEN FOR A WHILE. EXCEPT...
WELL, UNTIL TODAY. LOOK--
I'M STILL MAD AT YOU FOR NOT LISTENING TO ME BEFORE YOU DRAGGED ME OUT HERE. YOU MAY BE THE ONE DOCTOR RICHARDS CHOSE TO RUN THE FUTURE FOUNDATION, BUT I'M SMART TOO.
I'M SORRY. AND YEAH, YOU'VE LITERALLY ALWAYS BEEN SMARTER THAN ME. IN FACT, YOU'D PROBABLY DO MUCH BETTER AT THIS THAN ME.
FUNNY YOU SHOULD SAY THAT.
I'VE GOT NOTHING WORTH GOING BACK TO AT HOME, AND...I DON'T KNOW IF YOU KNOW THIS, BUT I WAS MAJORING IN EDUCATION.
OF COURSE I KNOW THAT. YOU'VE WANTED TO BE A TEACHER FOREVER!
WAIT! ARE YOU SAYING WHAT I THINK YOU'RE SAYING?
I'D LIKE TO HELP YOU RUN THE FUTURE FOUNDATION. I HAVE SOME IDEAS FOR--
ANYTHING YOU WANT! I REALLY UNDERESTIMATED HOW MUCH I DEPENDED ON YOU BACK IN THE POWER PACK DAYS. I COULD USE THE HELP.
ANYTHING I WANT?
CROSS MY HEART!
YOU GOTTA SHAVE THIS THING OFF. IT LOOKS LIKE YOU HAVE SOME KIND OF DISEASE.
OKAY, ANYTHING BUT THAT.

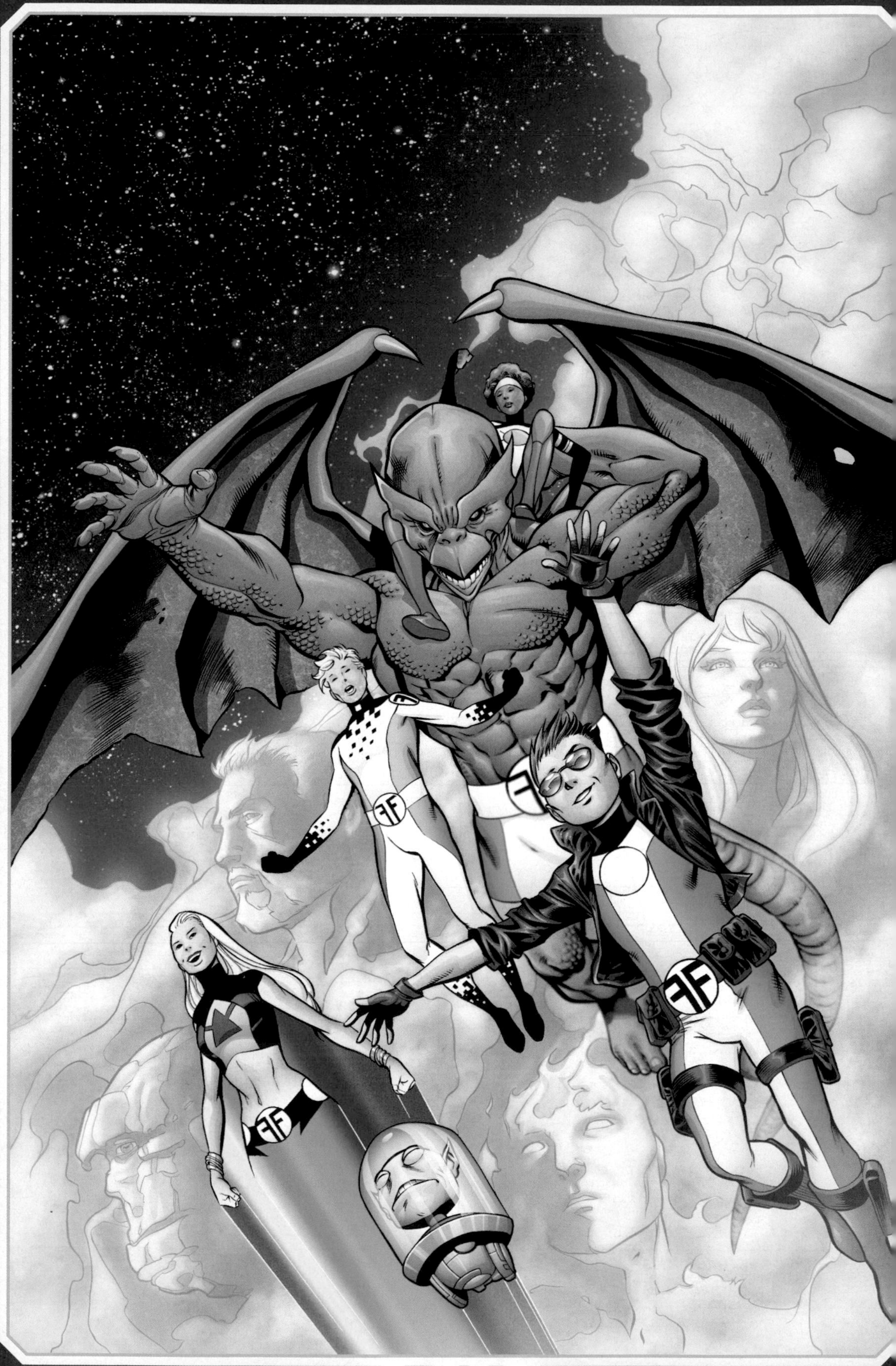

ONE

THE PLANET'S CALLED *L'AR GATH FIVE.*

L'AR GATH'S THE NAME OF AN ANCIENT GOD OF DEATH. THE SURFACE OF THE PLANET IS ENTIRELY CRYSTALLINE. IT HAS A BREATHABLE ATMOSPHERE BUT IS INCAPABLE OF SUSTAINING LIFE.

IT IS THE PERFECT PLACE FOR A *PRISON.*

THE GALAXY'S BIGGEST *PRIVATE* PRISON, IN FACT. THEY AIN'T GOTTA ANSWER TO NOBODY. IF YOU GOT A PRICE ON YOUR HEAD, THEY'LL TAKE YOU, NO QUESTIONS ASKED.

THEN THEY'LL *SELL* YOU TO WHOEVER'S WILLING TO PAY FOR YA. EVEN START A BIDDING WAR IF THEY CAN.

YONDU UDONTA.
SPACE MISCREANT.

YOU'RE WORTH A PRETTY PENNY, KID! YOU GOT ONE BOUNTY FROM THE ZN'RX, ONE FROM THE KYMELLIANS, A COUPLE MORE FROM SOME SHADIER-SOUNDING NAMES.

BUT THAT WASN'T WHAT WE TALKED ABOUT!

DON'T WORRY. THEY GOTTA PROCESS YOU FIRST. MAKE SURE YOU AIN'T A SKRULL OR A CLONE OR WHATEVER.

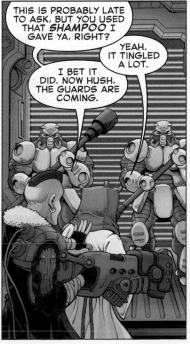

THIS IS PROBABLY LATE TO ASK, BUT YOU USED THAT *SHAMPOO* I GAVE YA, RIGHT?

YEAH. IT TINGLED A LOT.

I BET IT DID. NOW HUSH, THE GUARDS ARE COMING.

GENTLEMEN, I GOT A GOOD ONE FOR YOU TODAY!

YONDU UDONTA, LAST TIME I SAW YOU WAS *INSIDE* ONE OF OUR PRISON CELLS.

YEAH, WELL, I DON'T HOLD A GRUDGE WHEN THERE'S CASH TO BE MADE. PULL THAT BAG OFF AND TAKE A LOOK!

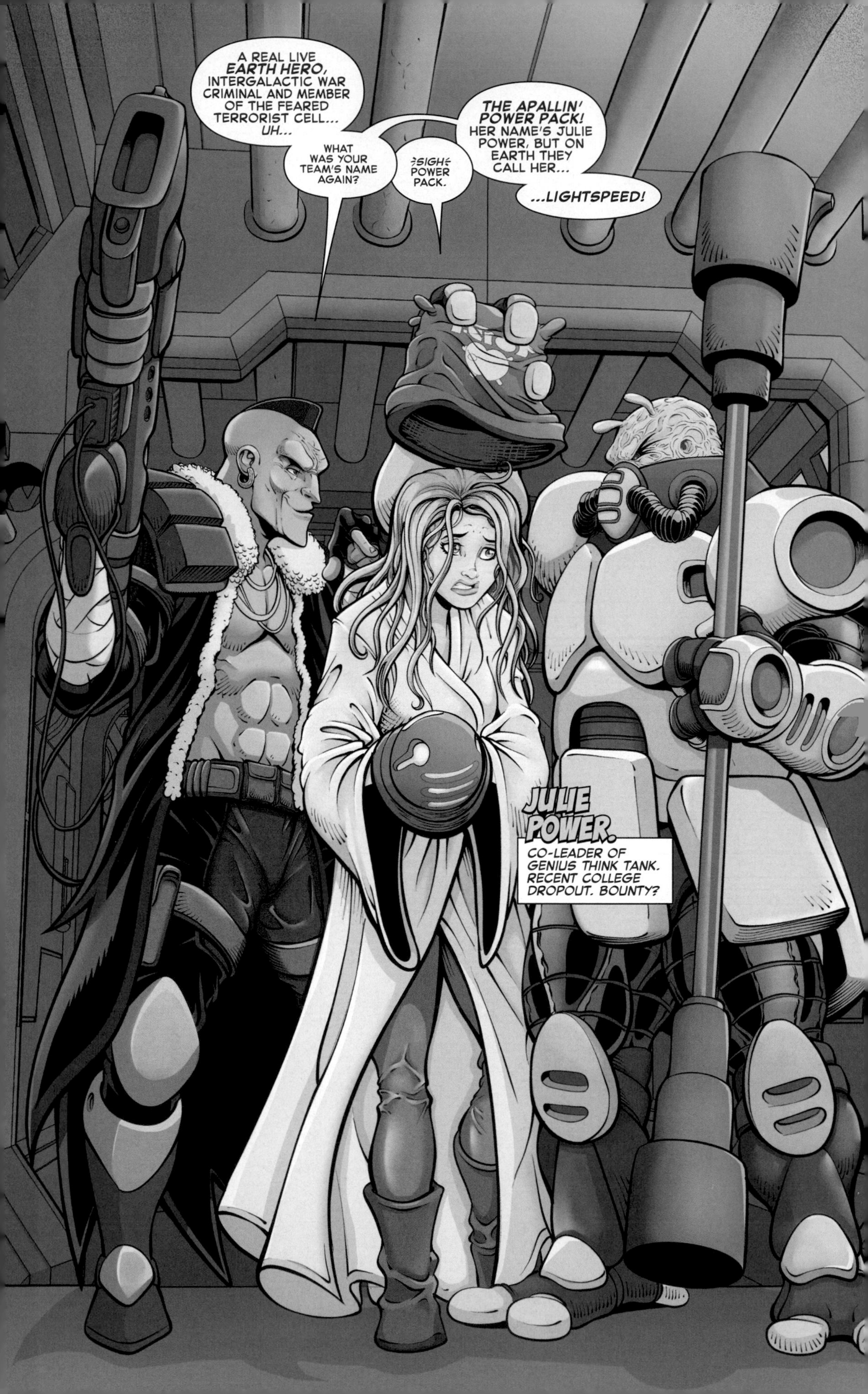
A REAL LIVE EARTH HERO, INTERGALACTIC WAR CRIMINAL AND MEMBER OF THE FEARED TERRORIST CELL... UH...
WHAT WAS YOUR TEAM'S NAME AGAIN?
SIGH POWER PACK.
THE APALLIN' POWER PACK! HER NAME'S JULIE POWER, BUT ON EARTH THEY CALL HER...
...LIGHTSPEED!
JULIE POWER.
CO-LEADER OF GENIUS THINK TANK. RECENT COLLEGE DROPOUT. BOUNTY?

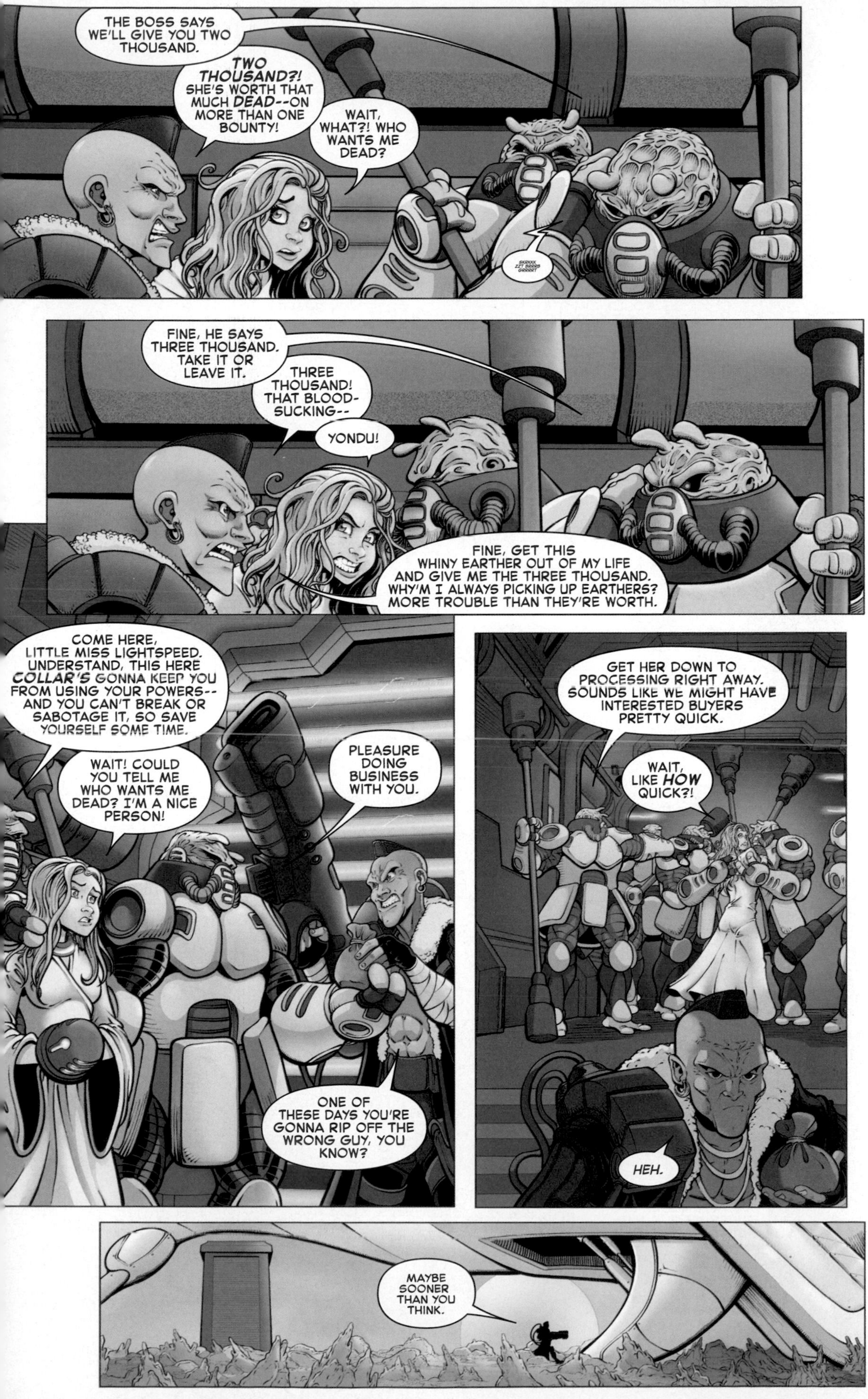
THE BOSS SAYS WE'LL GIVE YOU TWO THOUSAND.
TWO THOUSAND?! SHE'S WORTH THAT MUCH DEAD--ON MORE THAN ONE BOUNTY!
WAIT, WHAT?! WHO WANTS ME DEAD?
SKRKKK ZZT BRRRB GRRRRT
FINE, HE SAYS THREE THOUSAND. TAKE IT OR LEAVE IT.
THREE THOUSAND! THAT BLOOD-SUCKING--
YONDU!
FINE, GET THIS WHINY EARTHER OUT OF MY LIFE AND GIVE ME THE THREE THOUSAND. WHY'M I ALWAYS PICKING UP EARTHERS? MORE TROUBLE THAN THEY'RE WORTH.
COME HERE, LITTLE MISS LIGHTSPEED. UNDERSTAND, THIS HERE COLLAR'S GONNA KEEP YOU FROM USING YOUR POWERS--AND YOU CAN'T BREAK OR SABOTAGE IT, SO SAVE YOURSELF SOME TIME.
WAIT! COULD YOU TELL ME WHO WANTS ME DEAD? I'M A NICE PERSON!
PLEASURE DOING BUSINESS WITH YOU.
ONE OF THESE DAYS YOU'RE GONNA RIP OFF THE WRONG GUY, YOU KNOW?
GET HER DOWN TO PROCESSING RIGHT AWAY. SOUNDS LIKE WE MIGHT HAVE INTERESTED BUYERS PRETTY QUICK.
WAIT, LIKE HOW QUICK?!
HEH.
MAYBE SOONER THAN YOU THINK.

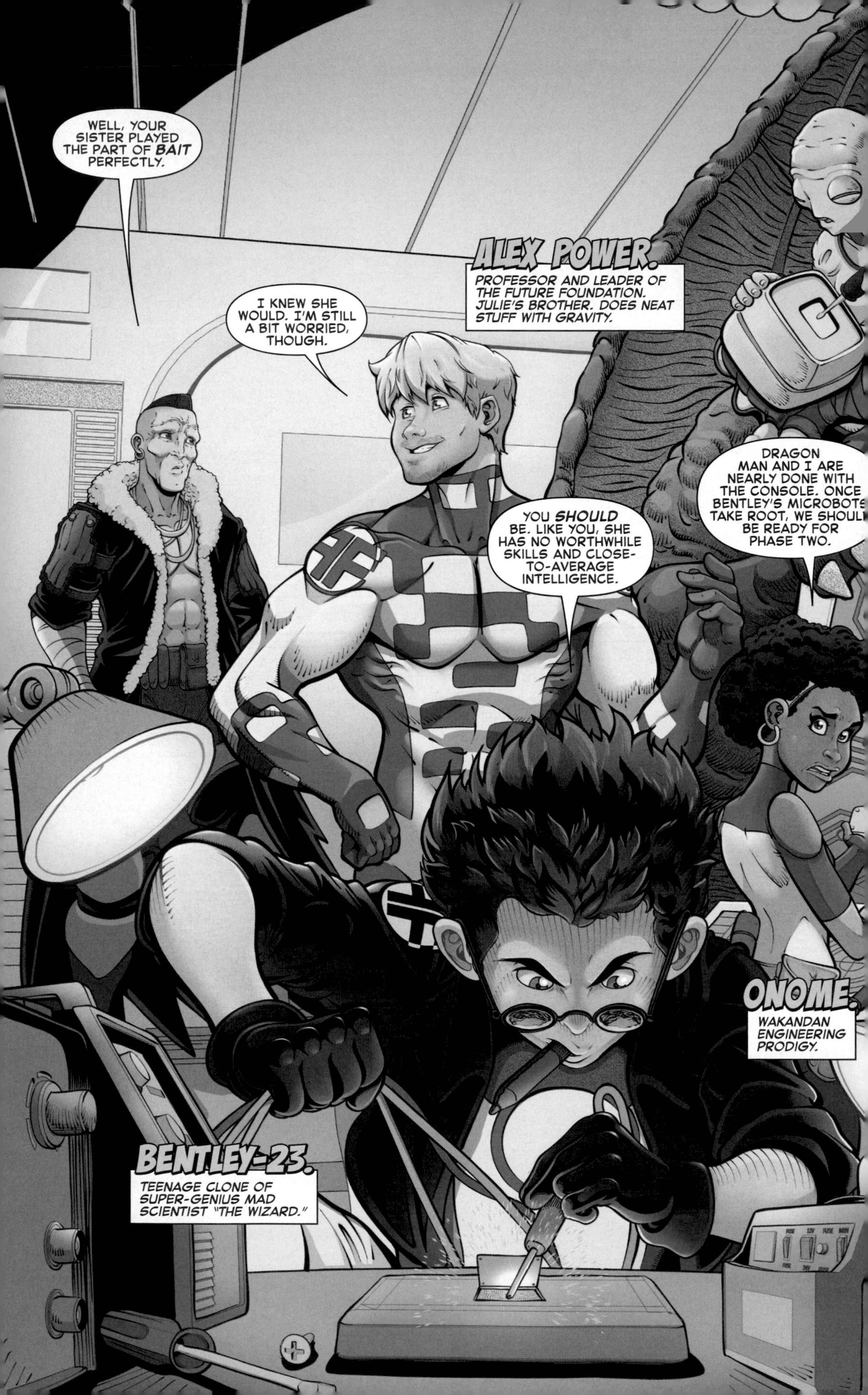

WELL, YOUR SISTER PLAYED THE PART OF BAIT PERFECTLY.
I KNEW SHE WOULD. I'M STILL A BIT WORRIED, THOUGH.
ALEX POWER.
PROFESSOR AND LEADER OF THE FUTURE FOUNDATION. JULIE'S BROTHER. DOES NEAT STUFF WITH GRAVITY.
YOU SHOULD BE. LIKE YOU, SHE HAS NO WORTHWHILE SKILLS AND CLOSE-TO-AVERAGE INTELLIGENCE.
DRAGON MAN AND I ARE NEARLY DONE WITH THE CONSOLE. ONCE BENTLEY'S MICROBOTS TAKE ROOT, WE SHOUL BE READY FOR PHASE TWO.
ONOME.
WAKANDAN ENGINEERING PRODIGY.
BENTLEY-23.
TEENAGE CLONE OF SUPER-GENIUS MAD SCIENTIST "THE WIZARD."

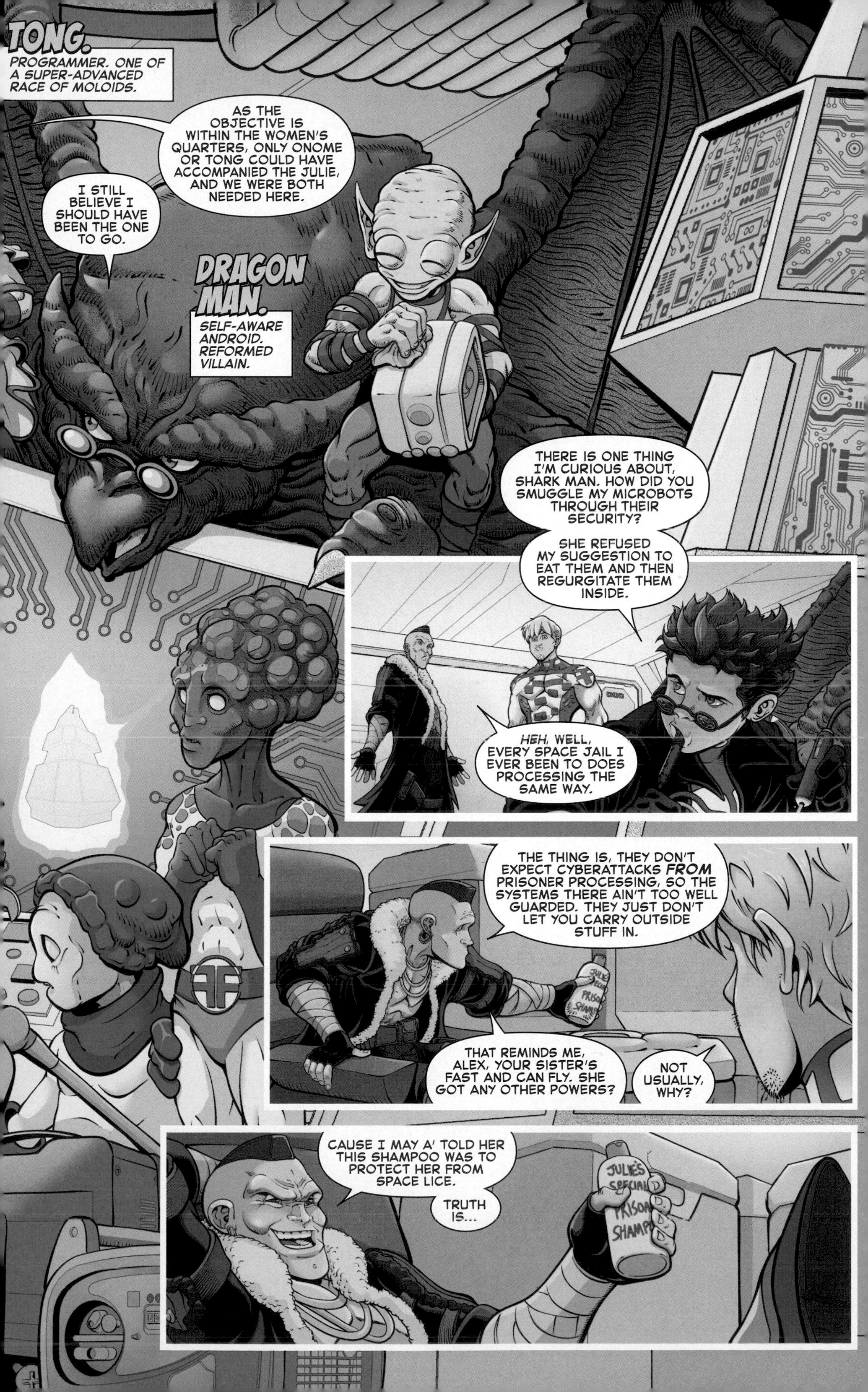
TONG.
PROGRAMMER. ONE OF A SUPER-ADVANCED RACE OF MOLOIDS.
AS THE OBJECTIVE IS WITHIN THE WOMEN'S QUARTERS, ONLY ONOME OR TONG COULD HAVE ACCOMPANIED THE JULIE, AND WE WERE BOTH NEEDED HERE.
I STILL BELIEVE I SHOULD HAVE BEEN THE ONE TO GO.
DRAGON MAN.
SELF-AWARE ANDROID. REFORMED VILLAIN.
THERE IS ONE THING I'M CURIOUS ABOUT, SHARK MAN. HOW DID YOU SMUGGLE MY MICROBOTS THROUGH THEIR SECURITY?
SHE REFUSED MY SUGGESTION TO EAT THEM AND THEN REGURGITATE THEM INSIDE.
HEH, WELL, EVERY SPACE JAIL I EVER BEEN TO DOES PROCESSING THE SAME WAY.
THE THING IS, THEY DON'T EXPECT CYBERATTACKS FROM PRISONER PROCESSING, SO THE SYSTEMS THERE AIN'T TOO WELL GUARDED. THEY JUST DON'T LET YOU CARRY OUTSIDE STUFF IN.
THAT REMINDS ME, ALEX, YOUR SISTER'S FAST AND CAN FLY. SHE GOT ANY OTHER POWERS?
NOT USUALLY, WHY?
CAUSE I MAY A' TOLD HER THIS SHAMPOO WAS TO PROTECT HER FROM SPACE LICE.
TRUTH IS...
JULIE'S SPECIAL PRISON SHAMPOO

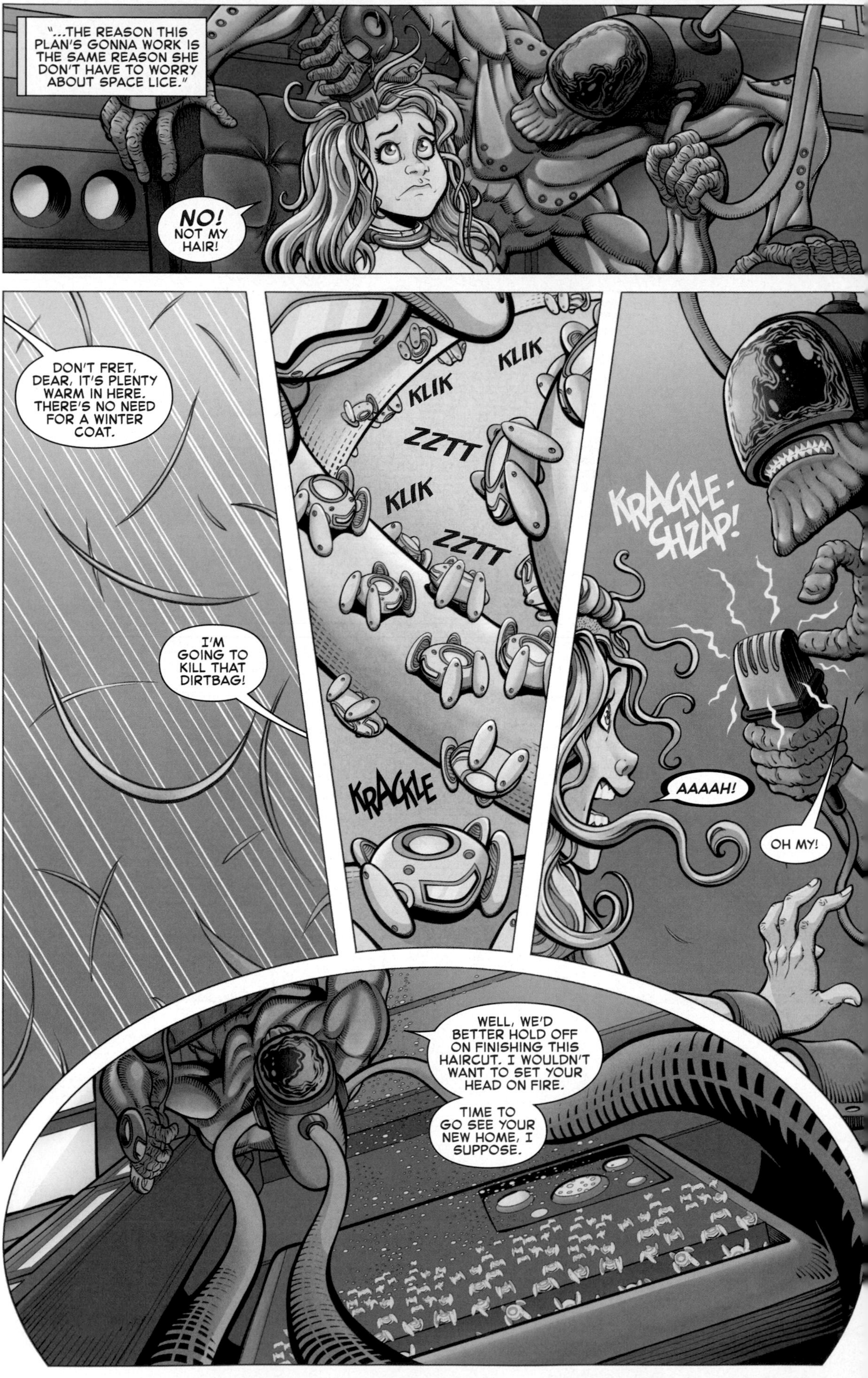
"...THE REASON THIS PLAN'S GONNA WORK IS THE SAME REASON SHE DON'T HAVE TO WORRY ABOUT SPACE LICE."
NO! NOT MY HAIR!
DON'T FRET, DEAR, IT'S PLENTY WARM IN HERE. THERE'S NO NEED FOR A WINTER COAT.
I'M GOING TO KILL THAT DIRTBAG!
KLIK
KLIK
ZZTT
KLIK
ZZTT
KRACKLE
KRACKLE-SHZAP!
AAAAH!
OH MY!
WELL, WE'D BETTER HOLD OFF ON FINISHING THIS HAIRCUT. I WOULDN'T WANT TO SET YOUR HEAD ON FIRE.
TIME TO GO SEE YOUR NEW HOME, I SUPPOSE.

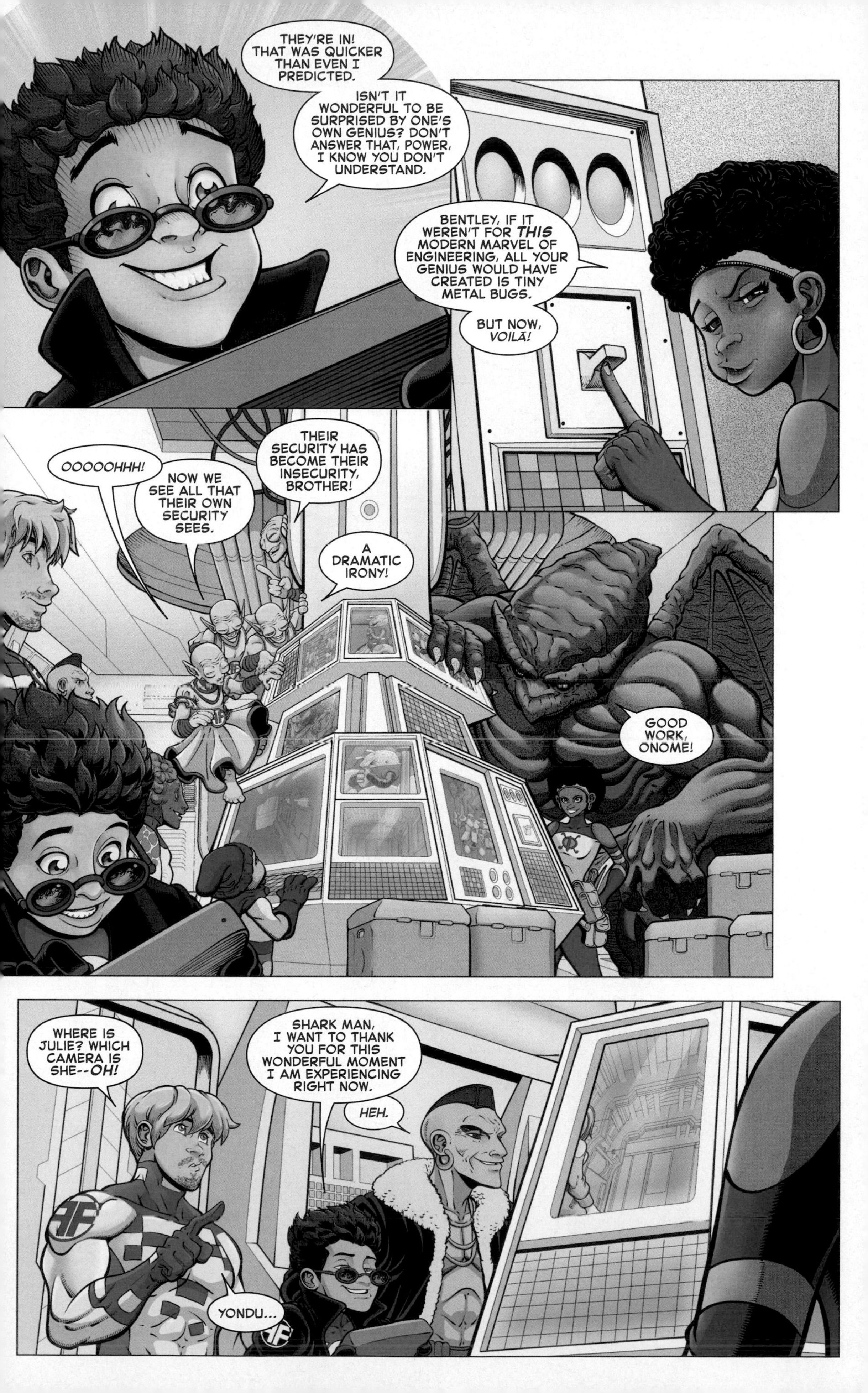
THEY'RE IN! THAT WAS QUICKER THAN EVEN I PREDICTED.
ISN'T IT WONDERFUL TO BE SURPRISED BY ONE'S OWN GENIUS? DON'T ANSWER THAT, POWER, I KNOW YOU DON'T UNDERSTAND.
BENTLEY, IF IT WEREN'T FOR THIS MODERN MARVEL OF ENGINEERING, ALL YOUR GENIUS WOULD HAVE CREATED IS TINY METAL BUGS.
BUT NOW, VOILÀ!
OOOOOHHH!
NOW WE SEE ALL THAT THEIR OWN SECURITY SEES.
THEIR SECURITY HAS BECOME THEIR INSECURITY, BROTHER!
A DRAMATIC IRONY!
GOOD WORK, ONOME!
WHERE IS JULIE? WHICH CAMERA IS SHE--OH!
SHARK MAN, I WANT TO THANK YOU FOR THIS WONDERFUL MOMENT I AM EXPERIENCING RIGHT NOW.
HEH.
YONDU...

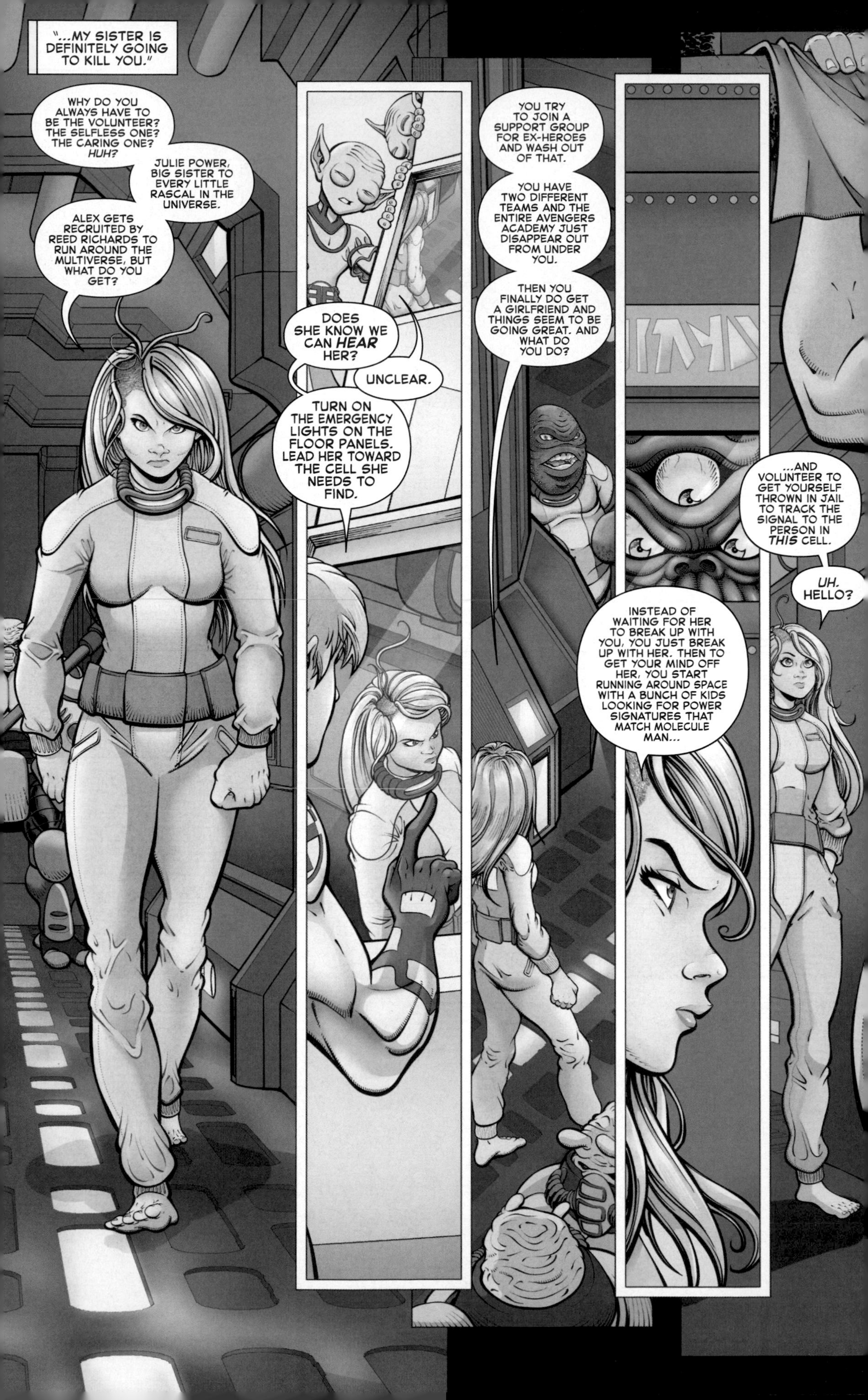
"...MY SISTER IS DEFINITELY GOING TO KILL YOU."
WHY DO YOU ALWAYS HAVE TO BE THE VOLUNTEER? THE SELFLESS ONE? THE CARING ONE? HUH?
JULIE POWER, BIG SISTER TO EVERY LITTLE RASCAL IN THE UNIVERSE.
ALEX GETS RECRUITED BY REED RICHARDS TO RUN AROUND THE MULTIVERSE, BUT WHAT DO YOU GET?
DOES SHE KNOW WE CAN HEAR HER?
UNCLEAR.
TURN ON THE EMERGENCY LIGHTS ON THE FLOOR PANELS. LEAD HER TOWARD THE CELL SHE NEEDS TO FIND.
YOU TRY TO JOIN A SUPPORT GROUP FOR EX-HEROES AND WASH OUT OF THAT.
YOU HAVE TWO DIFFERENT TEAMS AND THE ENTIRE AVENGERS ACADEMY JUST DISAPPEAR OUT FROM UNDER YOU.
THEN YOU FINALLY DO GET A GIRLFRIEND AND THINGS SEEM TO BE GOING GREAT. AND WHAT DO YOU DO?
INSTEAD OF WAITING FOR HER TO BREAK UP WITH YOU, YOU JUST BREAK UP WITH HER. THEN TO GET YOUR MIND OFF HER, YOU START RUNNING AROUND SPACE WITH A BUNCH OF KIDS LOOKING FOR POWER SIGNATURES THAT MATCH MOLECULE MAN...
...AND VOLUNTEER TO GET YOURSELF THROWN IN JAIL TO TRACK THE SIGNAL TO THE PERSON IN THIS CELL.
UH. HELLO?

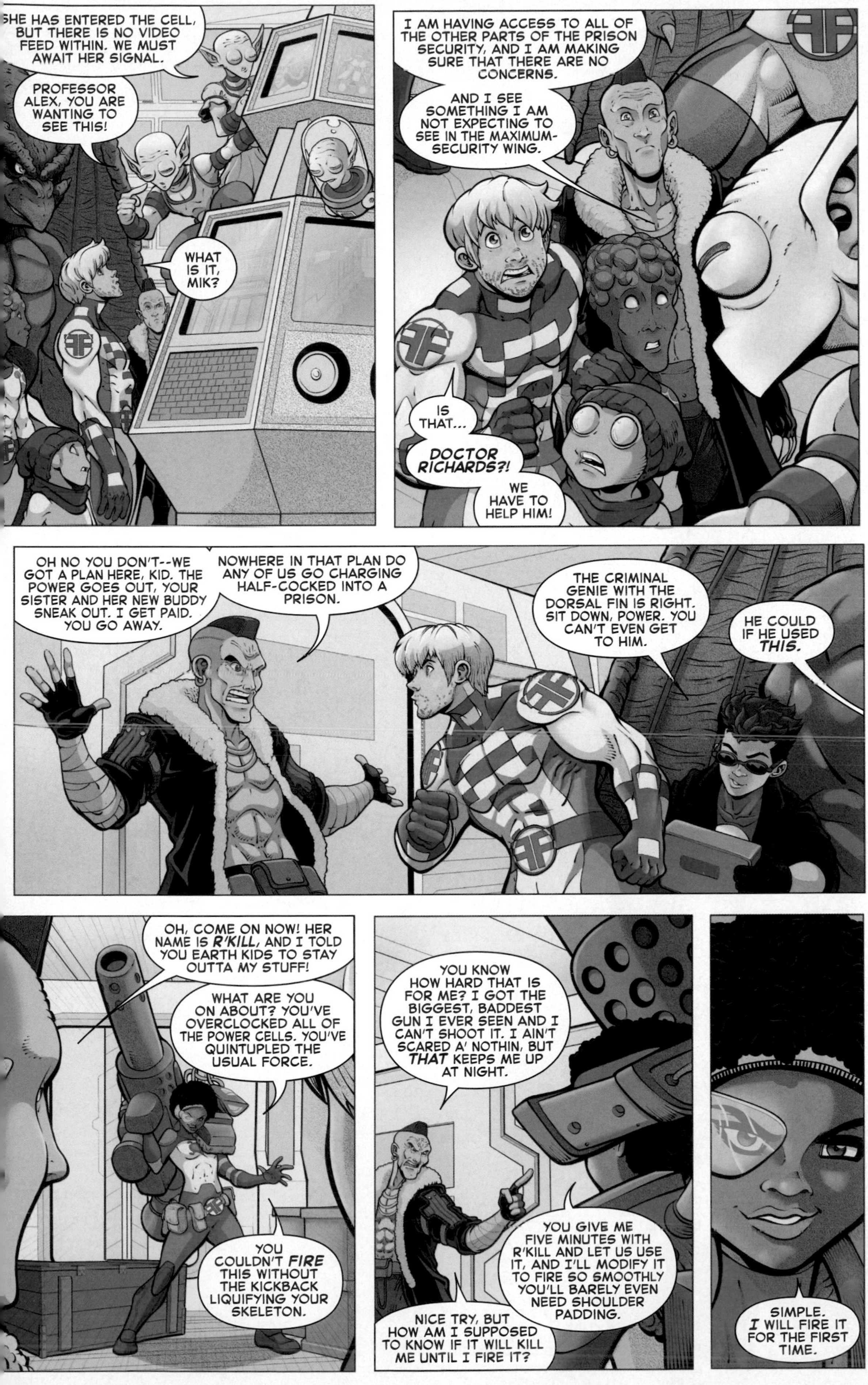
SHE HAS ENTERED THE CELL, BUT THERE IS NO VIDEO FEED WITHIN. WE MUST AWAIT HER SIGNAL.
PROFESSOR ALEX, YOU ARE WANTING TO SEE THIS!
WHAT IS IT, MIK?
I AM HAVING ACCESS TO ALL OF THE OTHER PARTS OF THE PRISON SECURITY, AND I AM MAKING SURE THAT THERE ARE NO CONCERNS.
AND I SEE SOMETHING I AM NOT EXPECTING TO SEE IN THE MAXIMUM-SECURITY WING.
IS THAT... *DOCTOR RICHARDS?!*
WE HAVE TO HELP HIM!
OH NO YOU DON'T--WE GOT A PLAN HERE, KID. THE POWER GOES OUT, YOUR SISTER AND HER NEW BUDDY SNEAK OUT. I GET PAID. YOU GO AWAY.
NOWHERE IN THAT PLAN DO ANY OF US GO CHARGING HALF-COCKED INTO A PRISON.
THE CRIMINAL GENIE WITH THE DORSAL FIN IS RIGHT. SIT DOWN, POWER. YOU CAN'T EVEN GET TO HIM.
HE COULD IF HE USED *THIS.*
OH, COME ON NOW! HER NAME IS *R'KILL,* AND I TOLD YOU EARTH KIDS TO STAY OUTTA MY STUFF!
WHAT ARE YOU ON ABOUT? YOU'VE OVERCLOCKED ALL OF THE POWER CELLS. YOU'VE QUINTUPLED THE USUAL FORCE.
YOU COULDN'T *FIRE* THIS WITHOUT THE KICKBACK LIQUIFYING YOUR SKELETON.
YOU KNOW HOW HARD THAT IS FOR ME? I GOT THE BIGGEST, BADDEST GUN I EVER SEEN AND I CAN'T SHOOT IT. I AIN'T SCARED A' NOTHIN, BUT *THAT* KEEPS ME UP AT NIGHT.
YOU GIVE ME FIVE MINUTES WITH R'KILL AND LET US USE IT, AND I'LL MODIFY IT TO FIRE SO SMOOTHLY YOU'LL BARELY EVEN NEED SHOULDER PADDING.
NICE TRY, BUT HOW AM I SUPPOSED TO KNOW IF IT WILL KILL ME UNTIL I FIRE IT?
SIMPLE. *I* WILL FIRE IT FOR THE FIRST TIME.

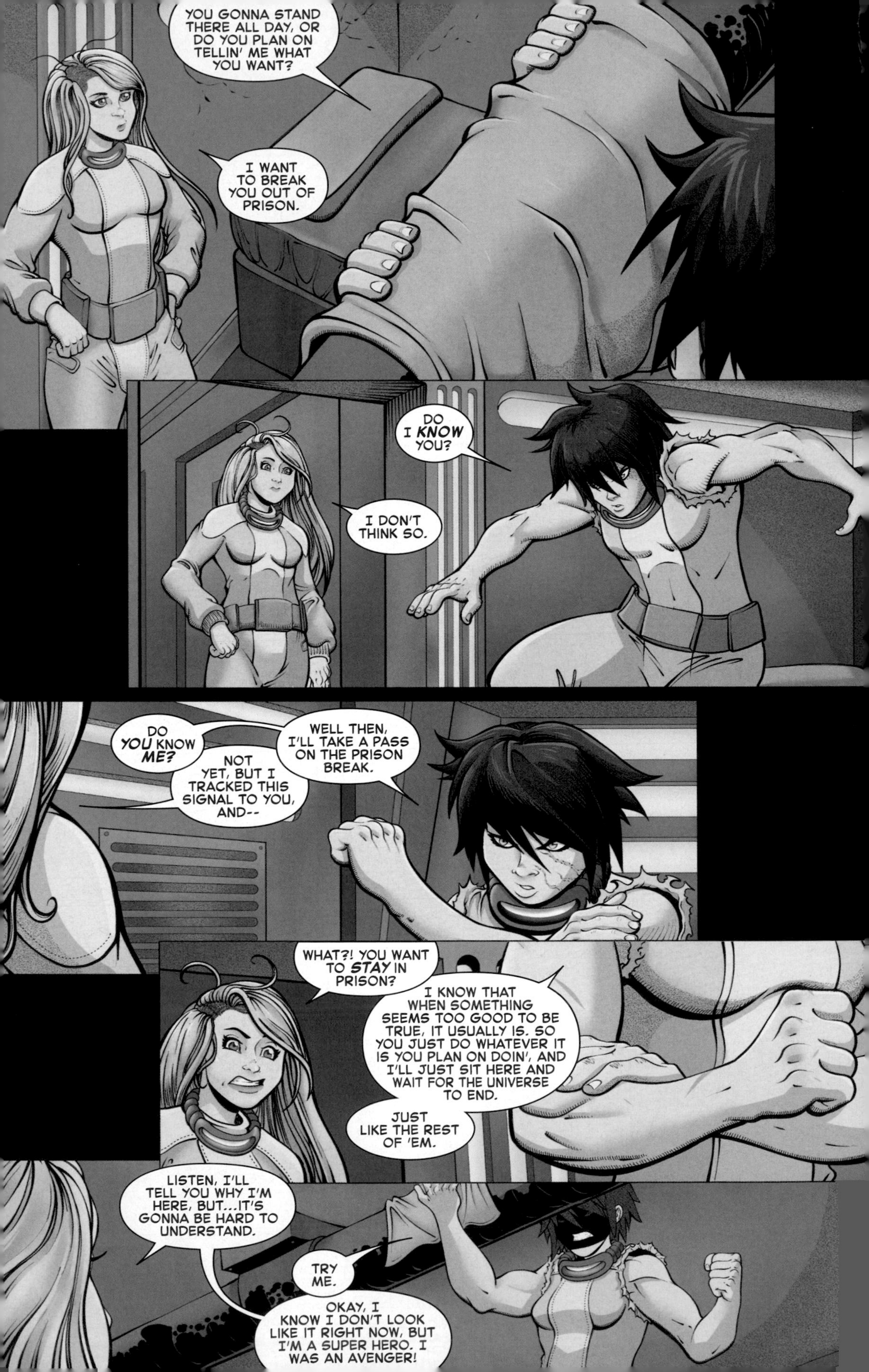

YOU GONNA STAND THERE ALL DAY, OR DO YOU PLAN ON TELLIN' ME WHAT YOU WANT?
I WANT TO BREAK YOU OUT OF PRISON.
DO I KNOW YOU?
I DON'T THINK SO.
DO YOU KNOW ME?
NOT YET, BUT I TRACKED THIS SIGNAL TO YOU, AND--
WELL THEN, I'LL TAKE A PASS ON THE PRISON BREAK.
WHAT?! YOU WANT TO STAY IN PRISON?
I KNOW THAT WHEN SOMETHING SEEMS TOO GOOD TO BE TRUE, IT USUALLY IS. SO YOU JUST DO WHATEVER IT IS YOU PLAN ON DOIN', AND I'LL JUST SIT HERE AND WAIT FOR THE UNIVERSE TO END.
JUST LIKE THE REST OF 'EM.
LISTEN, I'LL TELL YOU WHY I'M HERE, BUT...IT'S GONNA BE HARD TO UNDERSTAND.
TRY ME.
OKAY, I KNOW I DON'T LOOK LIKE IT RIGHT NOW, BUT I'M A SUPER HERO. I WAS AN AVENGER!

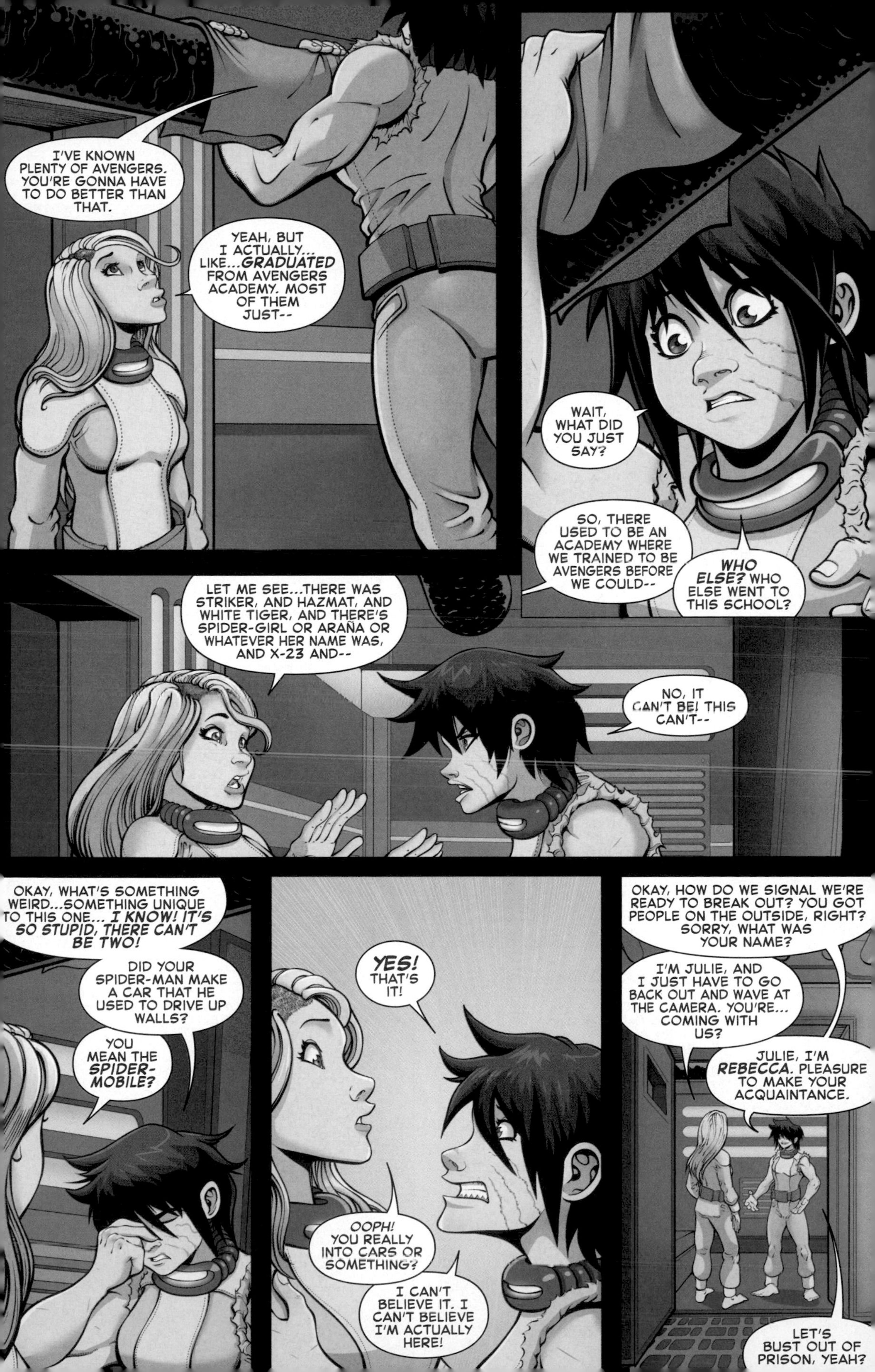

I'VE KNOWN PLENTY OF AVENGERS. YOU'RE GONNA HAVE TO DO BETTER THAN THAT.
YEAH, BUT I ACTUALLY... LIKE...GRADUATED FROM AVENGERS ACADEMY. MOST OF THEM JUST--
WAIT, WHAT DID YOU JUST SAY?
SO, THERE USED TO BE AN ACADEMY WHERE WE TRAINED TO BE AVENGERS BEFORE WE COULD--
WHO ELSE? WHO ELSE WENT TO THIS SCHOOL?
LET ME SEE...THERE WAS STRIKER, AND HAZMAT, AND WHITE TIGER, AND THERE'S SPIDER-GIRL OR ARAÑA OR WHATEVER HER NAME WAS, AND X-23 AND--
NO, IT CAN'T BE! THIS CAN'T--
OKAY, WHAT'S SOMETHING WEIRD...SOMETHING UNIQUE TO THIS ONE... I KNOW! IT'S SO STUPID, THERE CAN'T BE TWO!
DID YOUR SPIDER-MAN MAKE A CAR THAT HE USED TO DRIVE UP WALLS?
YOU MEAN THE SPIDER-MOBILE?
YES! THAT'S IT!
OOPH! YOU REALLY INTO CARS OR SOMETHING?
I CAN'T BELIEVE IT. I CAN'T BELIEVE I'M ACTUALLY HERE!
OKAY, HOW DO WE SIGNAL WE'RE READY TO BREAK OUT? YOU GOT PEOPLE ON THE OUTSIDE, RIGHT? SORRY, WHAT WAS YOUR NAME?
I'M JULIE, AND I JUST HAVE TO GO BACK OUT AND WAVE AT THE CAMERA. YOU'RE... COMING WITH US?
JULIE, I'M REBECCA. PLEASURE TO MAKE YOUR ACQUAINTANCE.
LET'S BUST OUT OF PRISON, YEAH?

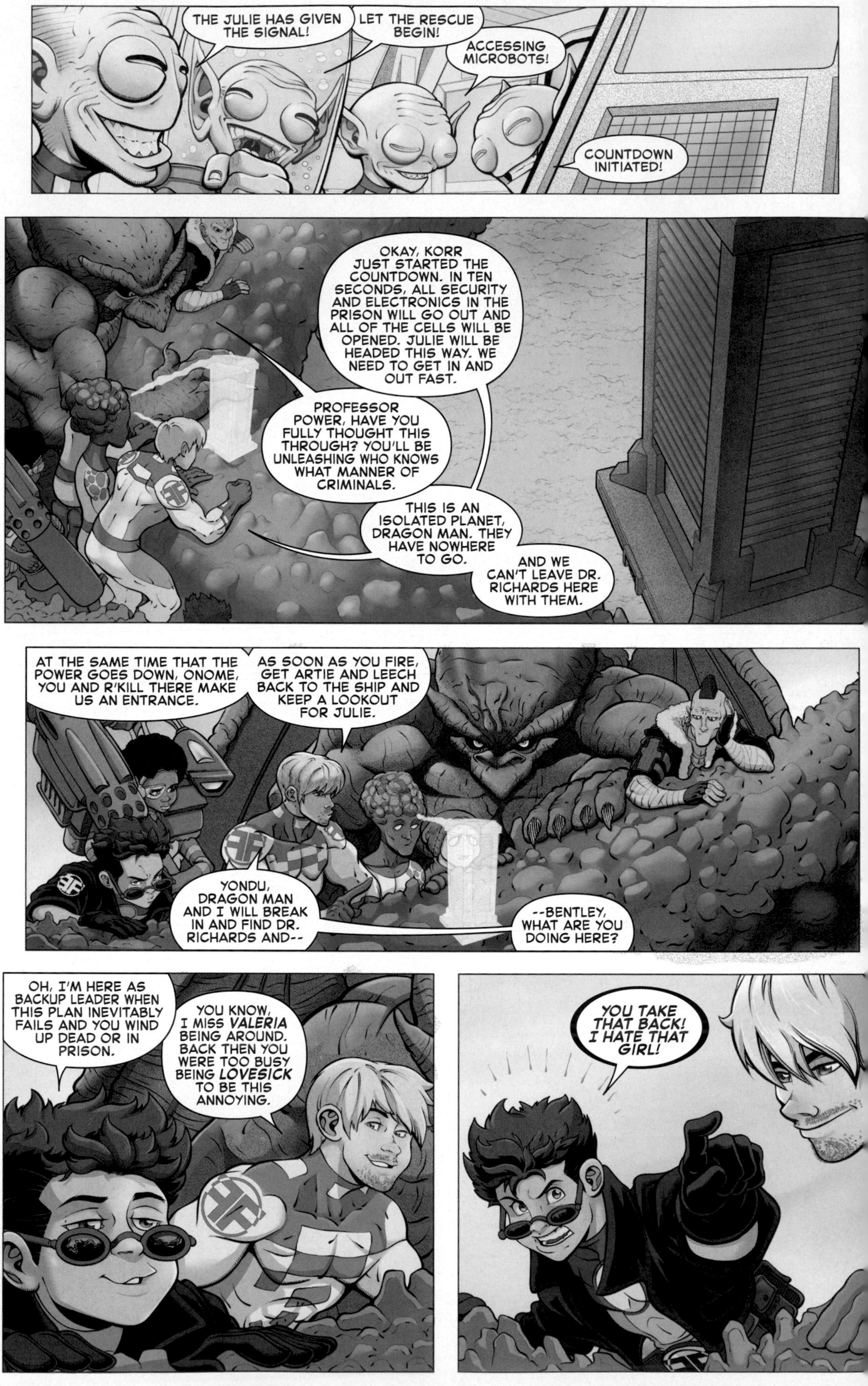
THE JULIE HAS GIVEN THE SIGNAL!
LET THE RESCUE BEGIN!
ACCESSING MICROBOTS!
COUNTDOWN INITIATED!
OKAY, KORR JUST STARTED THE COUNTDOWN. IN TEN SECONDS, ALL SECURITY AND ELECTRONICS IN THE PRISON WILL GO OUT AND ALL OF THE CELLS WILL BE OPENED. JULIE WILL BE HEADED THIS WAY. WE NEED TO GET IN AND OUT FAST.
PROFESSOR POWER, HAVE YOU FULLY THOUGHT THIS THROUGH? YOU'LL BE UNLEASHING WHO KNOWS WHAT MANNER OF CRIMINALS.
THIS IS AN ISOLATED PLANET, DRAGON MAN. THEY HAVE NOWHERE TO GO.
AND WE CAN'T LEAVE DR. RICHARDS HERE WITH THEM.
AT THE SAME TIME THAT THE POWER GOES DOWN, ONOME, YOU AND R'KILL THERE MAKE US AN ENTRANCE.
AS SOON AS YOU FIRE, GET ARTIE AND LEECH BACK TO THE SHIP AND KEEP A LOOKOUT FOR JULIE.
YONDU, DRAGON MAN AND I WILL BREAK IN AND FIND DR. RICHARDS AND--
--BENTLEY, WHAT ARE YOU DOING HERE?
OH, I'M HERE AS BACKUP LEADER WHEN THIS PLAN INEVITABLY FAILS AND YOU WIND UP DEAD OR IN PRISON.
YOU KNOW, I MISS VALERIA BEING AROUND. BACK THEN YOU WERE TOO BUSY BEING LOVESICK TO BE THIS ANNOYING.
YOU TAKE THAT BACK! I HATE THAT GIRL!

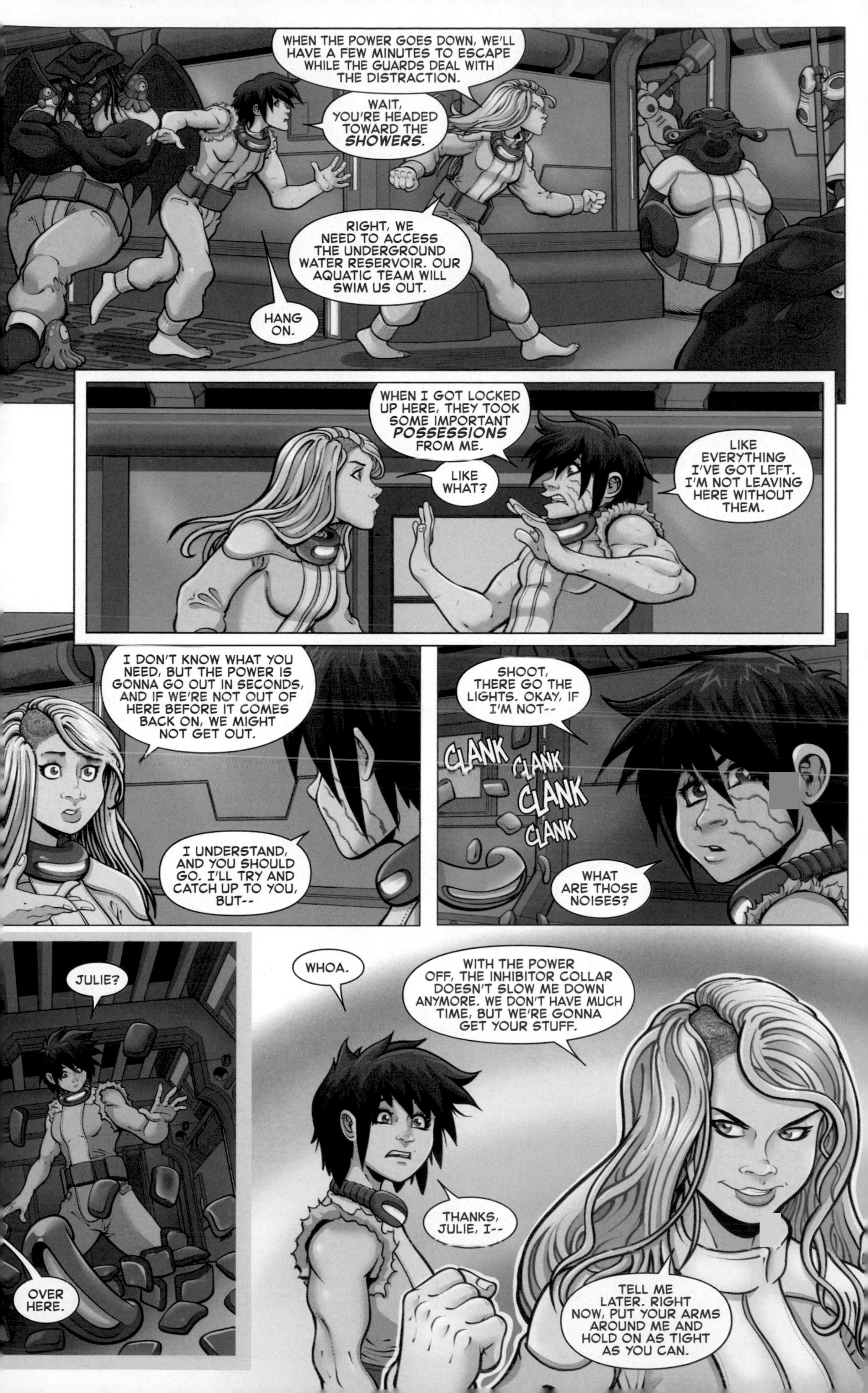
WHEN THE POWER GOES DOWN, WE'LL HAVE A FEW MINUTES TO ESCAPE WHILE THE GUARDS DEAL WITH THE DISTRACTION.
WAIT, YOU'RE HEADED TOWARD THE SHOWERS.
RIGHT, WE NEED TO ACCESS THE UNDERGROUND WATER RESERVOIR. OUR AQUATIC TEAM WILL SWIM US OUT.
HANG ON.
WHEN I GOT LOCKED UP HERE, THEY TOOK SOME IMPORTANT POSSESSIONS FROM ME.
LIKE WHAT?
LIKE EVERYTHING I'VE GOT LEFT. I'M NOT LEAVING HERE WITHOUT THEM.
I DON'T KNOW WHAT YOU NEED, BUT THE POWER IS GONNA GO OUT IN SECONDS, AND IF WE'RE NOT OUT OF HERE BEFORE IT COMES BACK ON, WE MIGHT NOT GET OUT.
I UNDERSTAND, AND YOU SHOULD GO. I'LL TRY AND CATCH UP TO YOU, BUT--
SHOOT, THERE GO THE LIGHTS. OKAY, IF I'M NOT--
CLANK CLANK CLANK CLANK
WHAT ARE THOSE NOISES?
JULIE?
OVER HERE.
WHOA.
WITH THE POWER OFF, THE INHIBITOR COLLAR DOESN'T SLOW ME DOWN ANYMORE. WE DON'T HAVE MUCH TIME, BUT WE'RE GONNA GET YOUR STUFF.
THANKS, JULIE, I--
TELL ME LATER. RIGHT NOW, PUT YOUR ARMS AROUND ME AND HOLD ON AS TIGHT AS YOU CAN.

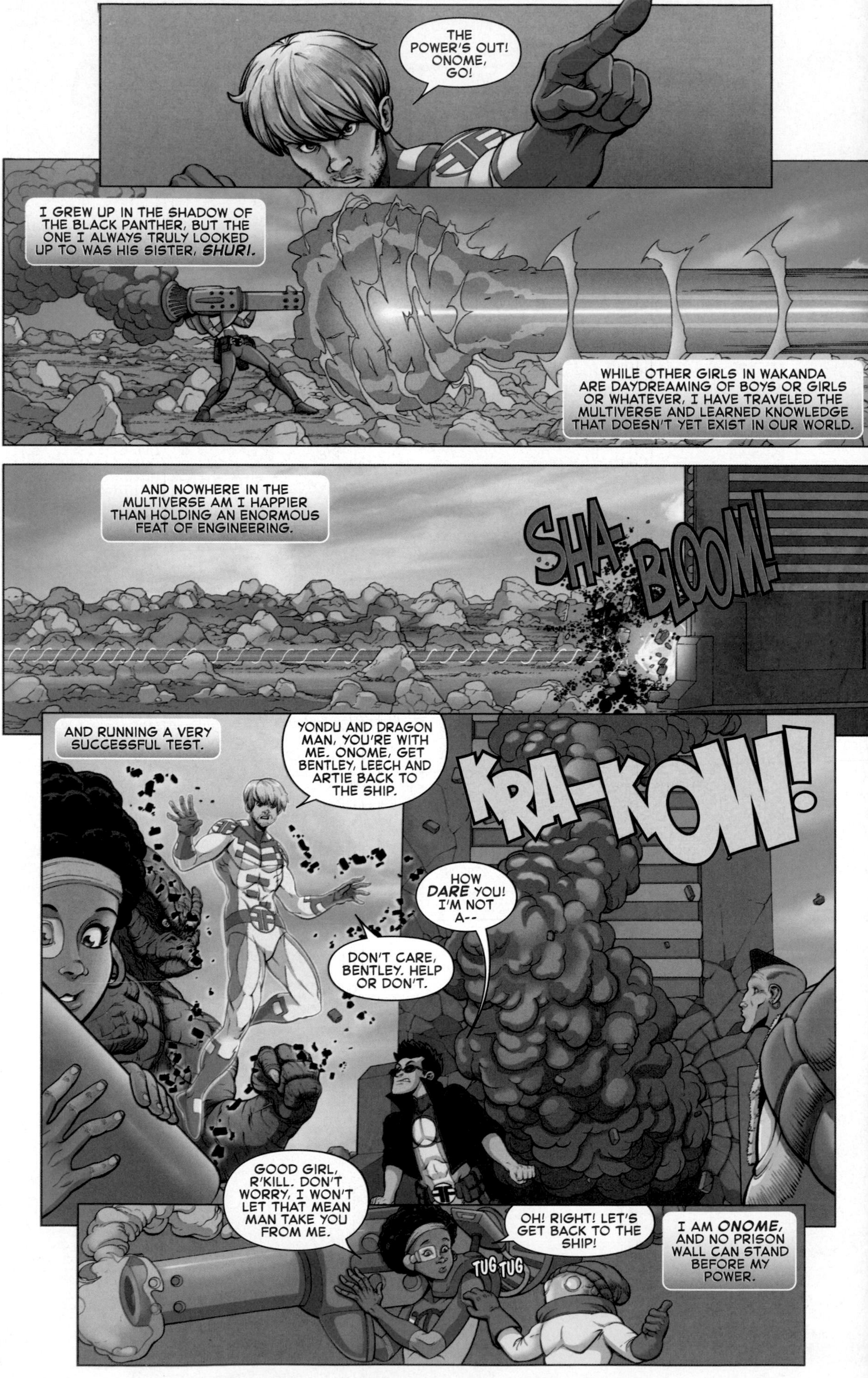

THE POWER'S OUT! ONOME, GO!
I GREW UP IN THE SHADOW OF THE BLACK PANTHER, BUT THE ONE I ALWAYS TRULY LOOKED UP TO WAS HIS SISTER, SHURI.
WHILE OTHER GIRLS IN WAKANDA ARE DAYDREAMING OF BOYS OR GIRLS OR WHATEVER, I HAVE TRAVELED THE MULTIVERSE AND LEARNED KNOWLEDGE THAT DOESN'T YET EXIST IN OUR WORLD.
AND NOWHERE IN THE MULTIVERSE AM I HAPPIER THAN HOLDING AN ENORMOUS FEAT OF ENGINEERING.
SHA-BLOOM!
AND RUNNING A VERY SUCCESSFUL TEST.
YONDU AND DRAGON MAN, YOU'RE WITH ME. ONOME, GET BENTLEY, LEECH AND ARTIE BACK TO THE SHIP.
KRA-KOW!
HOW DARE YOU! I'M NOT A--
DON'T CARE, BENTLEY. HELP OR DON'T.
GOOD GIRL, R'KILL. DON'T WORRY, I WON'T LET THAT MEAN MAN TAKE YOU FROM ME.
OH! RIGHT! LET'S GET BACK TO THE SHIP!
TUG TUG
I AM ONOME, AND NO PRISON WALL CAN STAND BEFORE MY POWER.

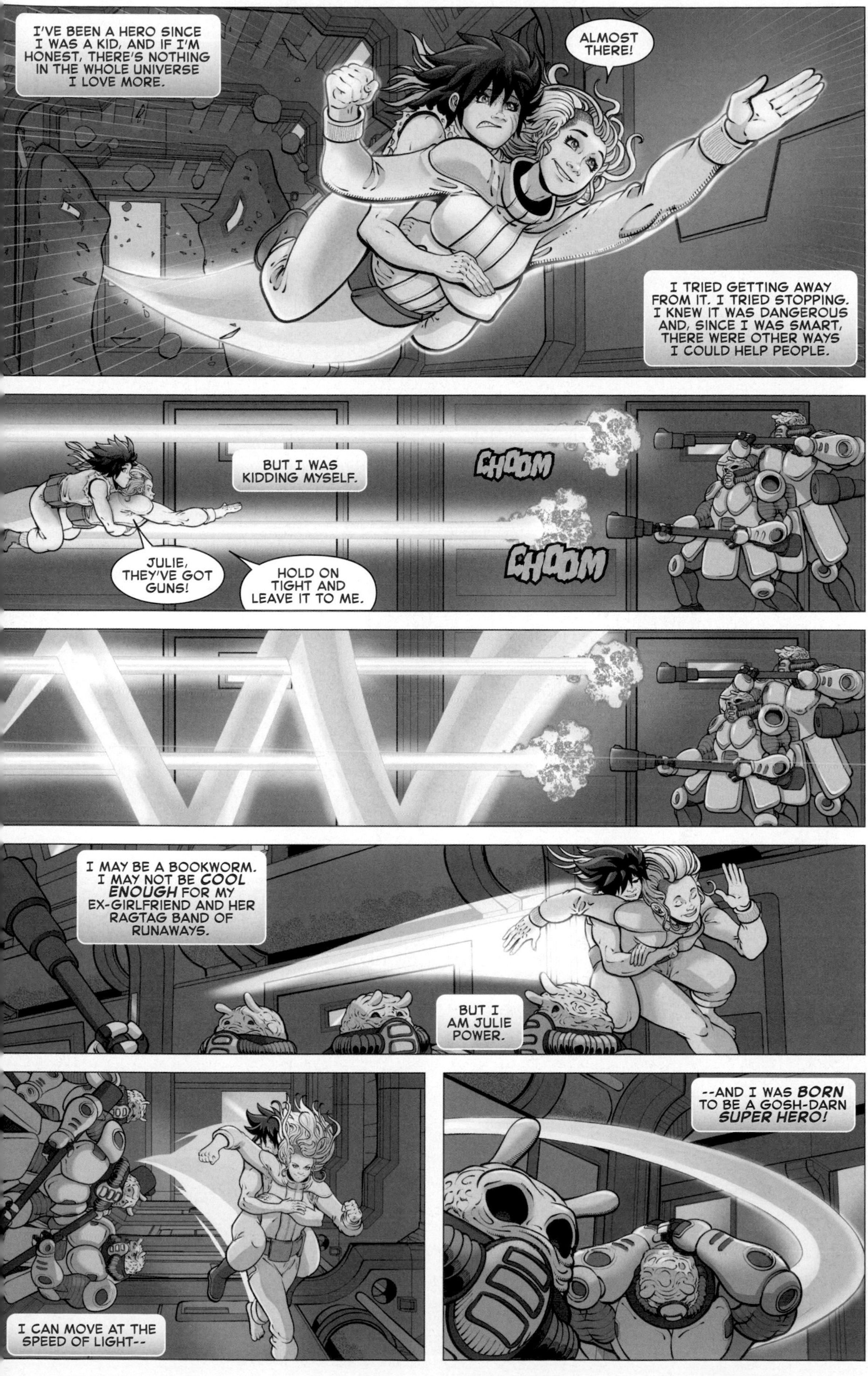
I'VE BEEN A HERO SINCE I WAS A KID, AND IF I'M HONEST, THERE'S NOTHING IN THE WHOLE UNIVERSE I LOVE MORE.
ALMOST THERE!
I TRIED GETTING AWAY FROM IT. I TRIED STOPPING. I KNEW IT WAS DANGEROUS AND, SINCE I WAS SMART, THERE WERE OTHER WAYS I COULD HELP PEOPLE.
BUT I WAS KIDDING MYSELF.
CHOOM
JULIE, THEY'VE GOT GUNS!
HOLD ON TIGHT AND LEAVE IT TO ME.
CHOOM
I MAY BE A BOOKWORM. I MAY NOT BE COOL ENOUGH FOR MY EX-GIRLFRIEND AND HER RAGTAG BAND OF RUNAWAYS.
BUT I AM JULIE POWER.
I CAN MOVE AT THE SPEED OF LIGHT--
--AND I WAS BORN TO BE A GOSH-DARN SUPER HERO!

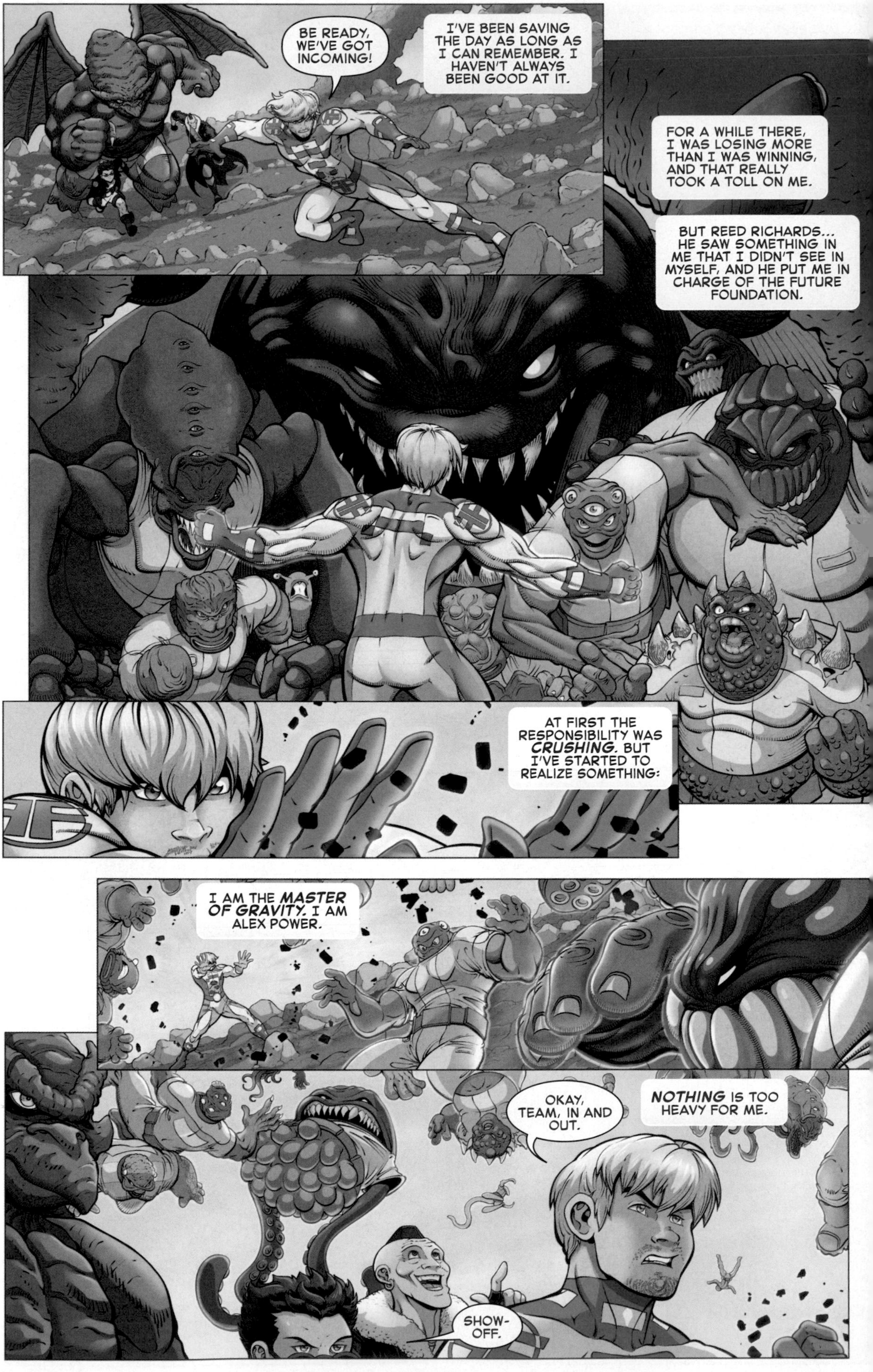
BE READY, WE'VE GOT INCOMING!
I'VE BEEN SAVING THE DAY AS LONG AS I CAN REMEMBER. I HAVEN'T ALWAYS BEEN GOOD AT IT.
FOR A WHILE THERE, I WAS LOSING MORE THAN I WAS WINNING, AND THAT REALLY TOOK A TOLL ON ME.
BUT REED RICHARDS... HE SAW SOMETHING IN ME THAT I DIDN'T SEE IN MYSELF, AND HE PUT ME IN CHARGE OF THE FUTURE FOUNDATION.
AT FIRST THE RESPONSIBILITY WAS CRUSHING. BUT I'VE STARTED TO REALIZE SOMETHING:
I AM THE MASTER OF GRAVITY. I AM ALEX POWER.
OKAY, TEAM, IN AND OUT.
NOTHING IS TOO HEAVY FOR ME.
SHOW-OFF.

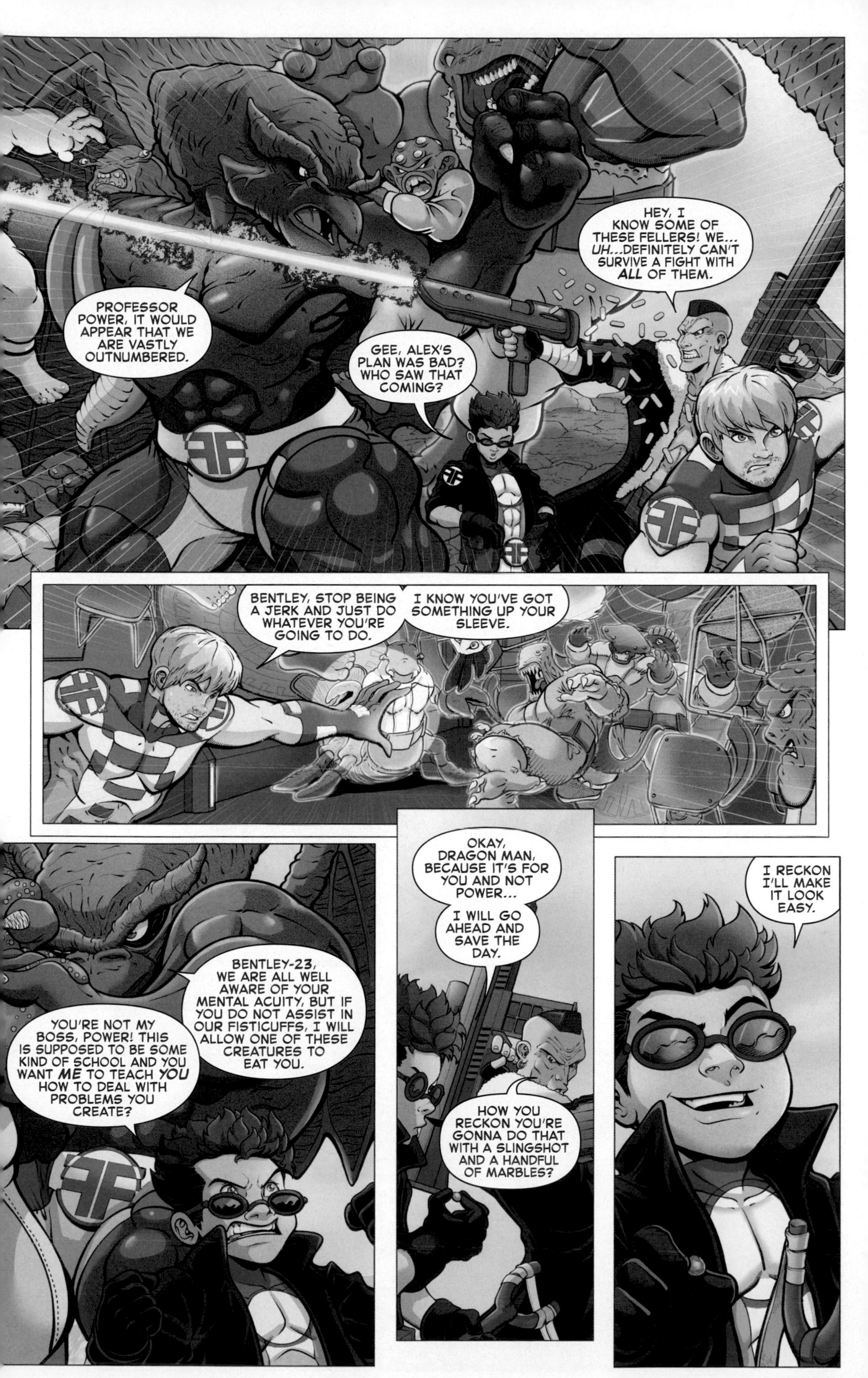
HEY, I KNOW SOME OF THESE FELLERS! WE... UH...DEFINITELY CAN'T SURVIVE A FIGHT WITH ALL OF THEM.
PROFESSOR POWER, IT WOULD APPEAR THAT WE ARE VASTLY OUTNUMBERED.
GEE, ALEX'S PLAN WAS BAD? WHO SAW THAT COMING?
BENTLEY, STOP BEING A JERK AND JUST DO WHATEVER YOU'RE GOING TO DO.
I KNOW YOU'VE GOT SOMETHING UP YOUR SLEEVE.
BENTLEY-23, WE ARE ALL WELL AWARE OF YOUR MENTAL ACUITY, BUT IF YOU DO NOT ASSIST IN OUR FISTICUFFS, I WILL ALLOW ONE OF THESE CREATURES TO EAT YOU.
YOU'RE NOT MY BOSS, POWER! THIS IS SUPPOSED TO BE SOME KIND OF SCHOOL AND YOU WANT ME TO TEACH YOU HOW TO DEAL WITH PROBLEMS YOU CREATE?
OKAY, DRAGON MAN, BECAUSE IT'S FOR YOU AND NOT POWER...
I WILL GO AHEAD AND SAVE THE DAY.
HOW YOU RECKON YOU'RE GONNA DO THAT WITH A SLINGSHOT AND A HANDFUL OF MARBLES?
I RECKON I'LL MAKE IT LOOK EASY.

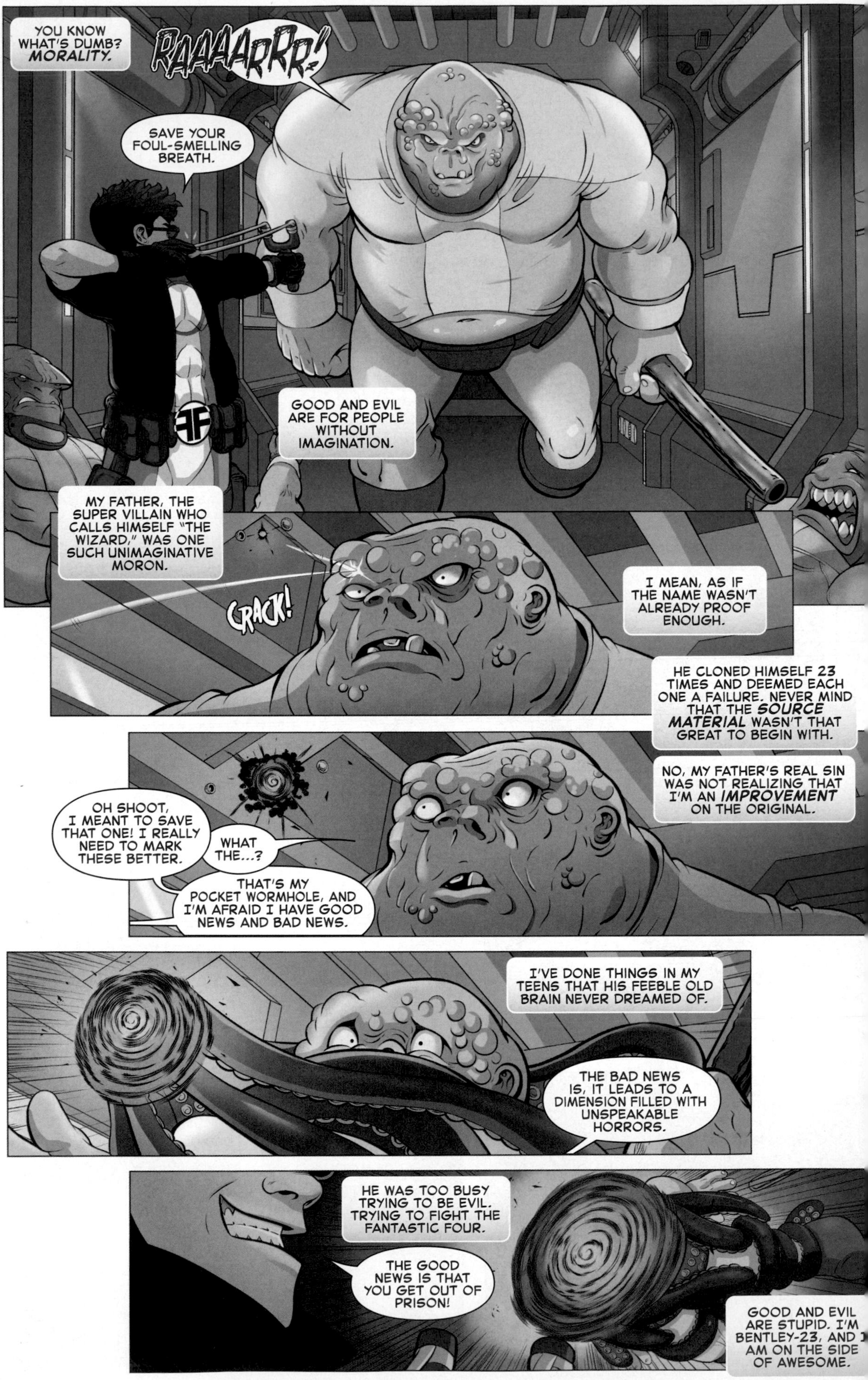

YOU KNOW WHAT'S DUMB? MORALITY.
RAAAAARRR!
SAVE YOUR FOUL-SMELLING BREATH.
GOOD AND EVIL ARE FOR PEOPLE WITHOUT IMAGINATION.
MY FATHER, THE SUPER VILLAIN WHO CALLS HIMSELF "THE WIZARD," WAS ONE SUCH UNIMAGINATIVE MORON.
CRACK!
I MEAN, AS IF THE NAME WASN'T ALREADY PROOF ENOUGH.
HE CLONED HIMSELF 23 TIMES AND DEEMED EACH ONE A FAILURE. NEVER MIND THAT THE SOURCE MATERIAL WASN'T THAT GREAT TO BEGIN WITH.
NO, MY FATHER'S REAL SIN WAS NOT REALIZING THAT I'M AN IMPROVEMENT ON THE ORIGINAL.
OH SHOOT, I MEANT TO SAVE THAT ONE! I REALLY NEED TO MARK THESE BETTER.
WHAT THE...?
THAT'S MY POCKET WORMHOLE, AND I'M AFRAID I HAVE GOOD NEWS AND BAD NEWS.
I'VE DONE THINGS IN MY TEENS THAT HIS FEEBLE OLD BRAIN NEVER DREAMED OF.
THE BAD NEWS IS, IT LEADS TO A DIMENSION FILLED WITH UNSPEAKABLE HORRORS.
HE WAS TOO BUSY TRYING TO BE EVIL. TRYING TO FIGHT THE FANTASTIC FOUR.
THE GOOD NEWS IS THAT YOU GET OUT OF PRISON!
GOOD AND EVIL ARE STUPID. I'M BENTLEY-23, AND I AM ON THE SIDE OF AWESOME.

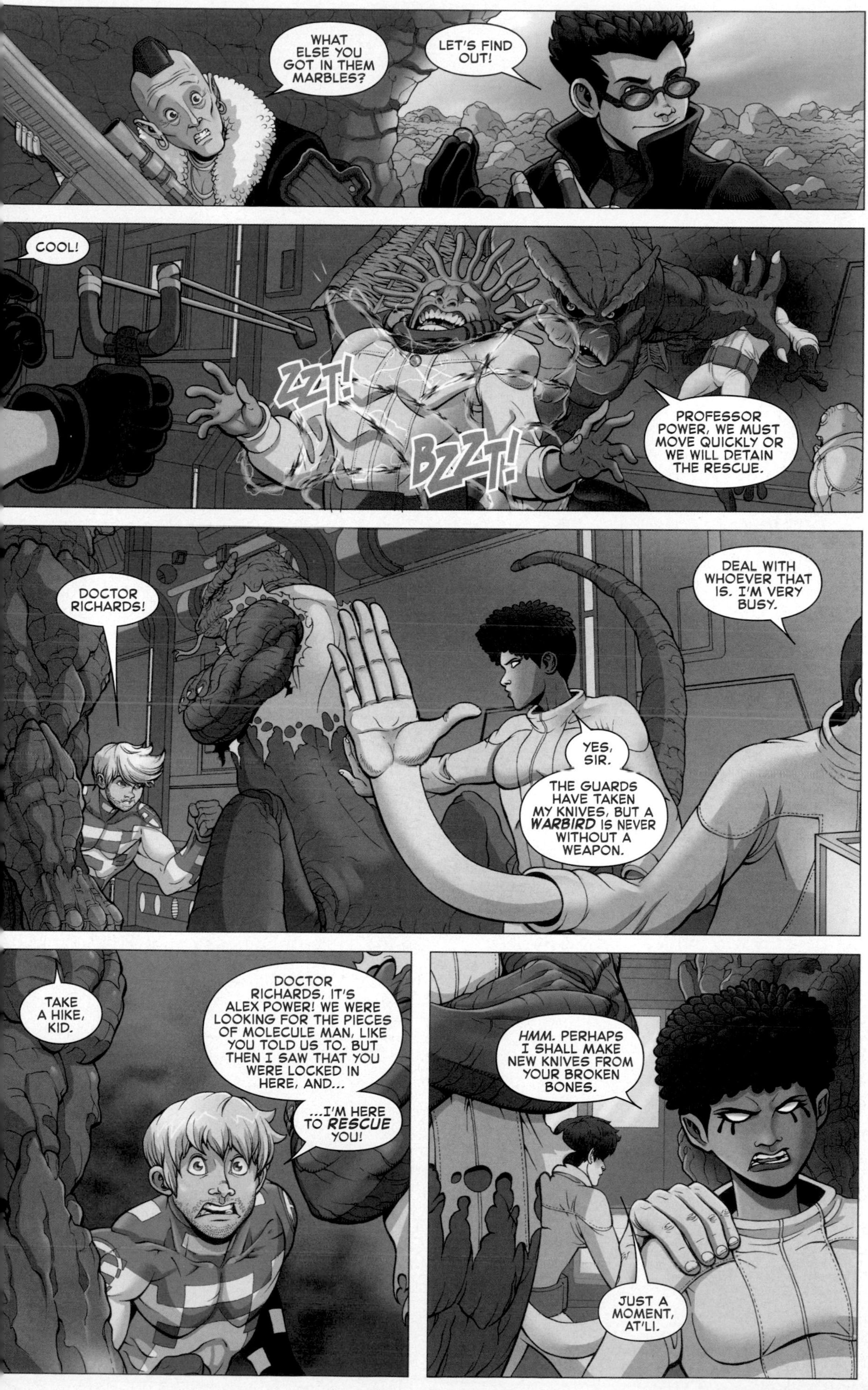
WHAT ELSE YOU GOT IN THEM MARBLES?
LET'S FIND OUT!
COOL!
ZZT!
BZZT!
PROFESSOR POWER, WE MUST MOVE QUICKLY OR WE WILL DETAIN THE RESCUE.
DOCTOR RICHARDS!
DEAL WITH WHOEVER THAT IS. I'M VERY BUSY.
YES, SIR.
THE GUARDS HAVE TAKEN MY KNIVES, BUT A WARBIRD IS NEVER WITHOUT A WEAPON.
TAKE A HIKE, KID.
DOCTOR RICHARDS, IT'S ALEX POWER! WE WERE LOOKING FOR THE PIECES OF MOLECULE MAN, LIKE YOU TOLD US TO. BUT THEN I SAW THAT YOU WERE LOCKED IN HERE, AND...
...I'M HERE TO RESCUE YOU!
HMM. PERHAPS I SHALL MAKE NEW KNIVES FROM YOUR BROKEN BONES.
JUST A MOMENT, AT'LI.

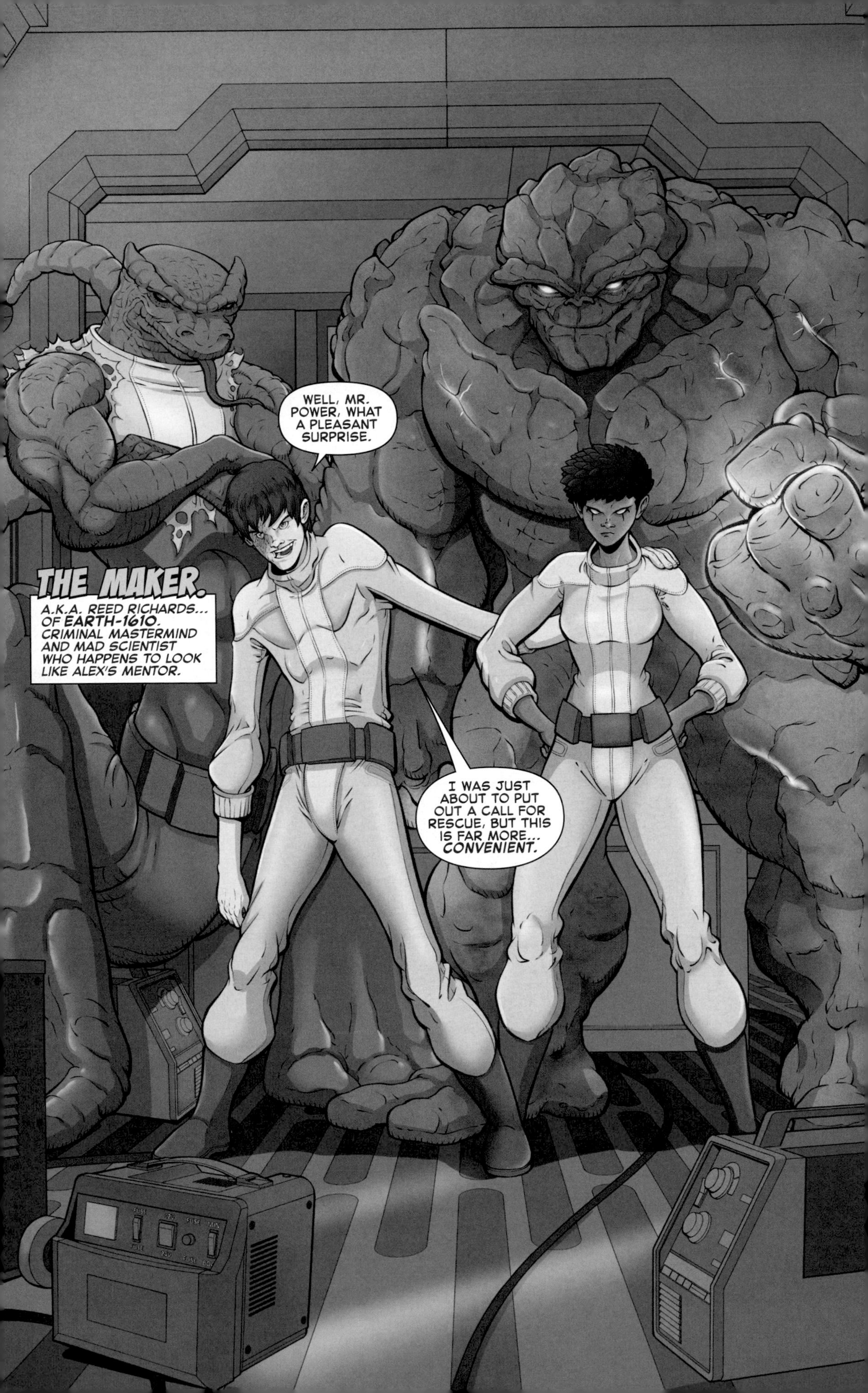
WELL, MR. POWER, WHAT A PLEASANT SURPRISE.
THE MAKER.
A.K.A. REED RICHARDS... OF EARTH-1610. CRIMINAL MASTERMIND AND MAD SCIENTIST WHO HAPPENS TO LOOK LIKE ALEX'S MENTOR.
I WAS JUST ABOUT TO PUT OUT A CALL FOR RESCUE, BUT THIS IS FAR MORE... CONVENIENT.

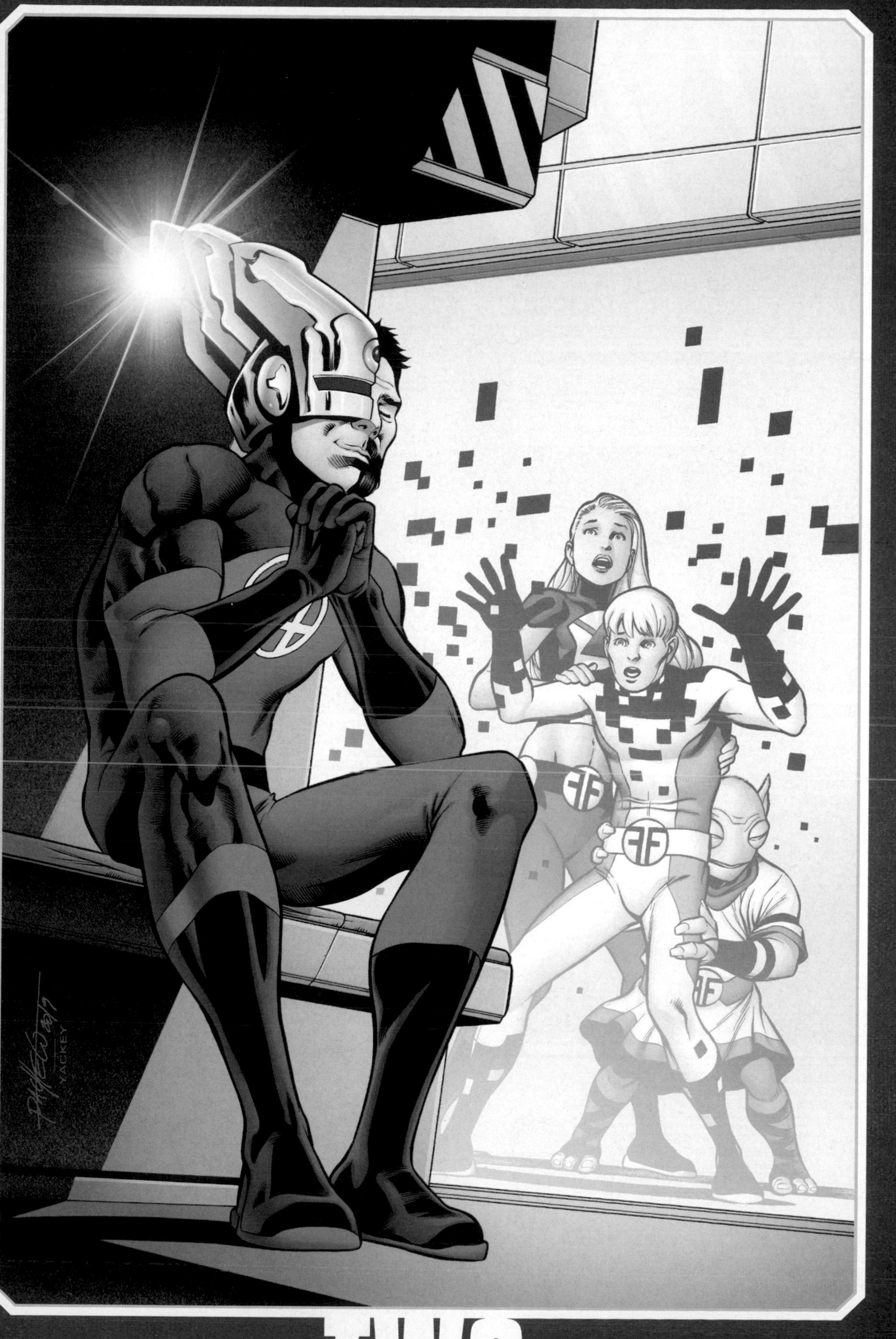
YACKEY

TWO

ONCE UPON A TIME, THERE WAS A BOY GENIUS NAMED REED RICHARDS.

HIS FATHER, NATHANIEL, NURTURED HIS BRILLIANCE. REED EARNED FIVE PHDS BY AGE 16.

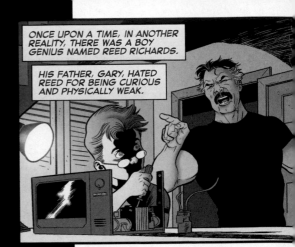

ONCE UPON A TIME, IN ANOTHER REALITY, THERE WAS A BOY GENIUS NAMED REED RICHARDS.

HIS FATHER, GARY, HATED REED FOR BEING CURIOUS AND PHYSICALLY WEAK.

ONE OF NATHANIEL'S SON'S EXPERIMENTS WENT AWRY, AND HE AND HIS FRIENDS GAINED POWERS AND BECAME THE **FANTASTIC FOUR.**

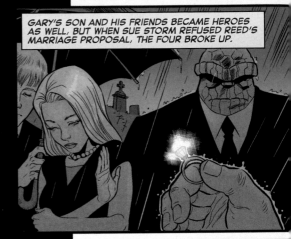

GARY'S SON AND HIS FRIENDS BECAME HEROES AS WELL, BUT WHEN SUE STORM REFUSED REED'S MARRIAGE PROPOSAL, THE FOUR BROKE UP.

NATHANIEL'S SON ALSO PROPOSED TO HIS SUE...AND THEY GOT MARRIED AND HAD TWO KIDS.

THE FANTASTIC FOUR BECAME THE MOST BELOVED TEAM OF SUPER HEROES ON THE PLANET.

SUE DISCOVERED GARY'S SON ATTEMPTING TO EXECUTE A PLAN TO RULE THE WORLD AND TRIED TO STOP HIM.

HE CAPTURED AND TORTURED HER. SUE'S BROTHER BURNED REED, LEAVING A FACIAL SCAR THAT NEVER HEALED.

NATHANIEL'S SON SAVED THE WORLD A HUNDRED TIMES OVER AND CREATED A LEGACY.

HE BROUGHT TOGETHER THE GREATEST YOUNG GENIUSES IN THE UNIVERSE. HE CALLED THEM THE **FUTURE FOUNDATION.**

GARY'S SON WAS CONCERNED WITH LEGACY TOO. HE CHRISTENED HIMSELF THE MAKER AND CREATED A RACE OF SUPER-EVOLVED HUMANS CALLED THE **CHILDREN OF TOMORROW.**

THEY WERE TWO BRILLIANT MEN ON PARALLEL PATHS, UNTIL...

...THE TWO REALITIES COLLIDED.

NATHANIEL'S SON TRIED TO SAVE HIS WORLD.

AND SO DID GARY'S SON.

BUT NEITHER OF THEM WOULD SAVE THE WORLD THAT DAY. THERE WAS ONLY **ONE** MAN WHO COULD.

HIS NAME WAS **VICTOR VON DOOM.** IN BOTH WORLDS, HE HAD BEEN REED'S GREATEST ENEMY-- SO GREAT THAT GARY'S SON HAD HIS DOOM KILLED.

VICTOR CREATED BATTLEWORLD FROM THE RUBBLE OF THE CATACLYSM, AND MUCH OF HIS OWN WORLD SURVIVED. THE VICTOR-LESS WORLD WAS LESS FORTUNATE.

VICTOR HELD BATTLEWORLD TOGETHER WITH THE HELP OF A MAN NAMED OWEN REECE, A.K.A. MOLECULE MAN.

BUT VICTOR'S GRASP BEGAN TO SLIP, AND EACH REED APPROACHED OWEN WITH A PLAN TO RESTORE THE MULTIVERSE.

OWEN CHOSE NATHANIEL'S SON'S PLAN.

AND GARY'S SON...HE CHOSE TO CUT INTO PIECES.

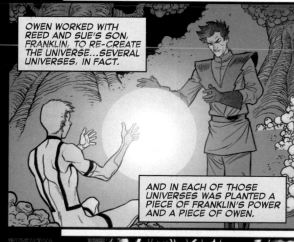

OWEN WORKED WITH REED AND SUE'S SON, FRANKLIN, TO RE-CREATE THE UNIVERSE...SEVERAL UNIVERSES, IN FACT.

AND IN EACH OF THOSE UNIVERSES WAS PLANTED A PIECE OF FRANKLIN'S POWER AND A PIECE OF OWEN.

AND IN EACH OF THOSE UNIVERSES, OWEN LEFT A PIECE OF A MAN HE HAD DESTROYED.

THE MAKER BECAME A BEING WITH A THOUSAND BODIES AND ONE MIND, CONNECTED ACROSS REALITIES.

BUT ONLY OWEN REECE UNDERSTOOD THIS, AND OWEN WAS DESTROYED.

THE FUTURE FOUNDATION DECIDED TO FIND AND REASSEMBLE THE PIECES OF OWEN LEFT BEHIND. A MISSION THAT LED THEM TO:

L'AR GATH FIVE.
THE PRISON PLANET.

DOCTOR RICHARDS, WHAT HAPPENED TO YOUR FACE?

YOUNG ALEX, I'M AFRAID I SUSTAINED A NASTY BURN.

BUT...WITH YOUR POWERS... CAN'T YOU JUST HEAL UP?

I MEAN, YOU'VE BEEN HURT BEFORE, AND I DON'T REMEMBER YOU HAVING ANY SCARS.

MY DEAR BOY, NORMALLY YOU'RE ABSOLUTELY RIGHT.

UNFORTUNATELY, WITH THESE COLLARS I WASN'T ABLE TO ACCESS MY POWERS. YOU SEE, I HAD TO DEPEND ON A FEW FRIENDS I MADE TO PROTECT ME.

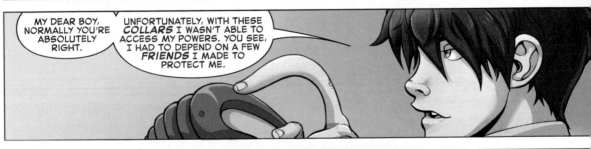

ALLOW ME TO INTRODUCE FORMER SHI'AR WARBIRD, AL'TI VIDUA.

THE MASSEIN KRONAN BARBARIAN KNOWN SIMPLY AS PHYLLIS.

AND KL'RATH OF THE ZN'RX.

I GUESS I HAVE A SOFT SPOT FOR GROUPS OF FOUR.

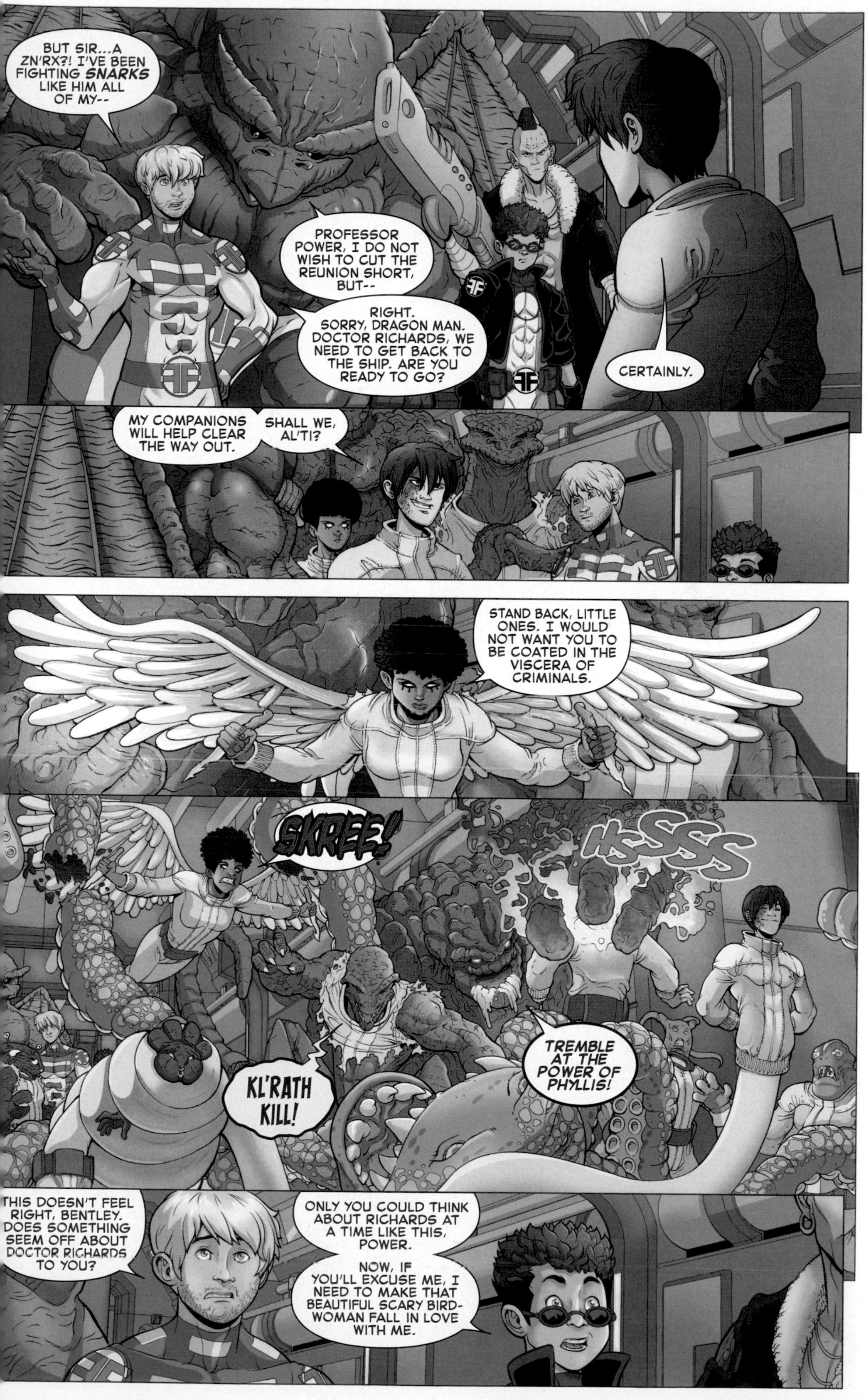
BUT SIR...A ZN'RX?! I'VE BEEN FIGHTING SNARKS LIKE HIM ALL OF MY--
PROFESSOR POWER, I DO NOT WISH TO CUT THE REUNION SHORT, BUT--
RIGHT. SORRY, DRAGON MAN. DOCTOR RICHARDS, WE NEED TO GET BACK TO THE SHIP. ARE YOU READY TO GO?
CERTAINLY.
MY COMPANIONS WILL HELP CLEAR THE WAY OUT.
SHALL WE, AL'TI?
STAND BACK, LITTLE ONES. I WOULD NOT WANT YOU TO BE COATED IN THE VISCERA OF CRIMINALS.
SKREE!
HSSSS
TREMBLE AT THE POWER OF PHYLLIS!
KL'RATH KILL!
THIS DOESN'T FEEL RIGHT, BENTLEY. DOES SOMETHING SEEM OFF ABOUT DOCTOR RICHARDS TO YOU?
ONLY YOU COULD THINK ABOUT RICHARDS AT A TIME LIKE THIS, POWER.
NOW, IF YOU'LL EXCUSE ME, I NEED TO MAKE THAT BEAUTIFUL SCARY BIRD-WOMAN FALL IN LOVE WITH ME.

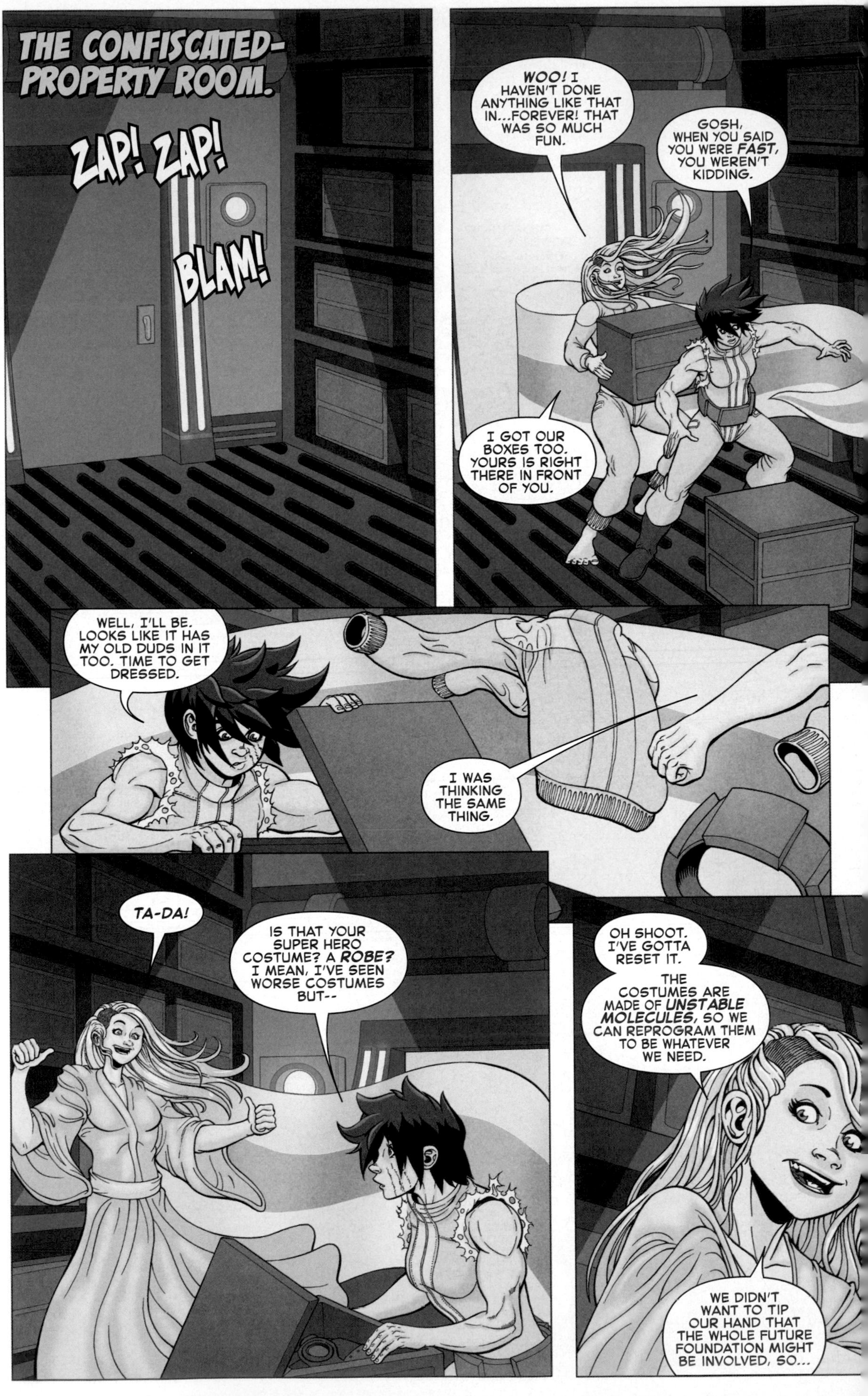
THE CONFISCATED-PROPERTY ROOM.
ZAP! ZAP!
BLAM!
WOO! I HAVEN'T DONE ANYTHING LIKE THAT IN...FOREVER! THAT WAS SO MUCH FUN.
GOSH, WHEN YOU SAID YOU WERE FAST, YOU WEREN'T KIDDING.
I GOT OUR BOXES TOO. YOURS IS RIGHT THERE IN FRONT OF YOU.
WELL, I'LL BE. LOOKS LIKE IT HAS MY OLD DUDS IN IT TOO. TIME TO GET DRESSED.
I WAS THINKING THE SAME THING.
TA-DA!
IS THAT YOUR SUPER HERO COSTUME? A ROBE? I MEAN, I'VE SEEN WORSE COSTUMES BUT--
OH SHOOT. I'VE GOTTA RESET IT.
THE COSTUMES ARE MADE OF UNSTABLE MOLECULES, SO WE CAN REPROGRAM THEM TO BE WHATEVER WE NEED.
WE DIDN'T WANT TO TIP OUR HAND THAT THE WHOLE FUTURE FOUNDATION MIGHT BE INVOLVED, SO...

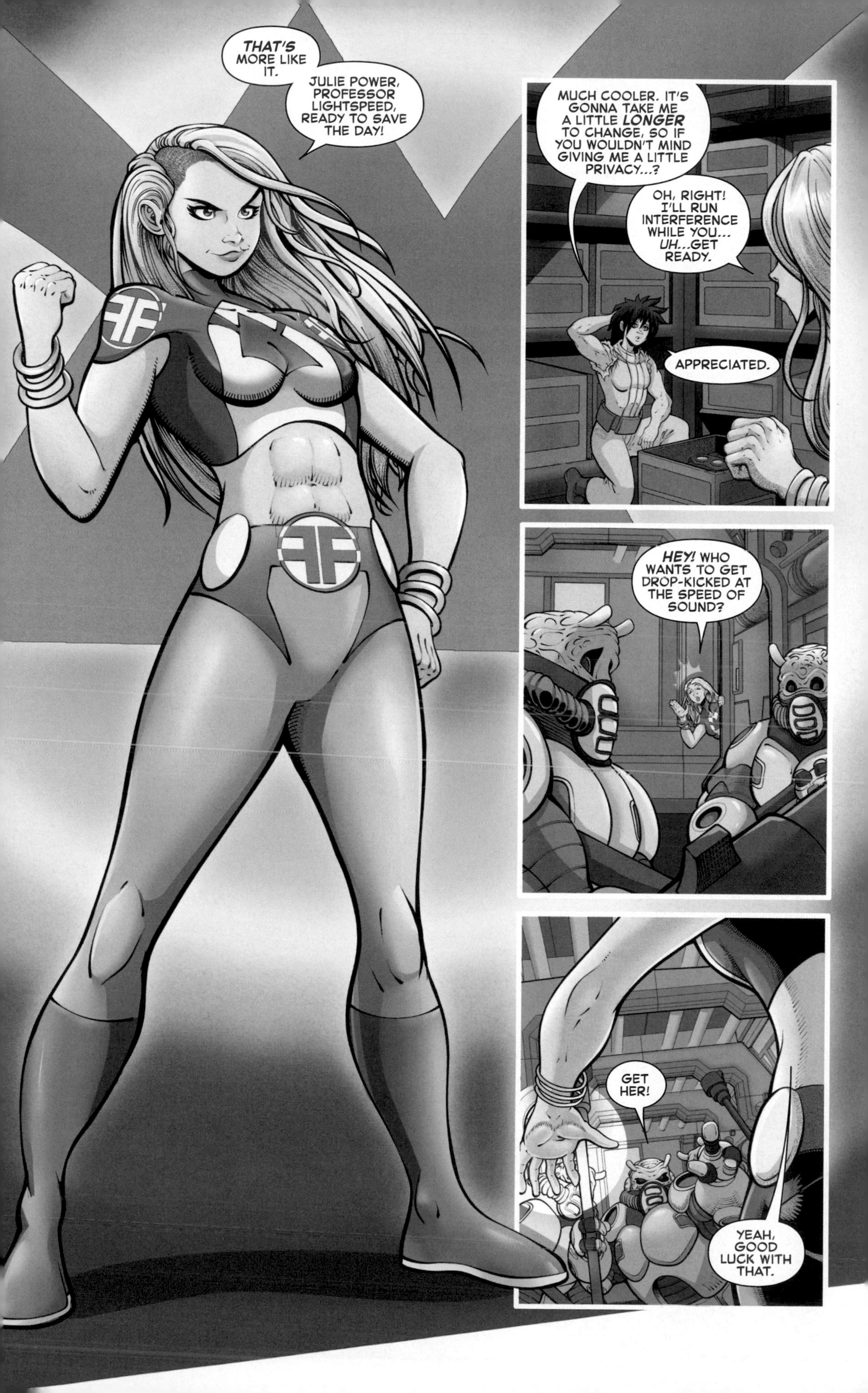
THAT'S MORE LIKE IT.
JULIE POWER, PROFESSOR LIGHTSPEED, READY TO SAVE THE DAY!
MUCH COOLER. IT'S GONNA TAKE ME A LITTLE LONGER TO CHANGE, SO IF YOU WOULDN'T MIND GIVING ME A LITTLE PRIVACY...?
OH, RIGHT! I'LL RUN INTERFERENCE WHILE YOU... UH...GET READY.
APPRECIATED.
HEY! WHO WANTS TO GET DROP-KICKED AT THE SPEED OF SOUND?
GET HER!
YEAH, GOOD LUCK WITH THAT.

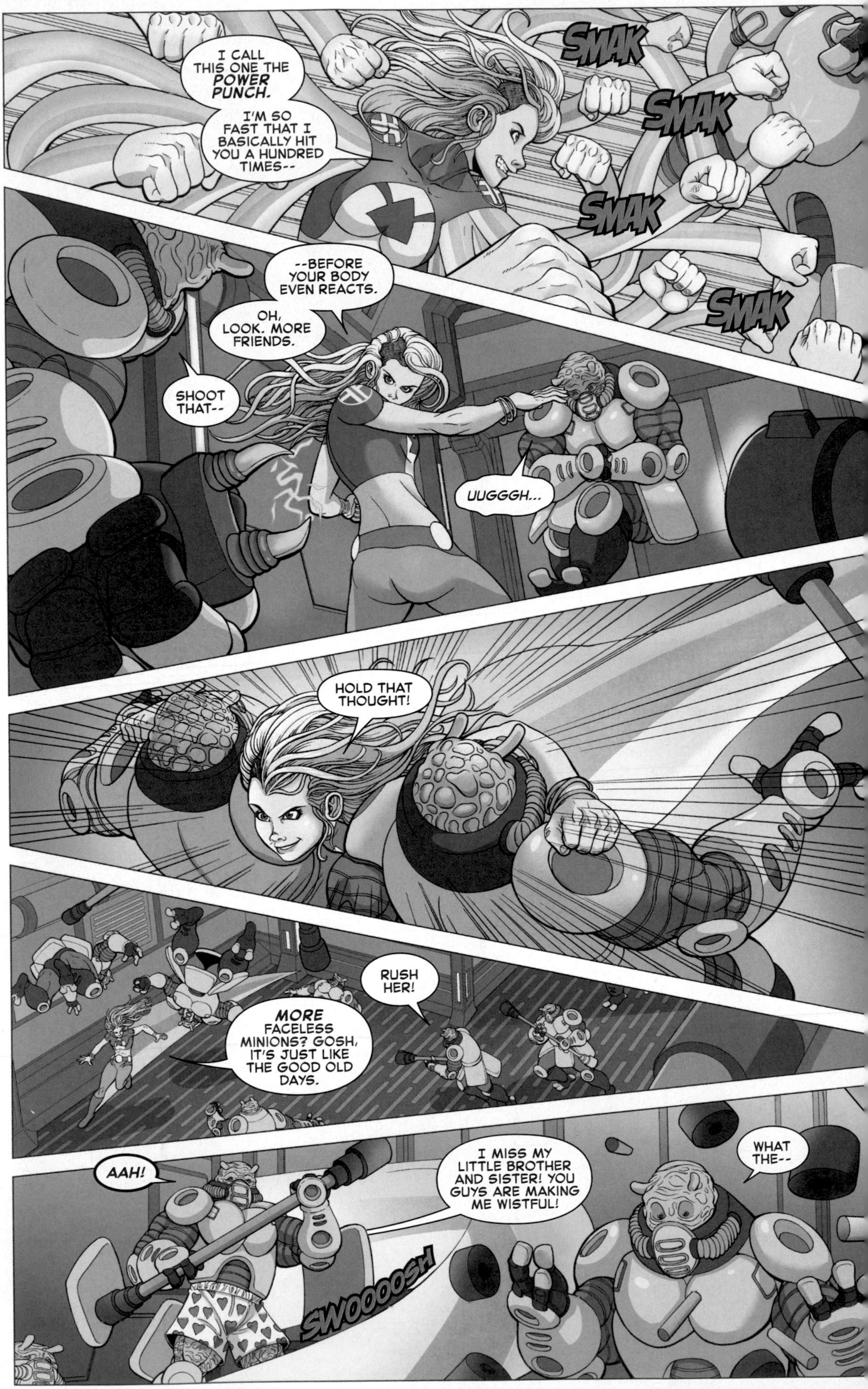

I CALL THIS ONE THE POWER PUNCH.
I'M SO FAST THAT I BASICALLY HIT YOU A HUNDRED TIMES--
SMAK
SMAK
SMAK
SMAK
--BEFORE YOUR BODY EVEN REACTS.
OH, LOOK. MORE FRIENDS.
SHOOT THAT--
UUGGGH...
HOLD THAT THOUGHT!
RUSH HER!
MORE FACELESS MINIONS? GOSH, IT'S JUST LIKE THE GOOD OLD DAYS.
AAH!
I MISS MY LITTLE BROTHER AND SISTER! YOU GUYS ARE MAKING ME WISTFUL!
WHAT THE--
SWOOOOSH

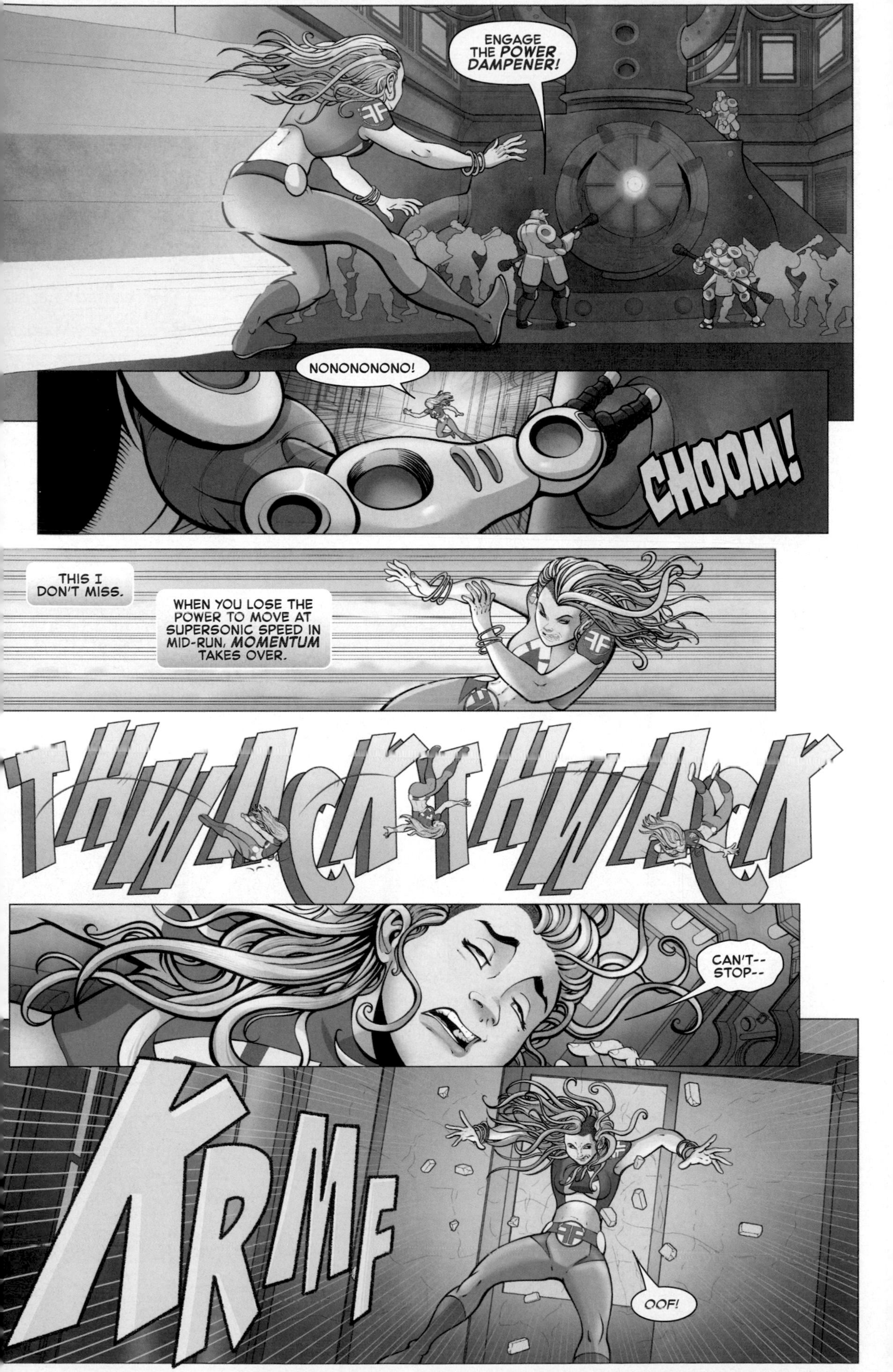
ENGAGE THE *POWER DAMPENER!*
NONONONONO!
CHOOM!
THIS I DON'T MISS.
WHEN YOU LOSE THE POWER TO MOVE AT SUPERSONIC SPEED IN MID-RUN, *MOMENTUM* TAKES OVER.
THWACK THWACK
CAN'T-- STOP--
KRMF
OOF!

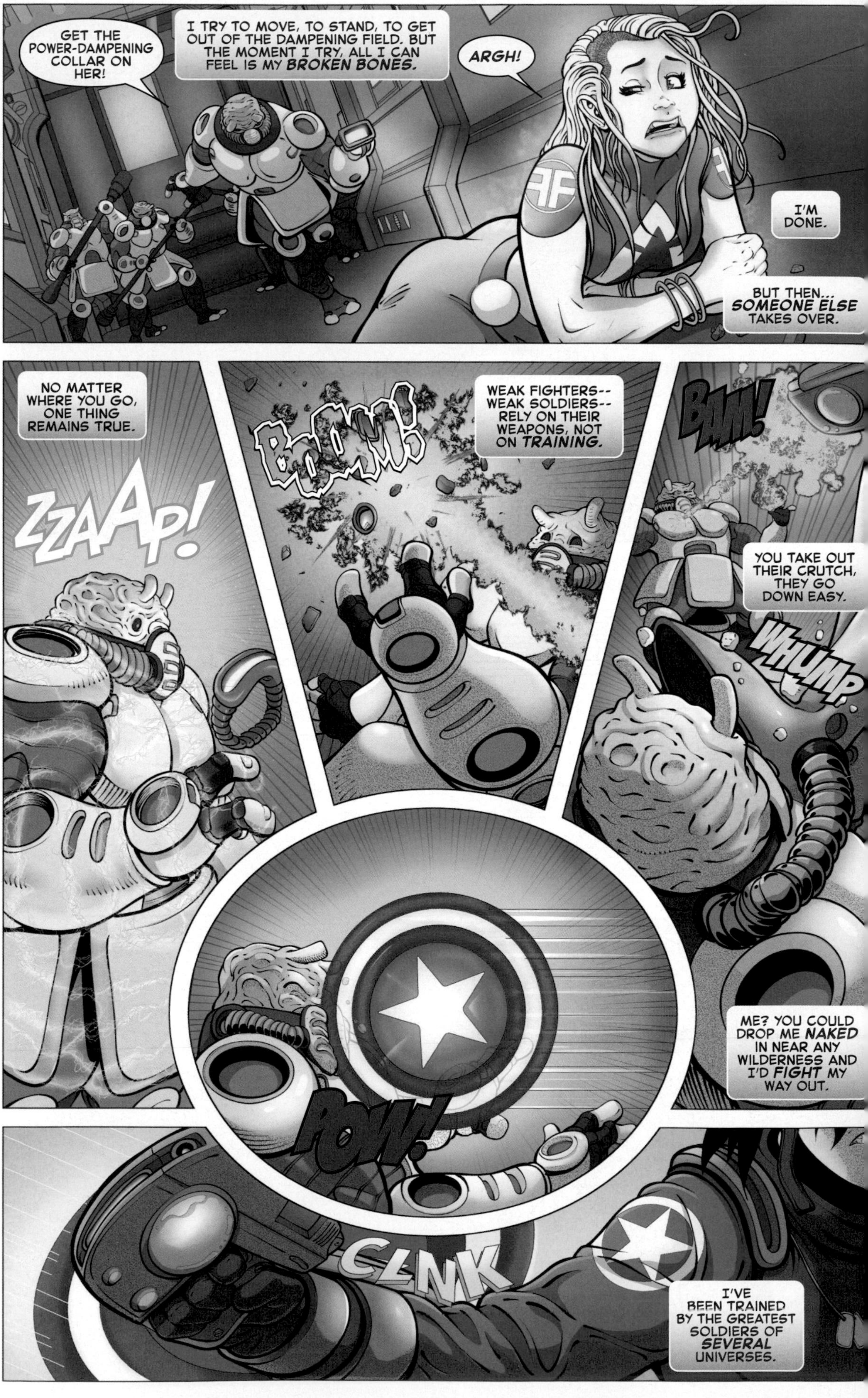
GET THE POWER-DAMPENING COLLAR ON HER!
I TRY TO MOVE, TO STAND, TO GET OUT OF THE DAMPENING FIELD. BUT THE MOMENT I TRY, ALL I CAN FEEL IS MY *BROKEN BONES.*
ARGH!
I'M DONE.
BUT THEN... *SOMEONE ELSE* TAKES OVER.
NO MATTER WHERE YOU GO, ONE THING REMAINS TRUE.
ZZAAP!
BOOM!
WEAK FIGHTERS-- WEAK SOLDIERS-- RELY ON THEIR WEAPONS, NOT ON *TRAINING.*
BAM!
YOU TAKE OUT THEIR CRUTCH, THEY GO DOWN EASY.
WHUMP!
POW!
ME? YOU COULD DROP ME *NAKED* IN NEAR ANY WILDERNESS AND I'D *FIGHT* MY WAY OUT.
CLNK
I'VE BEEN TRAINED BY THE GREATEST SOLDIERS OF *SEVERAL* UNIVERSES.

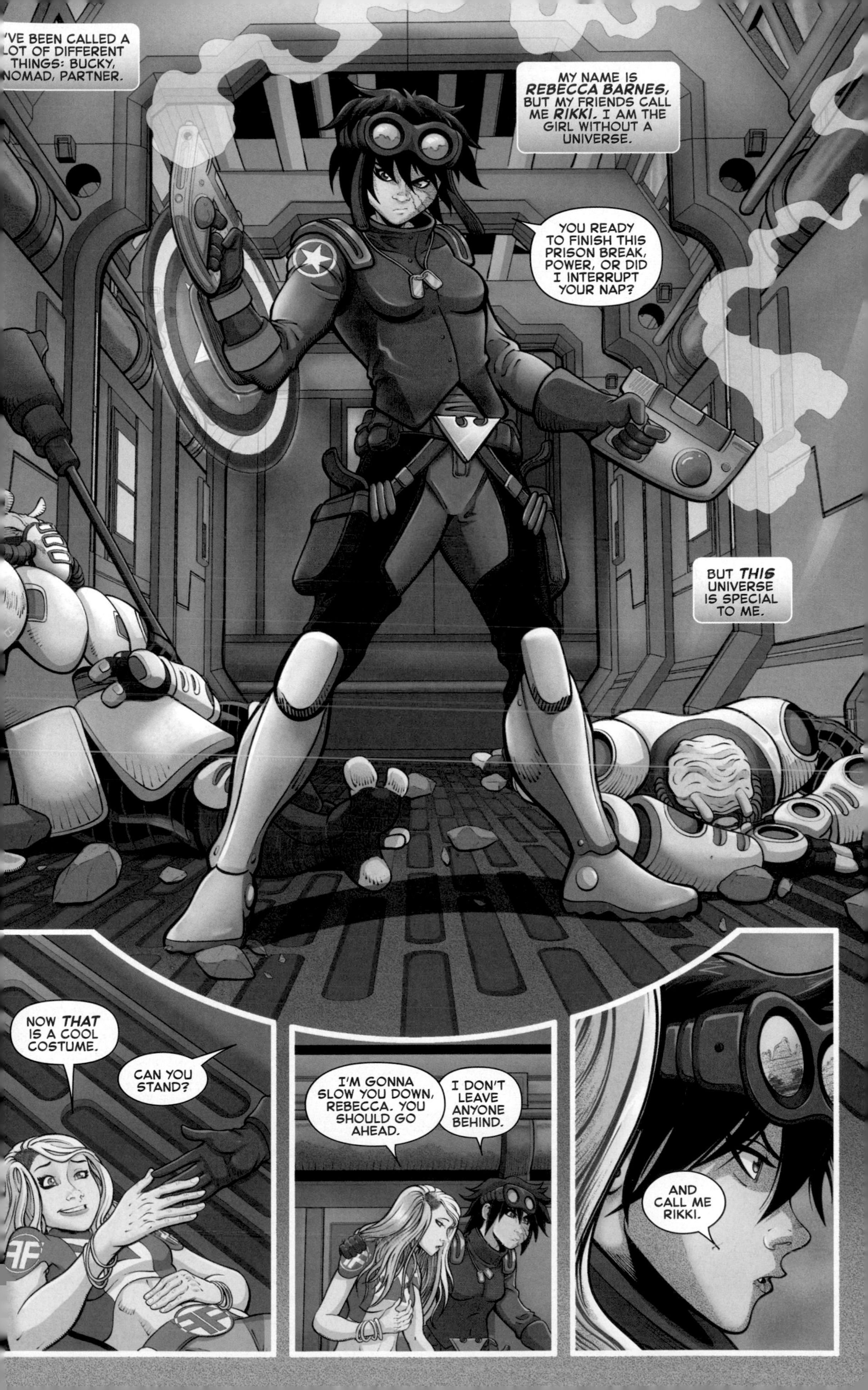

I'VE BEEN CALLED A LOT OF DIFFERENT THINGS: BUCKY, NOMAD, PARTNER.
MY NAME IS REBECCA BARNES, BUT MY FRIENDS CALL ME RIKKI. I AM THE GIRL WITHOUT A UNIVERSE.
YOU READY TO FINISH THIS PRISON BREAK, POWER, OR DID I INTERRUPT YOUR NAP?
BUT THIS UNIVERSE IS SPECIAL TO ME.
NOW THAT IS A COOL COSTUME.
CAN YOU STAND?
I'M GONNA SLOW YOU DOWN, REBECCA. YOU SHOULD GO AHEAD.
I DON'T LEAVE ANYONE BEHIND.
AND CALL ME RIKKI.

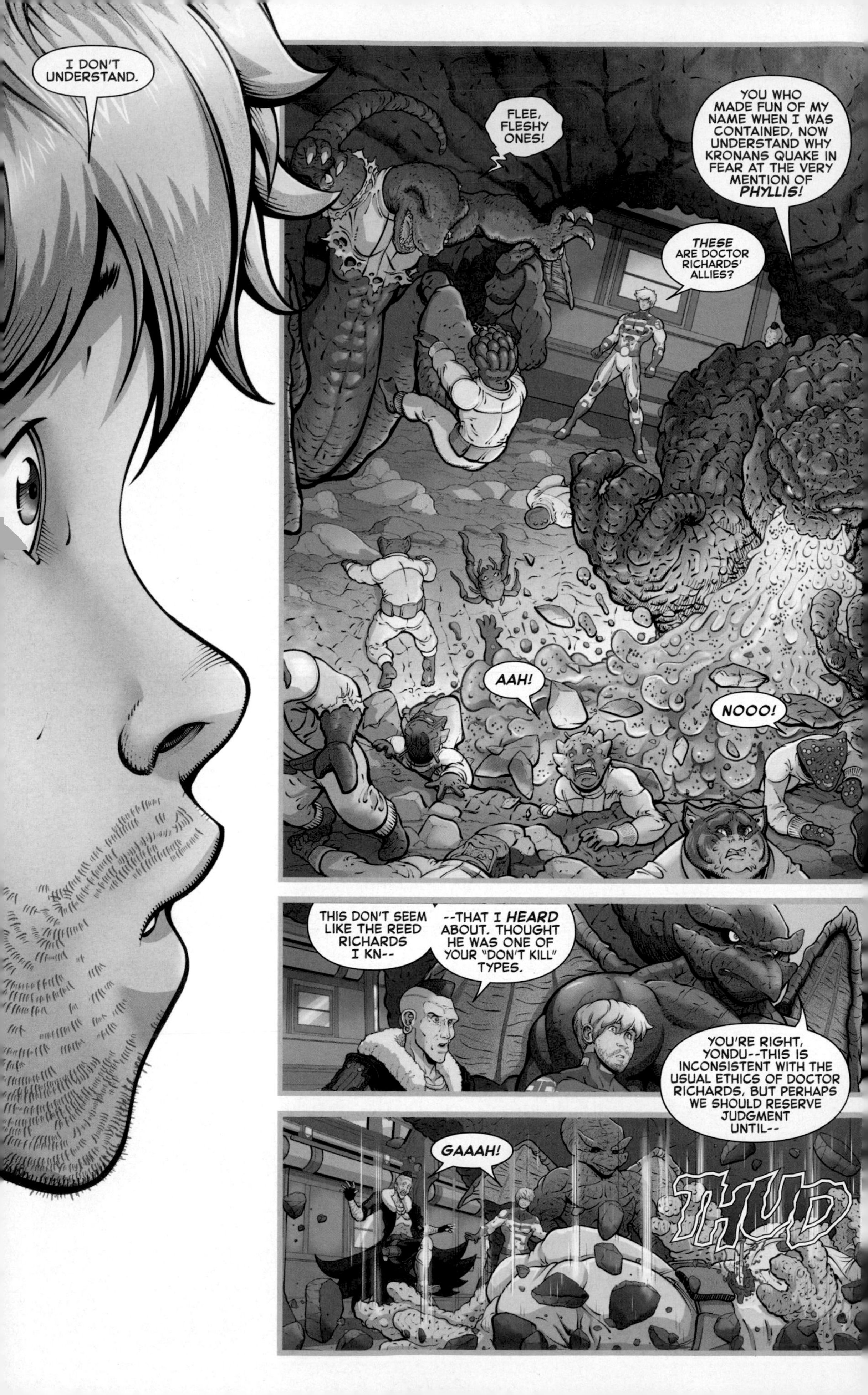
I DON'T UNDERSTAND.
FLEE, FLESHY ONES!
YOU WHO MADE FUN OF MY NAME WHEN I WAS CONTAINED, NOW UNDERSTAND WHY KRONANS QUAKE IN FEAR AT THE VERY MENTION OF PHYLLIS!
THESE ARE DOCTOR RICHARDS' ALLIES?
AAH!
NOOO!
THIS DON'T SEEM LIKE THE REED RICHARDS I KN--
--THAT I HEARD ABOUT. THOUGHT HE WAS ONE OF YOUR "DON'T KILL" TYPES.
YOU'RE RIGHT, YONDU--THIS IS INCONSISTENT WITH THE USUAL ETHICS OF DOCTOR RICHARDS, BUT PERHAPS WE SHOULD RESERVE JUDGMENT UNTIL--
GAAAH!
THUD

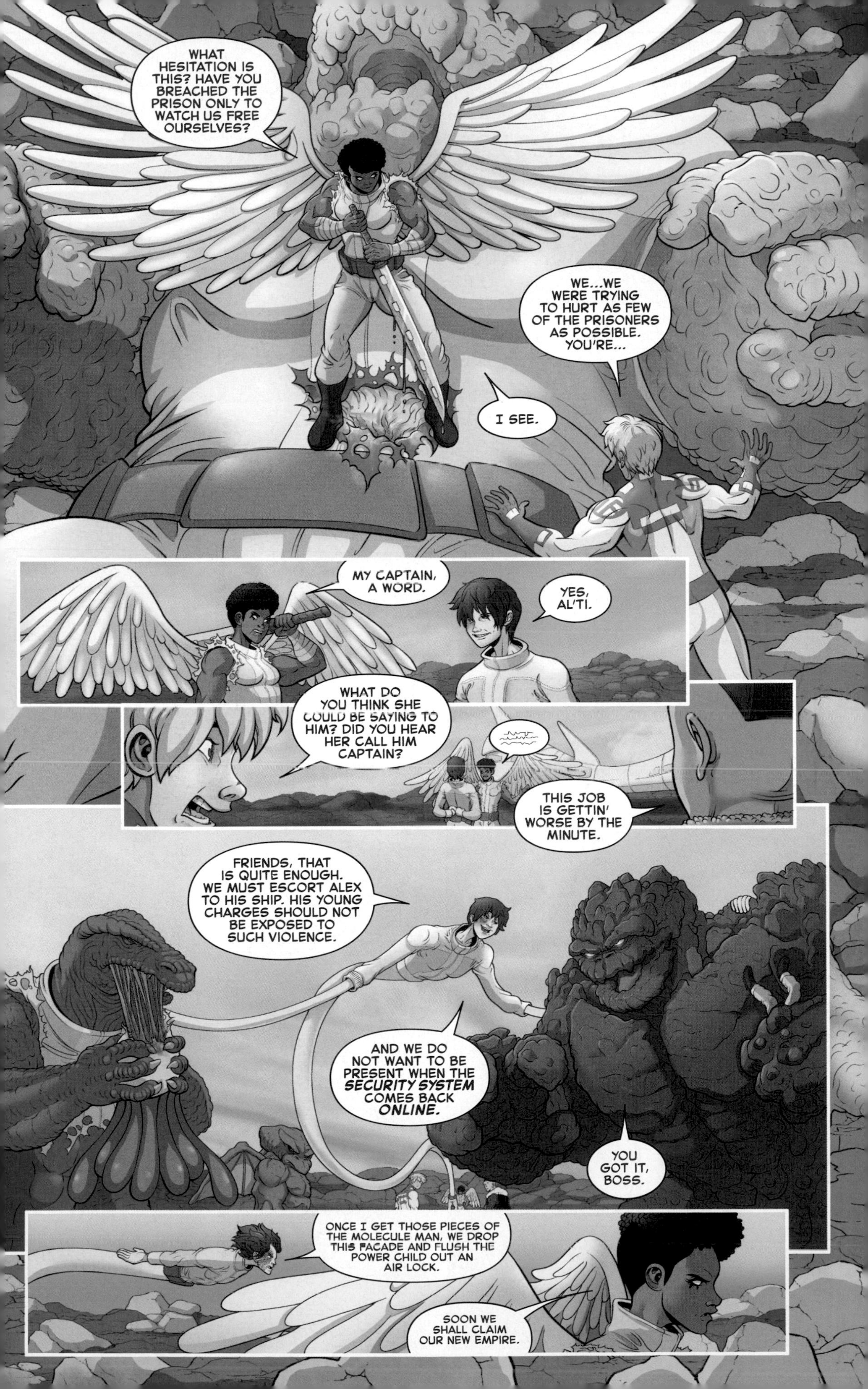
WHAT HESITATION IS THIS? HAVE YOU BREACHED THE PRISON ONLY TO WATCH US FREE OURSELVES?
WE...WE WERE TRYING TO HURT AS FEW OF THE PRISONERS AS POSSIBLE. YOU'RE...
I SEE.
MY CAPTAIN, A WORD.
YES, AL'TI.
WHAT DO YOU THINK SHE COULD BE SAYING TO HIM? DID YOU HEAR HER CALL HIM CAPTAIN?
THIS JOB IS GETTIN' WORSE BY THE MINUTE.
FRIENDS, THAT IS QUITE ENOUGH. WE MUST ESCORT ALEX TO HIS SHIP. HIS YOUNG CHARGES SHOULD NOT BE EXPOSED TO SUCH VIOLENCE.
AND WE DO NOT WANT TO BE PRESENT WHEN THE *SECURITY SYSTEM* COMES BACK *ONLINE.*
YOU GOT IT, BOSS.
ONCE I GET THOSE PIECES OF THE MOLECULE MAN, WE DROP THIS FACADE AND FLUSH THE POWER CHILD OUT AN AIR LOCK.
SOON WE SHALL CLAIM OUR NEW EMPIRE.

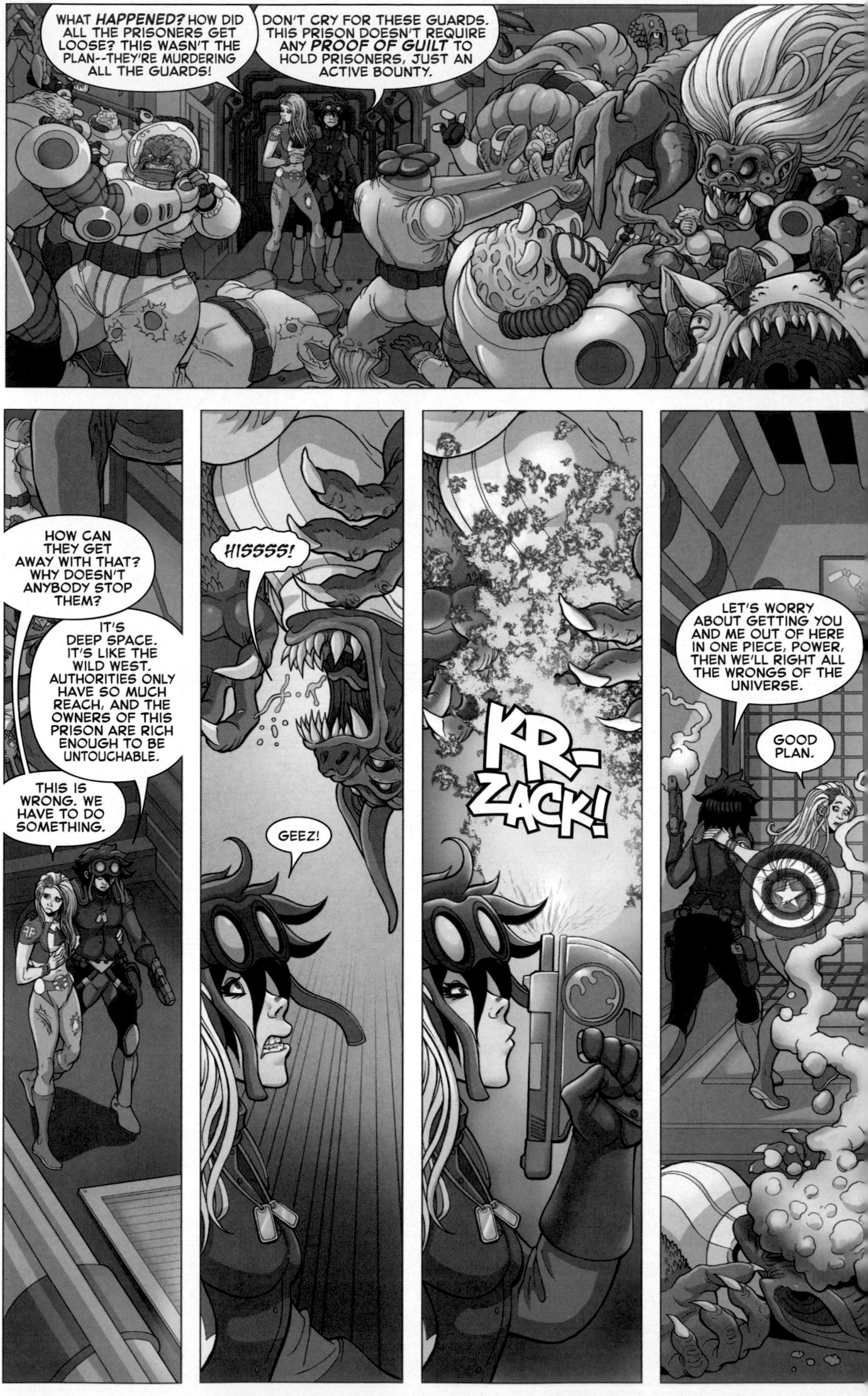
WHAT HAPPENED? HOW DID ALL THE PRISONERS GET LOOSE? THIS WASN'T THE PLAN--THEY'RE MURDERING ALL THE GUARDS!
DON'T CRY FOR THESE GUARDS. THIS PRISON DOESN'T REQUIRE ANY PROOF OF GUILT TO HOLD PRISONERS, JUST AN ACTIVE BOUNTY.
HOW CAN THEY GET AWAY WITH THAT? WHY DOESN'T ANYBODY STOP THEM?
IT'S DEEP SPACE. IT'S LIKE THE WILD WEST. AUTHORITIES ONLY HAVE SO MUCH REACH, AND THE OWNERS OF THIS PRISON ARE RICH ENOUGH TO BE UNTOUCHABLE.
THIS IS WRONG. WE HAVE TO DO SOMETHING.
HISSSS!
GEEZ!
KR-ZACK!
LET'S WORRY ABOUT GETTING YOU AND ME OUT OF HERE IN ONE PIECE, POWER, THEN WE'LL RIGHT ALL THE WRONGS OF THE UNIVERSE.
GOOD PLAN.

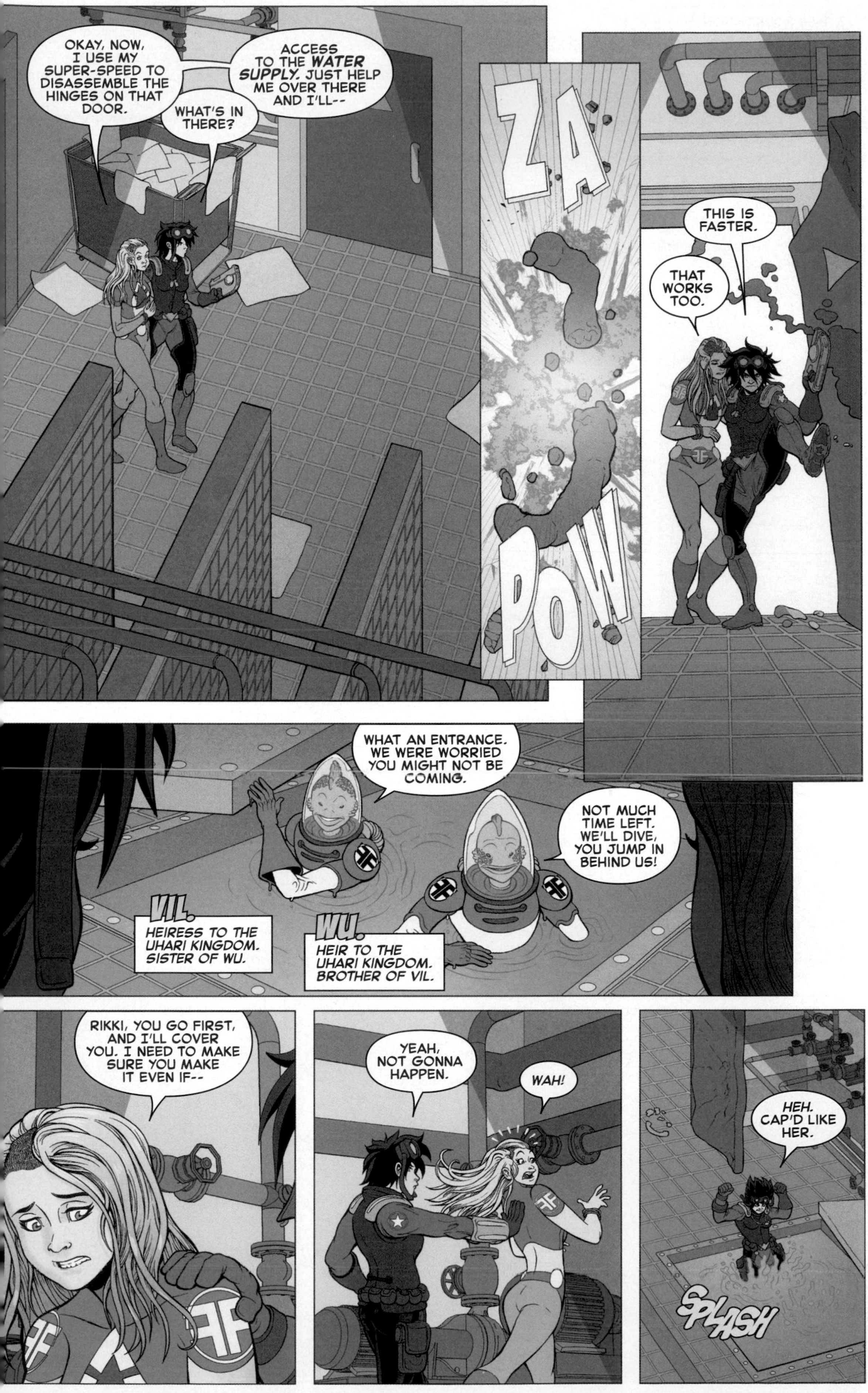
OKAY, NOW, I USE MY SUPER-SPEED TO DISASSEMBLE THE HINGES ON THAT DOOR.
WHAT'S IN THERE?
ACCESS TO THE WATER SUPPLY. JUST HELP ME OVER THERE AND I'LL--
ZA
POW
THIS IS FASTER.
THAT WORKS TOO.
WHAT AN ENTRANCE. WE WERE WORRIED YOU MIGHT NOT BE COMING.
NOT MUCH TIME LEFT. WE'LL DIVE, YOU JUMP IN BEHIND US!
VIL. HEIRESS TO THE UHARI KINGDOM. SISTER OF WU.
WU. HEIR TO THE UHARI KINGDOM. BROTHER OF VIL.
RIKKI, YOU GO FIRST, AND I'LL COVER YOU. I NEED TO MAKE SURE YOU MAKE IT EVEN IF--
YEAH, NOT GONNA HAPPEN.
WAH!
HEH. CAP'D LIKE HER.
SPLASH

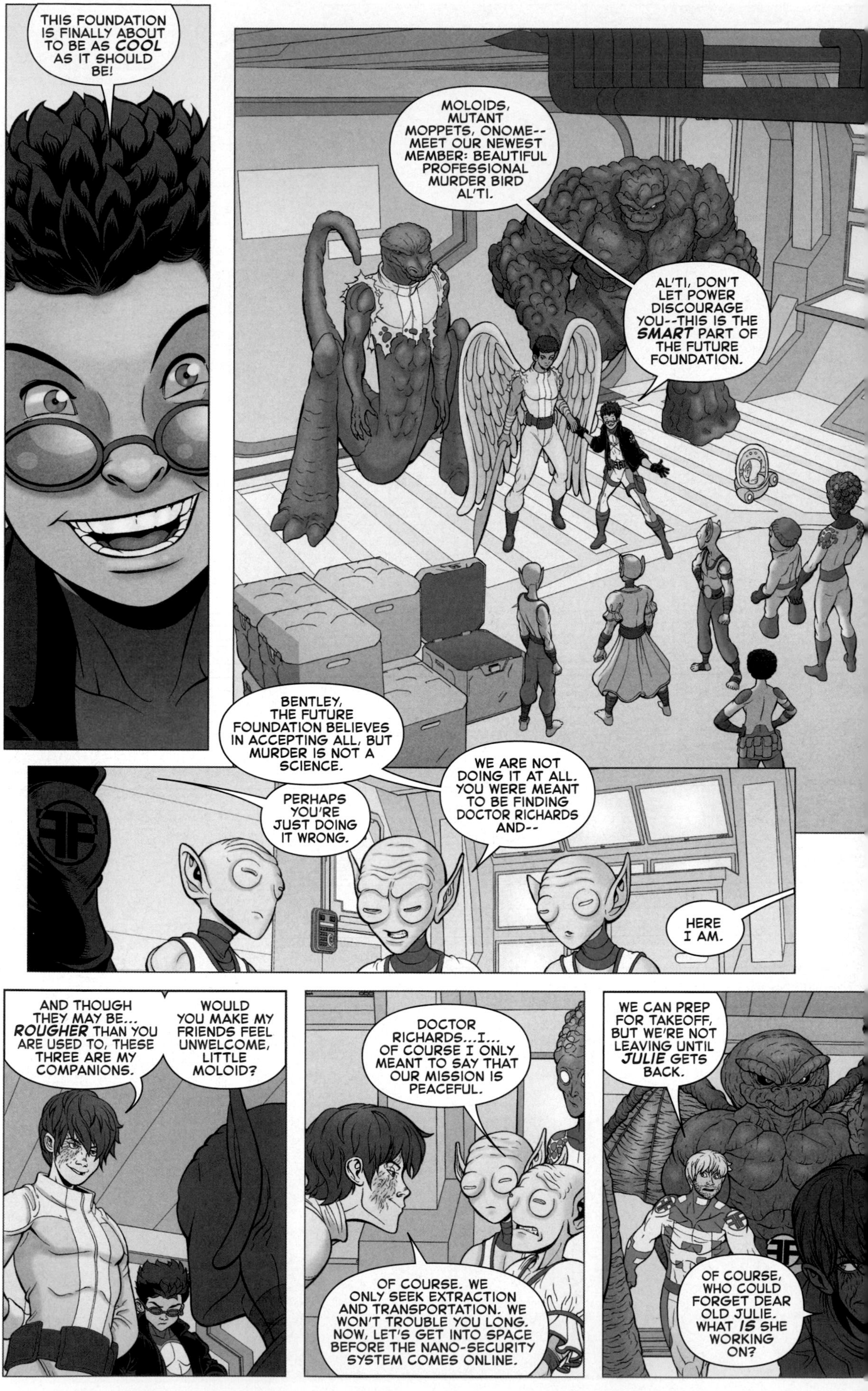
THIS FOUNDATION IS FINALLY ABOUT TO BE AS COOL AS IT SHOULD BE!
MOLOIDS, MUTANT MOPPETS, ONOME--MEET OUR NEWEST MEMBER: BEAUTIFUL PROFESSIONAL MURDER BIRD AL'TI.
AL'TI, DON'T LET POWER DISCOURAGE YOU--THIS IS THE SMART PART OF THE FUTURE FOUNDATION.
BENTLEY, THE FUTURE FOUNDATION BELIEVES IN ACCEPTING ALL, BUT MURDER IS NOT A SCIENCE.
PERHAPS YOU'RE JUST DOING IT WRONG.
WE ARE NOT DOING IT AT ALL. YOU WERE MEANT TO BE FINDING DOCTOR RICHARDS AND--
HERE I AM.
AND THOUGH THEY MAY BE... ROUGHER THAN YOU ARE USED TO, THESE THREE ARE MY COMPANIONS.
WOULD YOU MAKE MY FRIENDS FEEL UNWELCOME, LITTLE MOLOID?
DOCTOR RICHARDS...I... OF COURSE I ONLY MEANT TO SAY THAT OUR MISSION IS PEACEFUL.
OF COURSE. WE ONLY SEEK EXTRACTION AND TRANSPORTATION. WE WON'T TROUBLE YOU LONG. NOW, LET'S GET INTO SPACE BEFORE THE NANO-SECURITY SYSTEM COMES ONLINE.
WE CAN PREP FOR TAKEOFF, BUT WE'RE NOT LEAVING UNTIL JULIE GETS BACK.
OF COURSE, WHO COULD FORGET DEAR OLD JULIE. WHAT IS SHE WORKING ON?

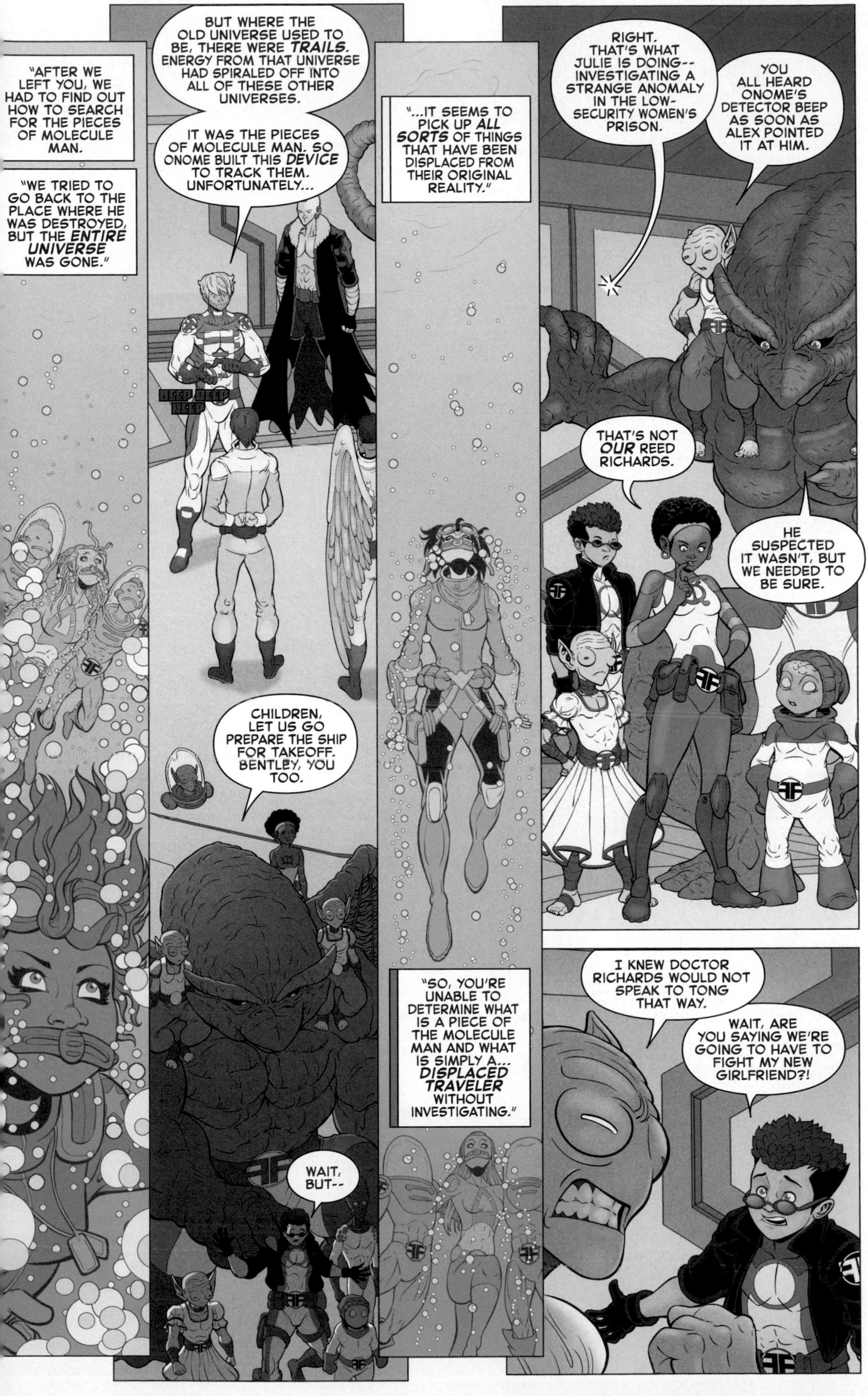
"AFTER WE LEFT YOU, WE HAD TO FIND OUT HOW TO SEARCH FOR THE PIECES OF MOLECULE MAN.
"WE TRIED TO GO BACK TO THE PLACE WHERE HE WAS DESTROYED, BUT THE ENTIRE UNIVERSE WAS GONE."
BUT WHERE THE OLD UNIVERSE USED TO BE, THERE WERE TRAILS. ENERGY FROM THAT UNIVERSE HAD SPIRALED OFF INTO ALL OF THESE OTHER UNIVERSES.
IT WAS THE PIECES OF MOLECULE MAN. SO ONOME BUILT THIS DEVICE TO TRACK THEM. UNFORTUNATELY...
BEEP BEEP BEEP
"...IT SEEMS TO PICK UP ALL SORTS OF THINGS THAT HAVE BEEN DISPLACED FROM THEIR ORIGINAL REALITY."
RIGHT. THAT'S WHAT JULIE IS DOING-- INVESTIGATING A STRANGE ANOMALY IN THE LOW-SECURITY WOMEN'S PRISON.
YOU ALL HEARD ONOME'S DETECTOR BEEP AS SOON AS ALEX POINTED IT AT HIM.
THAT'S NOT OUR REED RICHARDS.
HE SUSPECTED IT WASN'T, BUT WE NEEDED TO BE SURE.
CHILDREN, LET US GO PREPARE THE SHIP FOR TAKEOFF. BENTLEY, YOU TOO.
WAIT, BUT--
"SO, YOU'RE UNABLE TO DETERMINE WHAT IS A PIECE OF THE MOLECULE MAN AND WHAT IS SIMPLY A... DISPLACED TRAVELER WITHOUT INVESTIGATING."
I KNEW DOCTOR RICHARDS WOULD NOT SPEAK TO TONG THAT WAY.
WAIT, ARE YOU SAYING WE'RE GOING TO HAVE TO FIGHT MY NEW GIRLFRIEND?!

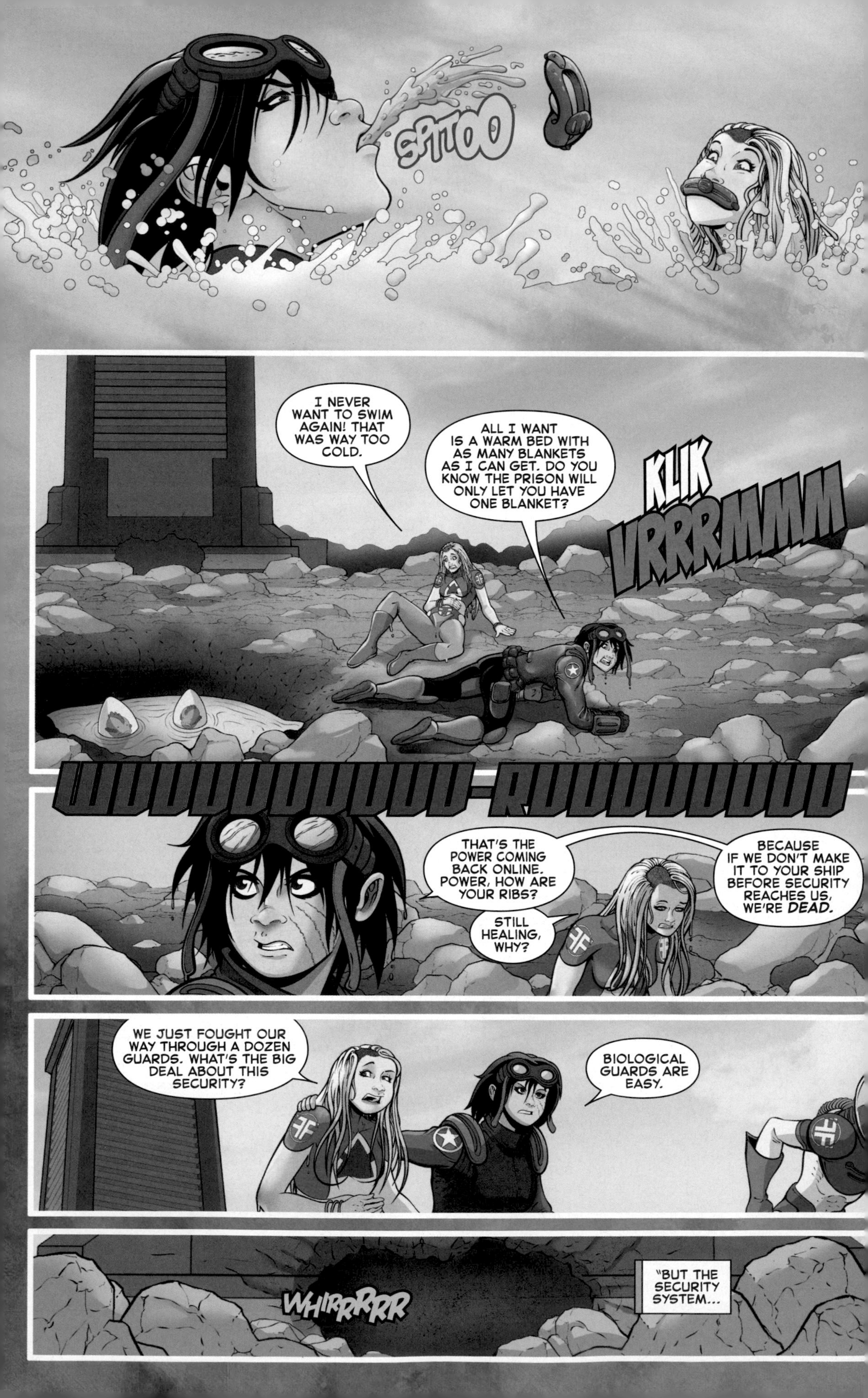
SPTOO
I NEVER WANT TO SWIM AGAIN! THAT WAS WAY TOO COLD.
ALL I WANT IS A WARM BED WITH AS MANY BLANKETS AS I CAN GET. DO YOU KNOW THE PRISON WILL ONLY LET YOU HAVE ONE BLANKET?
KLIK
VRRRMMM
WUUUUUUUUUU-RUUUUUUUUU
THAT'S THE POWER COMING BACK ONLINE. POWER, HOW ARE YOUR RIBS?
STILL HEALING, WHY?
BECAUSE IF WE DON'T MAKE IT TO YOUR SHIP BEFORE SECURITY REACHES US, WE'RE *DEAD.*
WE JUST FOUGHT OUR WAY THROUGH A DOZEN GUARDS. WHAT'S THE BIG DEAL ABOUT THIS SECURITY?
BIOLOGICAL GUARDS ARE EASY.
WHIRRRRR
"BUT THE SECURITY SYSTEM...

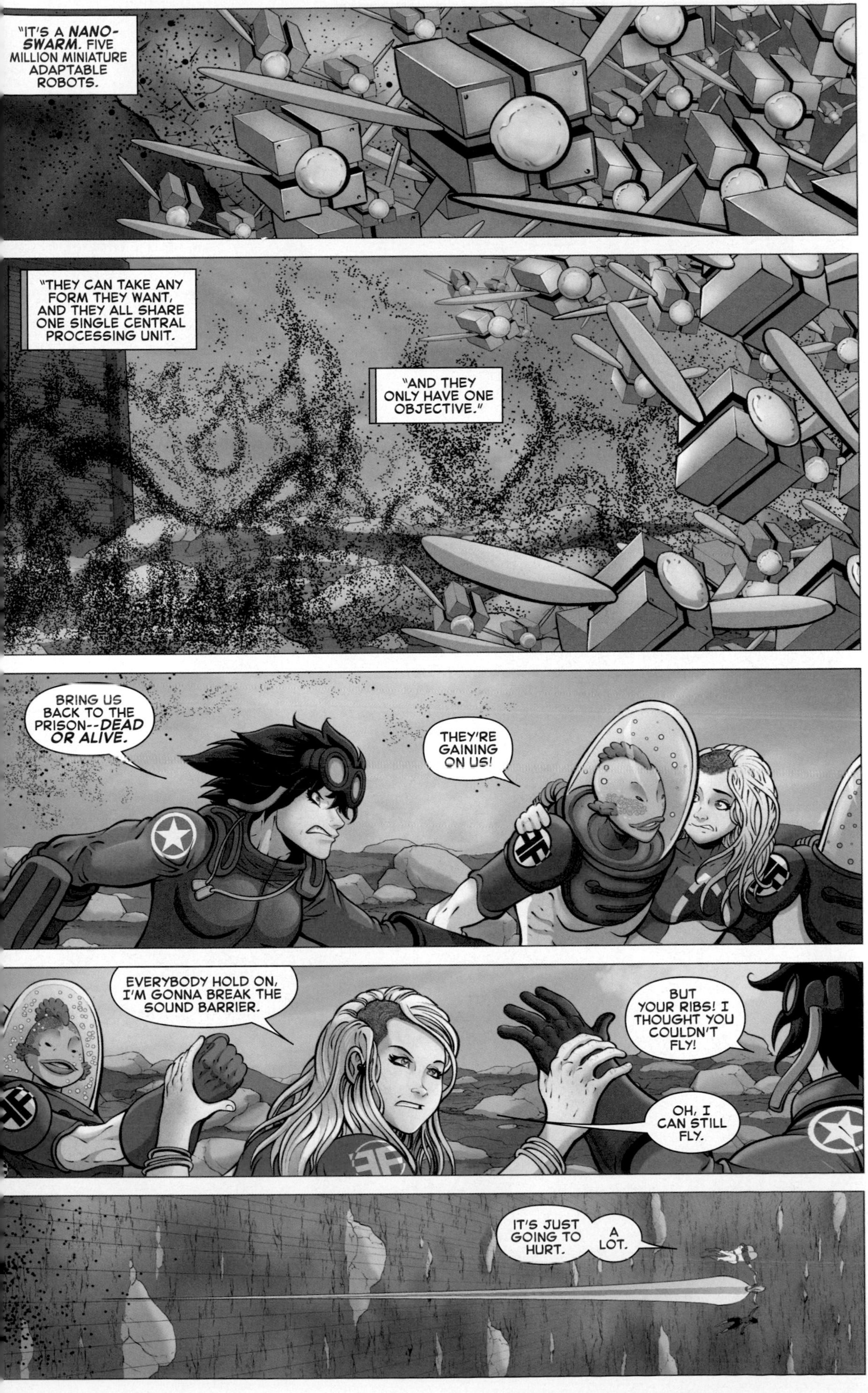
"IT'S A NANO-SWARM. FIVE MILLION MINIATURE ADAPTABLE ROBOTS.
"THEY CAN TAKE ANY FORM THEY WANT, AND THEY ALL SHARE ONE SINGLE CENTRAL PROCESSING UNIT.
"AND THEY ONLY HAVE ONE OBJECTIVE."
BRING US BACK TO THE PRISON--DEAD OR ALIVE.
THEY'RE GAINING ON US!
EVERYBODY HOLD ON, I'M GONNA BREAK THE SOUND BARRIER.
BUT YOUR RIBS! I THOUGHT YOU COULDN'T FLY!
OH, I CAN STILL FLY.
IT'S JUST GOING TO HURT.
A LOT.

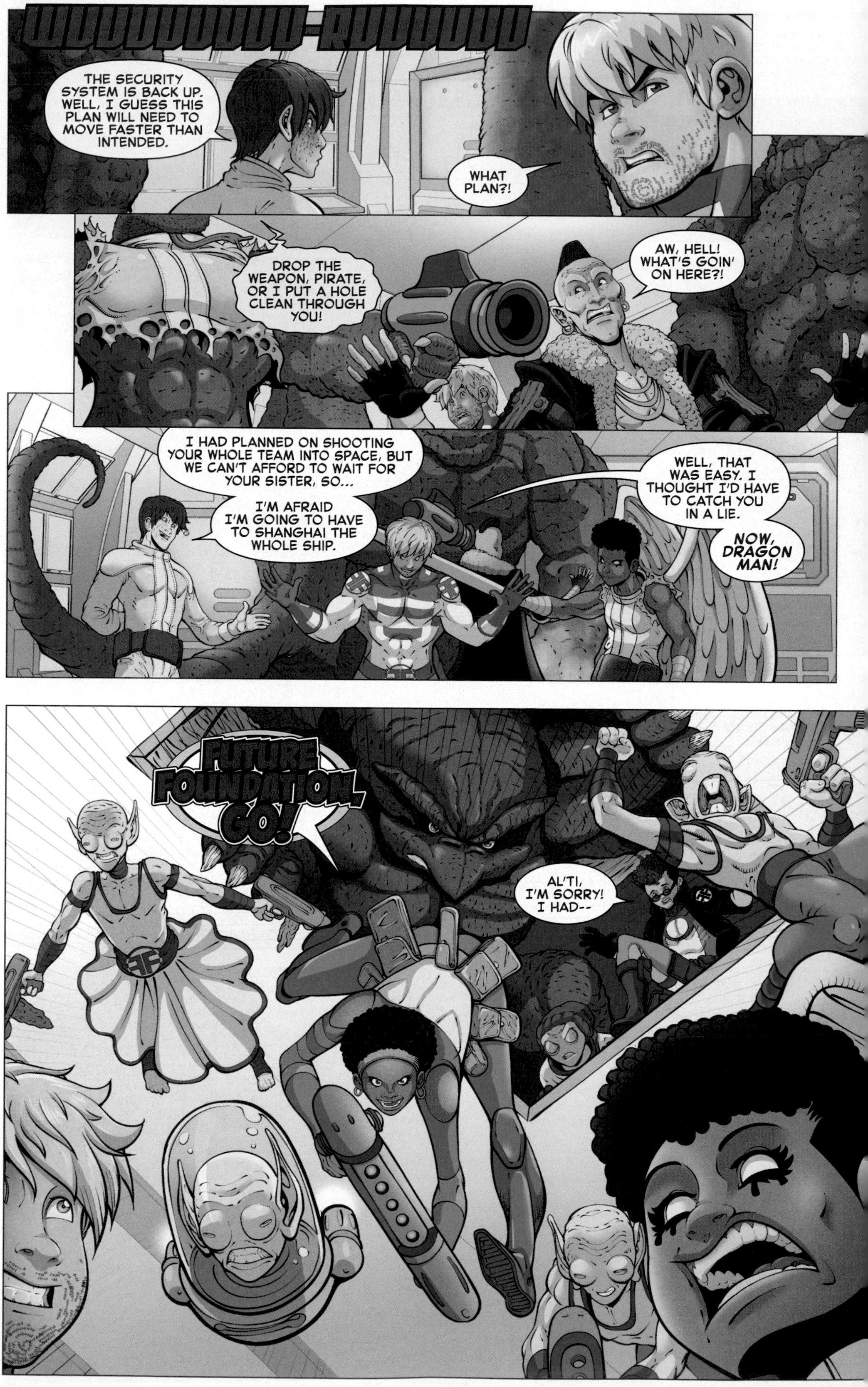
WUUUUUUUU-RUUUUUU
THE SECURITY SYSTEM IS BACK UP. WELL, I GUESS THIS PLAN WILL NEED TO MOVE FASTER THAN INTENDED.
WHAT PLAN?!
DROP THE WEAPON, PIRATE, OR I PUT A HOLE CLEAN THROUGH YOU!
AW, HELL! WHAT'S GOIN' ON HERE?!
I HAD PLANNED ON SHOOTING YOUR WHOLE TEAM INTO SPACE, BUT WE CAN'T AFFORD TO WAIT FOR YOUR SISTER, SO...
I'M AFRAID I'M GOING TO HAVE TO SHANGHAI THE WHOLE SHIP.
WELL, THAT WAS EASY. I THOUGHT I'D HAVE TO CATCH YOU IN A LIE.
NOW, DRAGON MAN!
FUTURE FOUNDATION, GO!
AL'TI, I'M SORRY! I HAD--

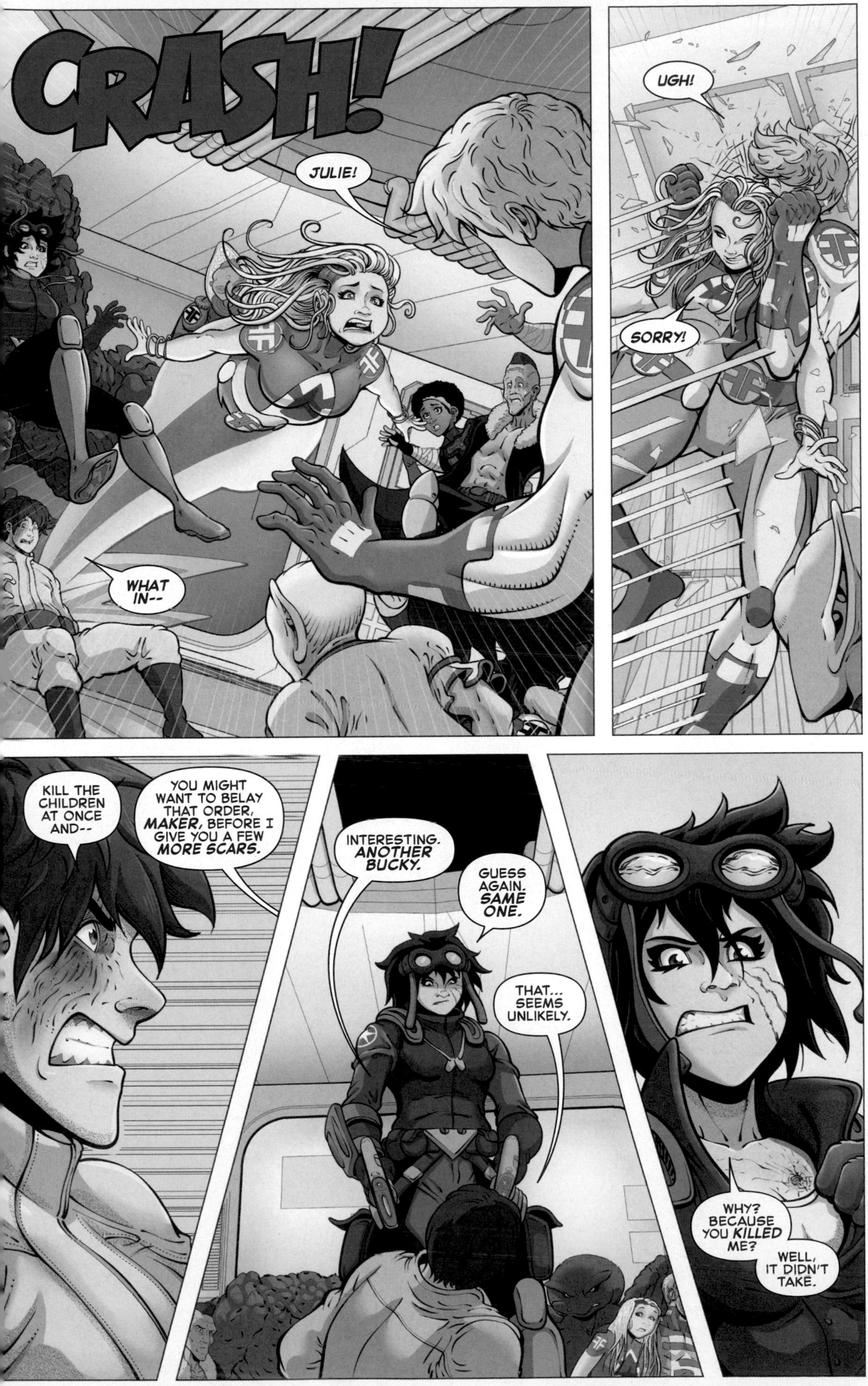
CRASH!
JULIE!
WHAT IN--
UGH!
SORRY!
KILL THE CHILDREN AT ONCE AND--
YOU MIGHT WANT TO BELAY THAT ORDER, MAKER, BEFORE I GIVE YOU A FEW MORE SCARS.
INTERESTING. ANOTHER BUCKY.
GUESS AGAIN. SAME ONE.
THAT... SEEMS UNLIKELY.
WHY? BECAUSE YOU KILLED ME?
WELL, IT DIDN'T TAKE.

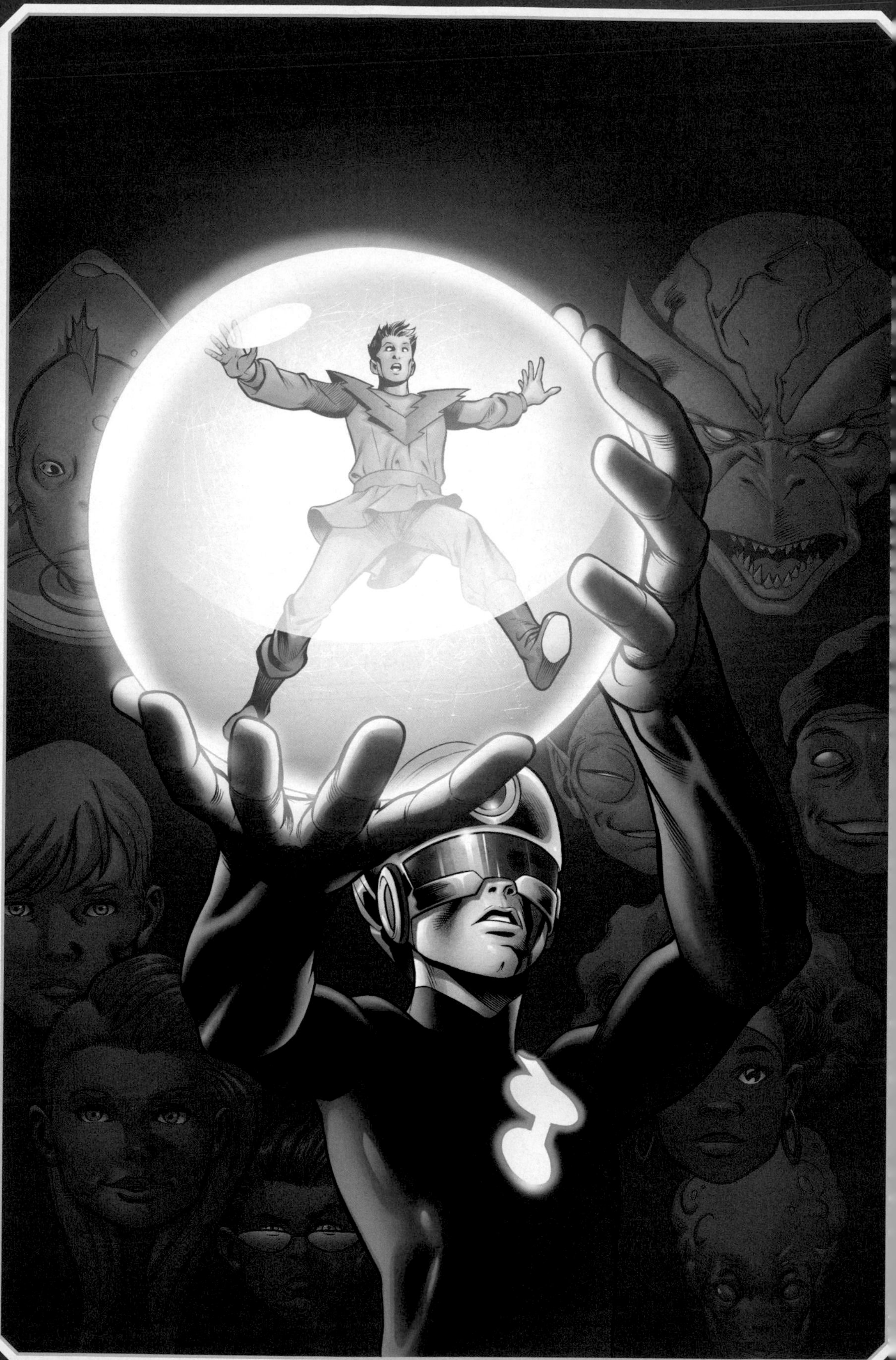

THREE

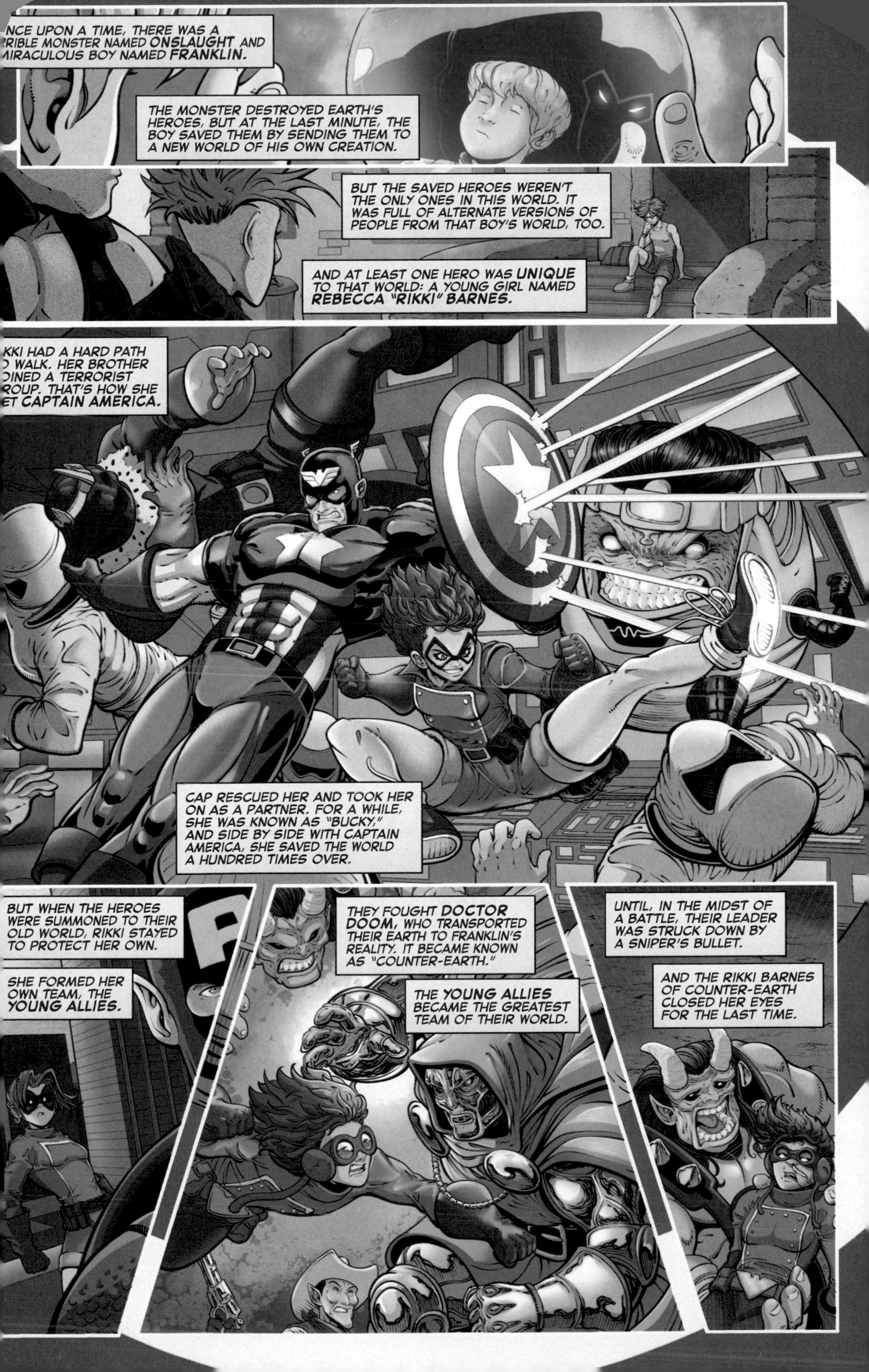
NCE UPON A TIME, THERE WAS A RRIBLE MONSTER NAMED ONSLAUGHT AND MIRACULOUS BOY NAMED FRANKLIN.
THE MONSTER DESTROYED EARTH'S HEROES, BUT AT THE LAST MINUTE, THE BOY SAVED THEM BY SENDING THEM TO A NEW WORLD OF HIS OWN CREATION.
BUT THE SAVED HEROES WEREN'T THE ONLY ONES IN THIS WORLD. IT WAS FULL OF ALTERNATE VERSIONS OF PEOPLE FROM THAT BOY'S WORLD, TOO.
AND AT LEAST ONE HERO WAS UNIQUE TO THAT WORLD: A YOUNG GIRL NAMED REBECCA "RIKKI" BARNES.
KKI HAD A HARD PATH WALK. HER BROTHER OINED A TERRORIST ROUP. THAT'S HOW SHE ET CAPTAIN AMERICA.
CAP RESCUED HER AND TOOK HER ON AS A PARTNER. FOR A WHILE, SHE WAS KNOWN AS "BUCKY," AND SIDE BY SIDE WITH CAPTAIN AMERICA, SHE SAVED THE WORLD A HUNDRED TIMES OVER.
BUT WHEN THE HEROES WERE SUMMONED TO THEIR OLD WORLD, RIKKI STAYED TO PROTECT HER OWN.
SHE FORMED HER OWN TEAM, THE YOUNG ALLIES.
THEY FOUGHT DOCTOR DOOM, WHO TRANSPORTED THEIR EARTH TO FRANKLIN'S REALITY. IT BECAME KNOWN AS "COUNTER-EARTH."
THE YOUNG ALLIES BECAME THE GREATEST TEAM OF THEIR WORLD.
UNTIL, IN THE MIDST OF A BATTLE, THEIR LEADER WAS STRUCK DOWN BY A SNIPER'S BULLET.
AND THE RIKKI BARNES OF COUNTER-EARTH CLOSED HER EYES FOR THE LAST TIME.

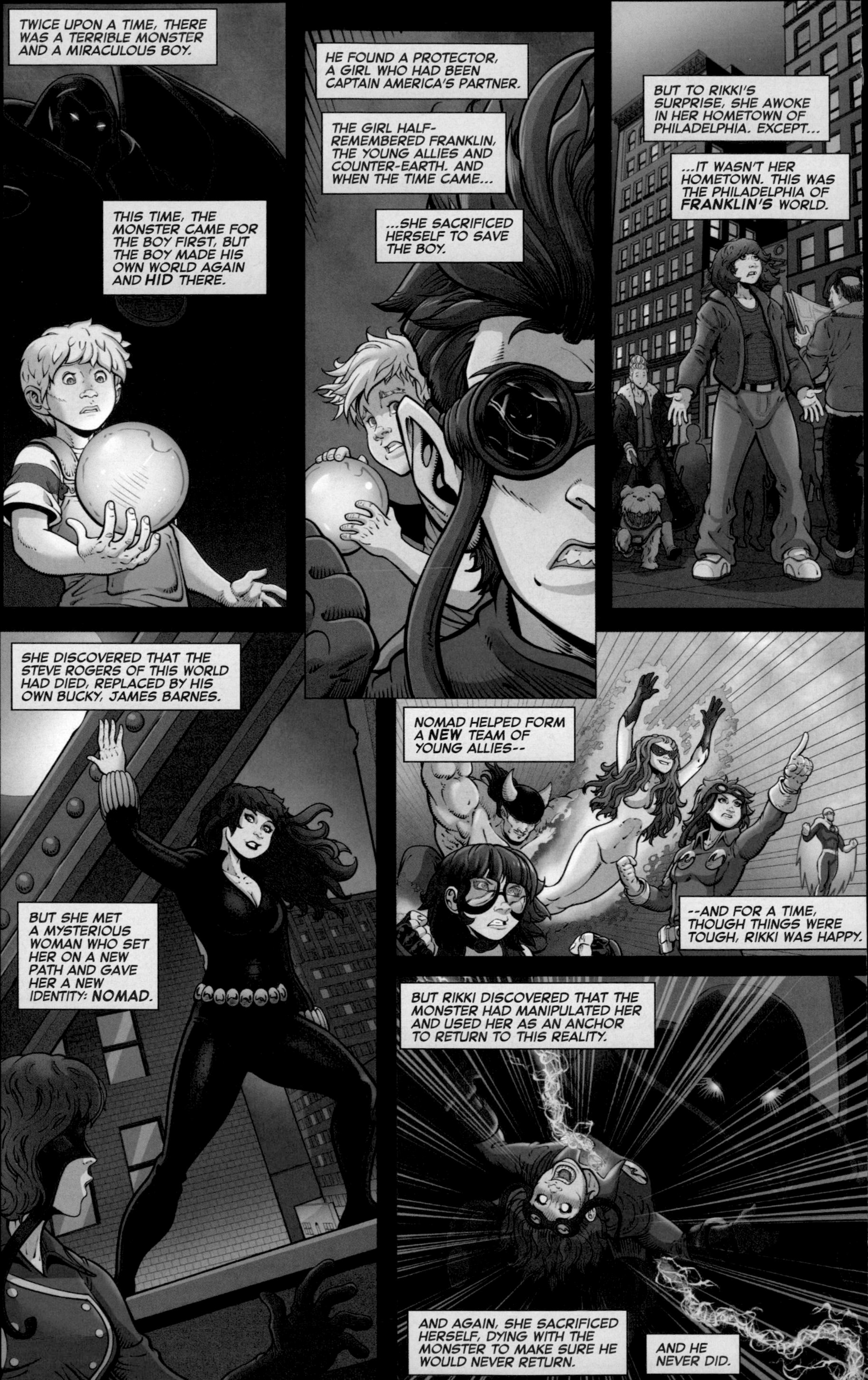

TWICE UPON A TIME, THERE WAS A TERRIBLE MONSTER AND A MIRACULOUS BOY.
THIS TIME, THE MONSTER CAME FOR THE BOY FIRST, BUT THE BOY MADE HIS OWN WORLD AGAIN AND HID THERE.
HE FOUND A PROTECTOR, A GIRL WHO HAD BEEN CAPTAIN AMERICA'S PARTNER.
THE GIRL HALF-REMEMBERED FRANKLIN, THE YOUNG ALLIES AND COUNTER-EARTH. AND WHEN THE TIME CAME...
...SHE SACRIFICED HERSELF TO SAVE THE BOY.
BUT TO RIKKI'S SURPRISE, SHE AWOKE IN HER HOMETOWN OF PHILADELPHIA. EXCEPT...
...IT WASN'T HER HOMETOWN. THIS WAS THE PHILADELPHIA OF FRANKLIN'S WORLD.
SHE DISCOVERED THAT THE STEVE ROGERS OF THIS WORLD HAD DIED, REPLACED BY HIS OWN BUCKY, JAMES BARNES.
BUT SHE MET A MYSTERIOUS WOMAN WHO SET HER ON A NEW PATH AND GAVE HER A NEW IDENTITY: NOMAD.
NOMAD HELPED FORM A NEW TEAM OF YOUNG ALLIES--
--AND FOR A TIME, THOUGH THINGS WERE TOUGH, RIKKI WAS HAPPY.
BUT RIKKI DISCOVERED THAT THE MONSTER HAD MANIPULATED HER AND USED HER AS AN ANCHOR TO RETURN TO THIS REALITY.
AND AGAIN, SHE SACRIFICED HERSELF, DYING WITH THE MONSTER TO MAKE SURE HE WOULD NEVER RETURN.
AND HE NEVER DID.

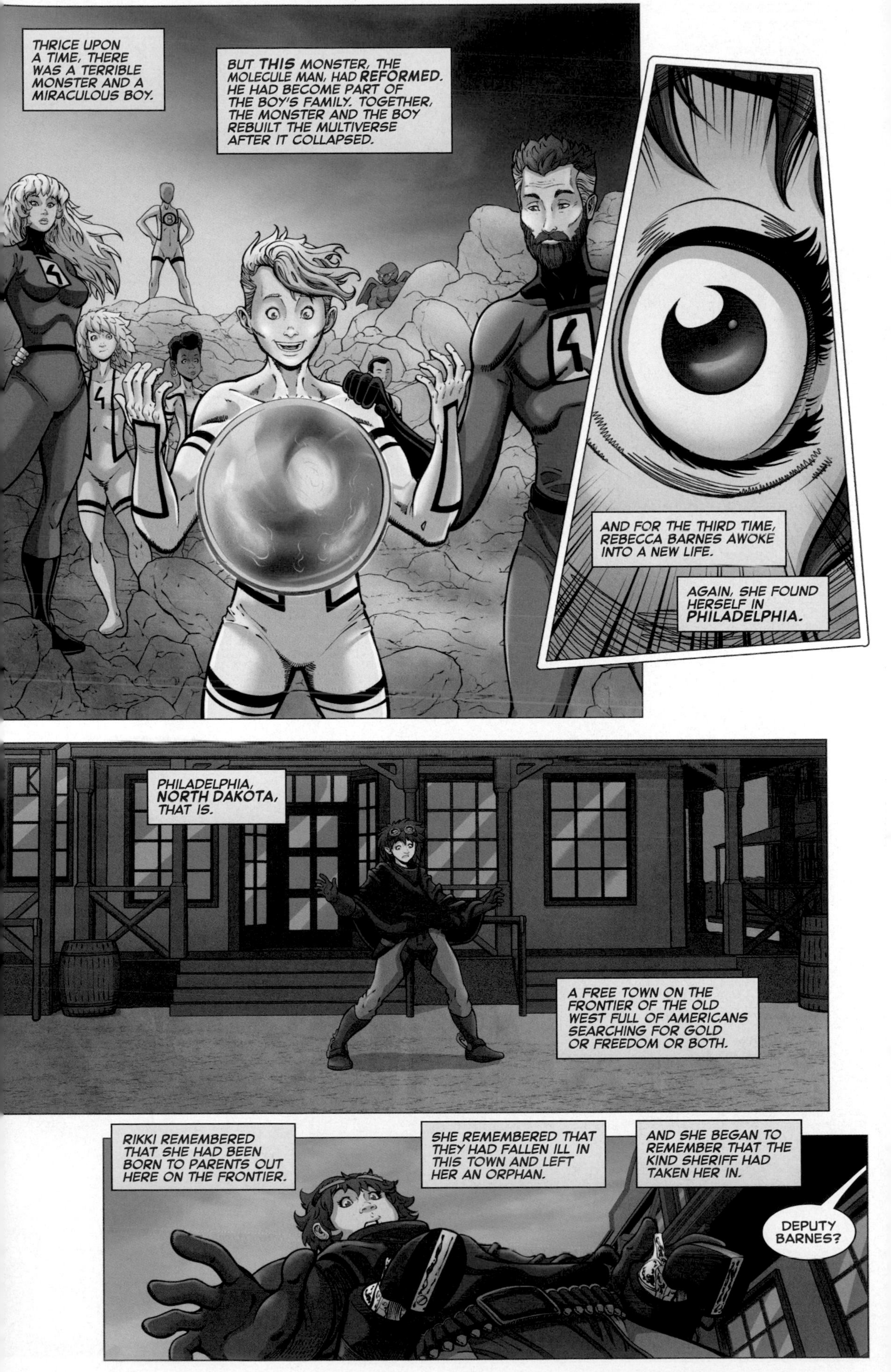
THRICE UPON A TIME, THERE WAS A TERRIBLE MONSTER AND A MIRACULOUS BOY.
BUT THIS MONSTER, THE MOLECULE MAN, HAD REFORMED. HE HAD BECOME PART OF THE BOY'S FAMILY. TOGETHER, THE MONSTER AND THE BOY REBUILT THE MULTIVERSE AFTER IT COLLAPSED.
AND FOR THE THIRD TIME, REBECCA BARNES AWOKE INTO A NEW LIFE.
AGAIN, SHE FOUND HERSELF IN PHILADELPHIA.
PHILADELPHIA, NORTH DAKOTA, THAT IS.
A FREE TOWN ON THE FRONTIER OF THE OLD WEST FULL OF AMERICANS SEARCHING FOR GOLD OR FREEDOM OR BOTH.
RIKKI REMEMBERED THAT SHE HAD BEEN BORN TO PARENTS OUT HERE ON THE FRONTIER.
SHE REMEMBERED THAT THEY HAD FALLEN ILL IN THIS TOWN AND LEFT HER AN ORPHAN.
AND SHE BEGAN TO REMEMBER THAT THE KIND SHERIFF HAD TAKEN HER IN.
DEPUTY BARNES?

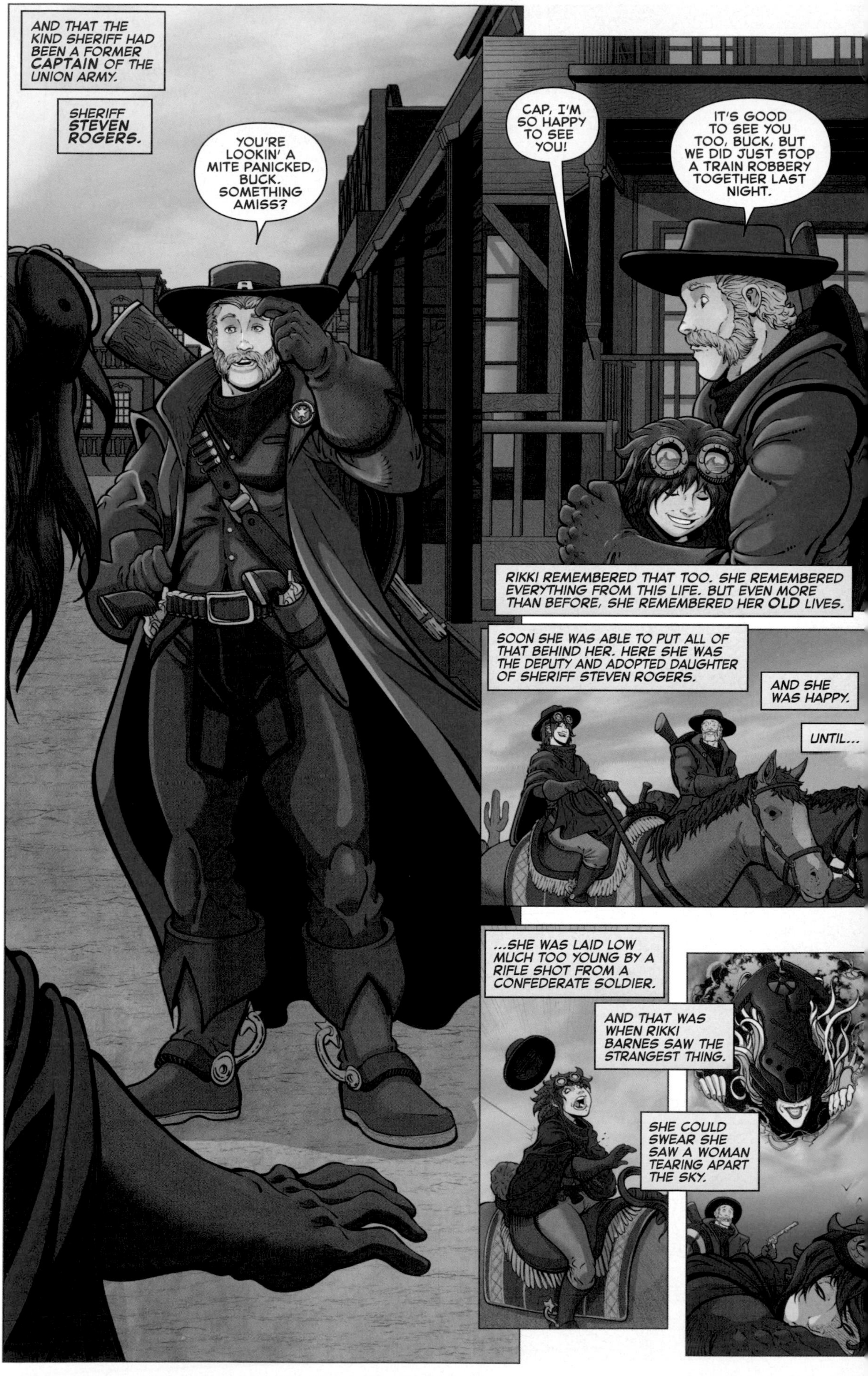
AND THAT THE KIND SHERIFF HAD BEEN A FORMER CAPTAIN OF THE UNION ARMY.
SHERIFF STEVEN ROGERS.
YOU'RE LOOKIN' A MITE PANICKED, BUCK. SOMETHING AMISS?
CAP, I'M SO HAPPY TO SEE YOU!
IT'S GOOD TO SEE YOU TOO, BUCK, BUT WE DID JUST STOP A TRAIN ROBBERY TOGETHER LAST NIGHT.
RIKKI REMEMBERED THAT TOO. SHE REMEMBERED EVERYTHING FROM THIS LIFE. BUT EVEN MORE THAN BEFORE, SHE REMEMBERED HER OLD LIVES.
SOON SHE WAS ABLE TO PUT ALL OF THAT BEHIND HER. HERE SHE WAS THE DEPUTY AND ADOPTED DAUGHTER OF SHERIFF STEVEN ROGERS.
AND SHE WAS HAPPY.
UNTIL...
...SHE WAS LAID LOW MUCH TOO YOUNG BY A RIFLE SHOT FROM A CONFEDERATE SOLDIER.
AND THAT WAS WHEN RIKKI BARNES SAW THE STRANGEST THING.
SHE COULD SWEAR SHE SAW A WOMAN TEARING APART THE SKY.

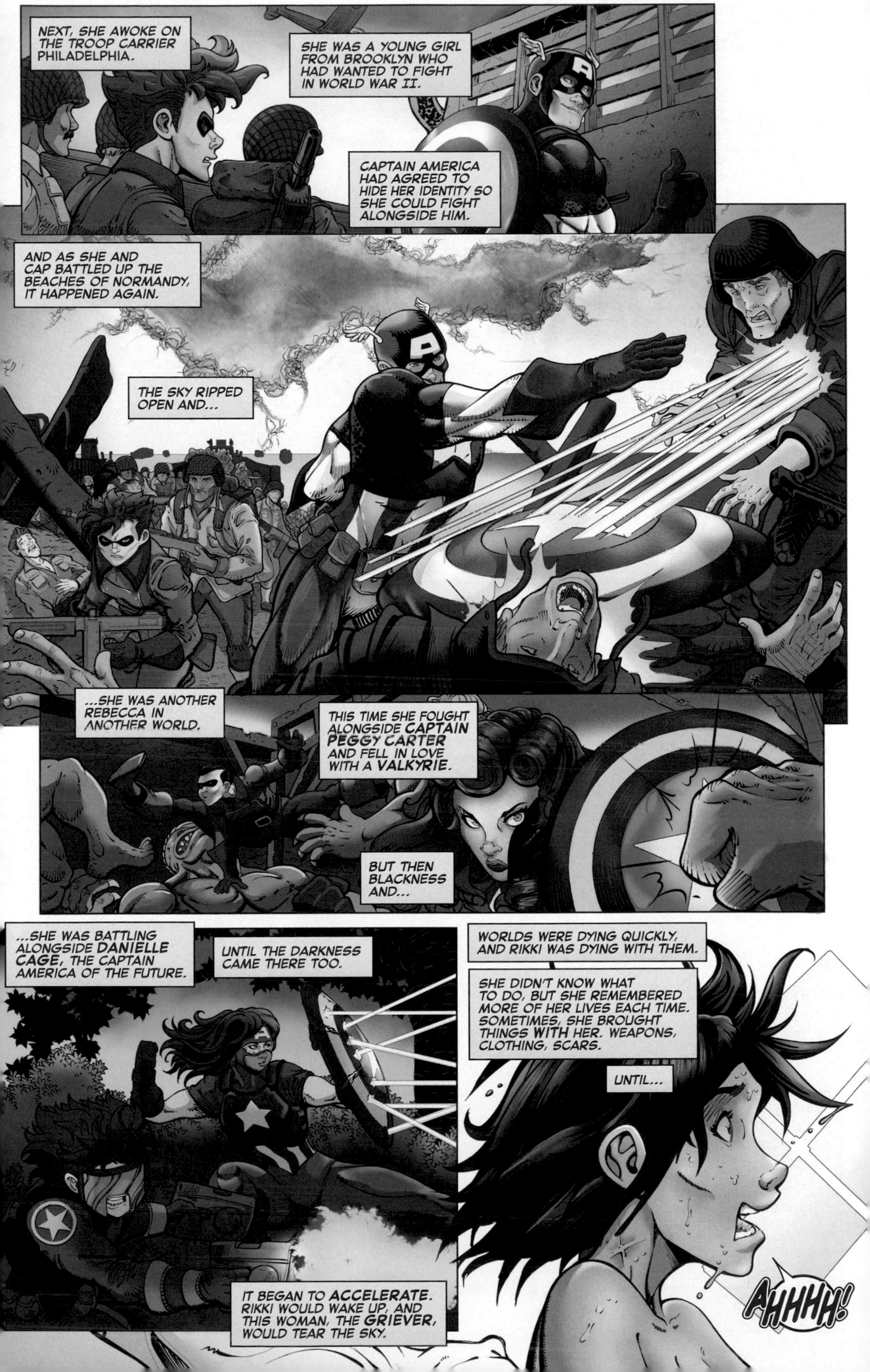
NEXT, SHE AWOKE ON THE TROOP CARRIER PHILADELPHIA.
SHE WAS A YOUNG GIRL FROM BROOKLYN WHO HAD WANTED TO FIGHT IN WORLD WAR II.
CAPTAIN AMERICA HAD AGREED TO HIDE HER IDENTITY SO SHE COULD FIGHT ALONGSIDE HIM.
AND AS SHE AND CAP BATTLED UP THE BEACHES OF NORMANDY, IT HAPPENED AGAIN.
THE SKY RIPPED OPEN AND...
...SHE WAS ANOTHER REBECCA IN ANOTHER WORLD.
THIS TIME SHE FOUGHT ALONGSIDE CAPTAIN PEGGY CARTER AND FELL IN LOVE WITH A VALKYRIE.
BUT THEN BLACKNESS AND...
...SHE WAS BATTLING ALONGSIDE DANIELLE CAGE, THE CAPTAIN AMERICA OF THE FUTURE.
UNTIL THE DARKNESS CAME THERE TOO.
IT BEGAN TO ACCELERATE. RIKKI WOULD WAKE UP, AND THIS WOMAN, THE GRIEVER, WOULD TEAR THE SKY.
WORLDS WERE DYING QUICKLY, AND RIKKI WAS DYING WITH THEM.
SHE DIDN'T KNOW WHAT TO DO, BUT SHE REMEMBERED MORE OF HER LIVES EACH TIME. SOMETIMES, SHE BROUGHT THINGS WITH HER. WEAPONS, CLOTHING, SCARS.
UNTIL...
AHHHH!

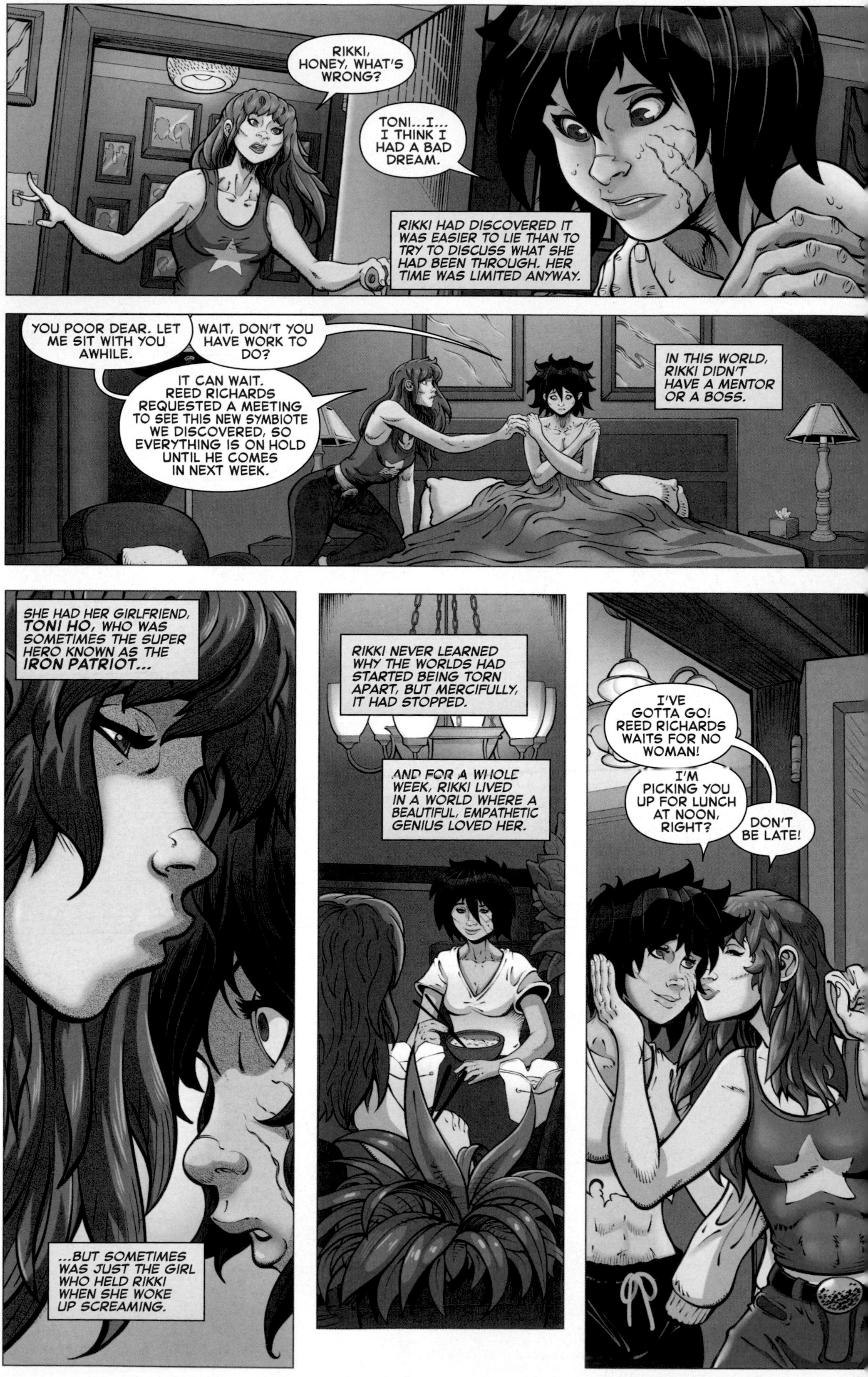
RIKKI, HONEY, WHAT'S WRONG?
TONI...I... I THINK I HAD A BAD DREAM.
RIKKI HAD DISCOVERED IT WAS EASIER TO LIE THAN TO TRY TO DISCUSS WHAT SHE HAD BEEN THROUGH. HER TIME WAS LIMITED ANYWAY.
YOU POOR DEAR. LET ME SIT WITH YOU AWHILE.
WAIT, DON'T YOU HAVE WORK TO DO?
IT CAN WAIT. REED RICHARDS REQUESTED A MEETING TO SEE THIS NEW SYMBIOTE WE DISCOVERED, SO EVERYTHING IS ON HOLD UNTIL HE COMES IN NEXT WEEK.
IN THIS WORLD, RIKKI DIDN'T HAVE A MENTOR OR A BOSS.
SHE HAD HER GIRLFRIEND, TONI HO, WHO WAS SOMETIMES THE SUPER HERO KNOWN AS THE IRON PATRIOT...
...BUT SOMETIMES WAS JUST THE GIRL WHO HELD RIKKI WHEN SHE WOKE UP SCREAMING.
RIKKI NEVER LEARNED WHY THE WORLDS HAD STARTED BEING TORN APART, BUT MERCIFULLY, IT HAD STOPPED.
AND FOR A WHOLE WEEK, RIKKI LIVED IN A WORLD WHERE A BEAUTIFUL, EMPATHETIC GENIUS LOVED HER.
I'VE GOTTA GO! REED RICHARDS WAITS FOR NO WOMAN!
I'M PICKING YOU UP FOR LUNCH AT NOON, RIGHT?
DON'T BE LATE!

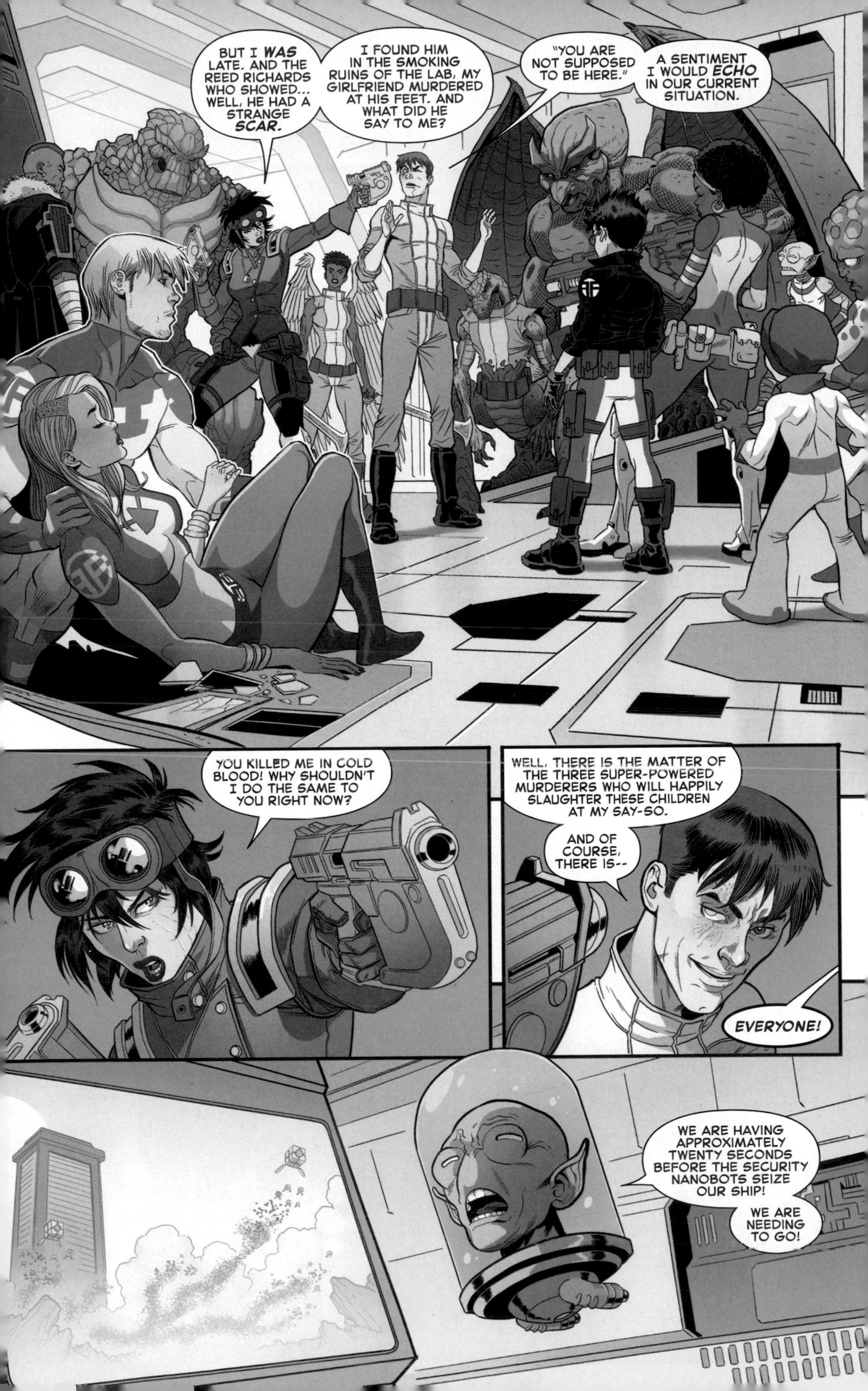
BUT I WAS LATE. AND THE REED RICHARDS WHO SHOWED... WELL, HE HAD A STRANGE SCAR.
I FOUND HIM IN THE SMOKING RUINS OF THE LAB, MY GIRLFRIEND MURDERED AT HIS FEET. AND WHAT DID HE SAY TO ME?
"YOU ARE NOT SUPPOSED TO BE HERE."
A SENTIMENT I WOULD ECHO IN OUR CURRENT SITUATION.
YOU KILLED ME IN COLD BLOOD! WHY SHOULDN'T I DO THE SAME TO YOU RIGHT NOW?
WELL, THERE IS THE MATTER OF THE THREE SUPER-POWERED MURDERERS WHO WILL HAPPILY SLAUGHTER THESE CHILDREN AT MY SAY-SO.
AND OF COURSE, THERE IS--
EVERYONE!
WE ARE HAVING APPROXIMATELY TWENTY SECONDS BEFORE THE SECURITY NANOBOTS SEIZE OUR SHIP!
WE ARE NEEDING TO GO!

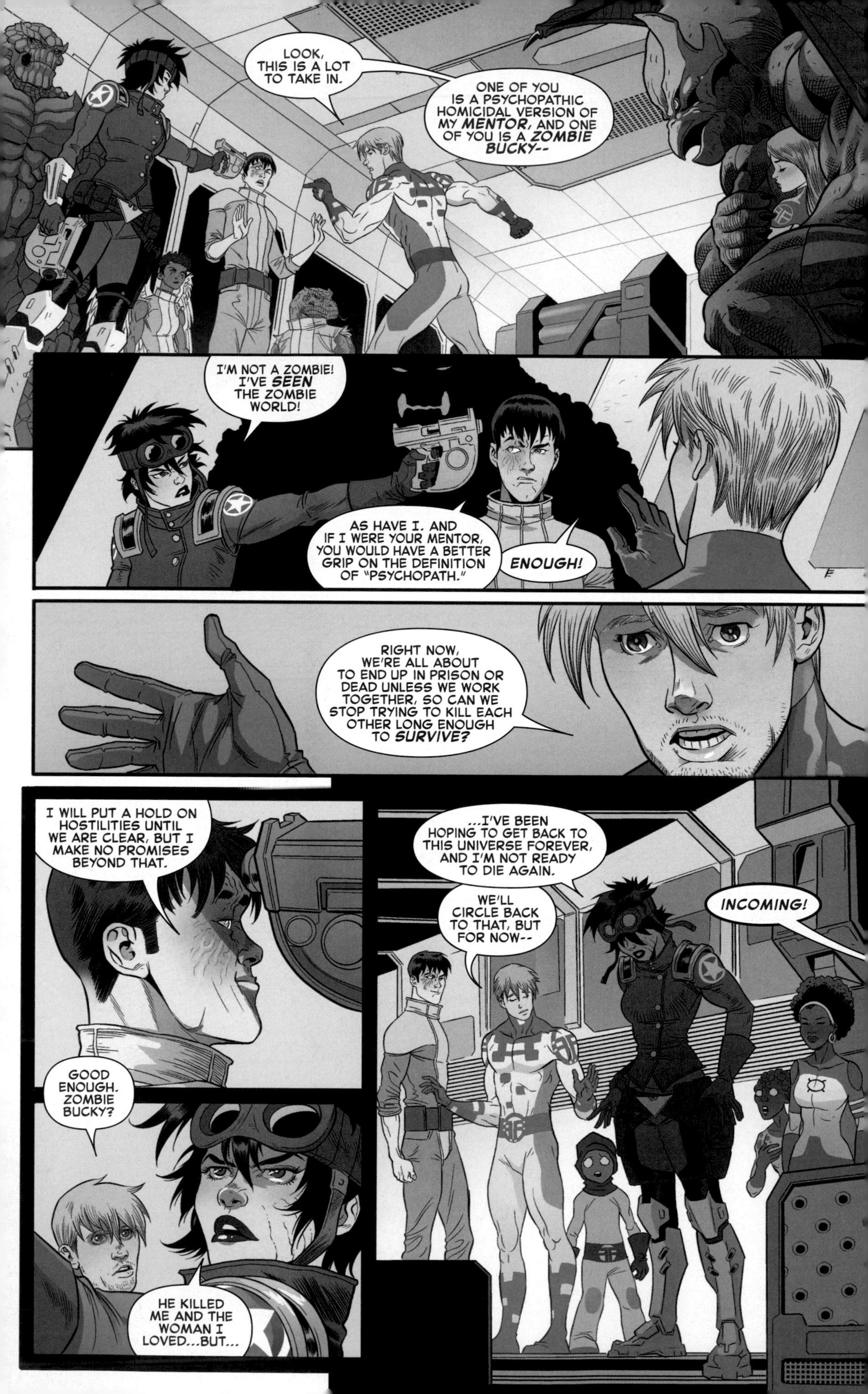
LOOK, THIS IS A LOT TO TAKE IN.
ONE OF YOU IS A PSYCHOPATHIC HOMICIDAL VERSION OF MY MENTOR, AND ONE OF YOU IS A ZOMBIE BUCKY--
I'M NOT A ZOMBIE! I'VE SEEN THE ZOMBIE WORLD!
AS HAVE I. AND IF I WERE YOUR MENTOR, YOU WOULD HAVE A BETTER GRIP ON THE DEFINITION OF "PSYCHOPATH."
ENOUGH!
RIGHT NOW, WE'RE ALL ABOUT TO END UP IN PRISON OR DEAD UNLESS WE WORK TOGETHER, SO CAN WE STOP TRYING TO KILL EACH OTHER LONG ENOUGH TO SURVIVE?
I WILL PUT A HOLD ON HOSTILITIES UNTIL WE ARE CLEAR, BUT I MAKE NO PROMISES BEYOND THAT.
GOOD ENOUGH. ZOMBIE BUCKY?
HE KILLED ME AND THE WOMAN I LOVED...BUT...
...I'VE BEEN HOPING TO GET BACK TO THIS UNIVERSE FOREVER, AND I'M NOT READY TO DIE AGAIN.
WE'LL CIRCLE BACK TO THAT, BUT FOR NOW--
INCOMING!

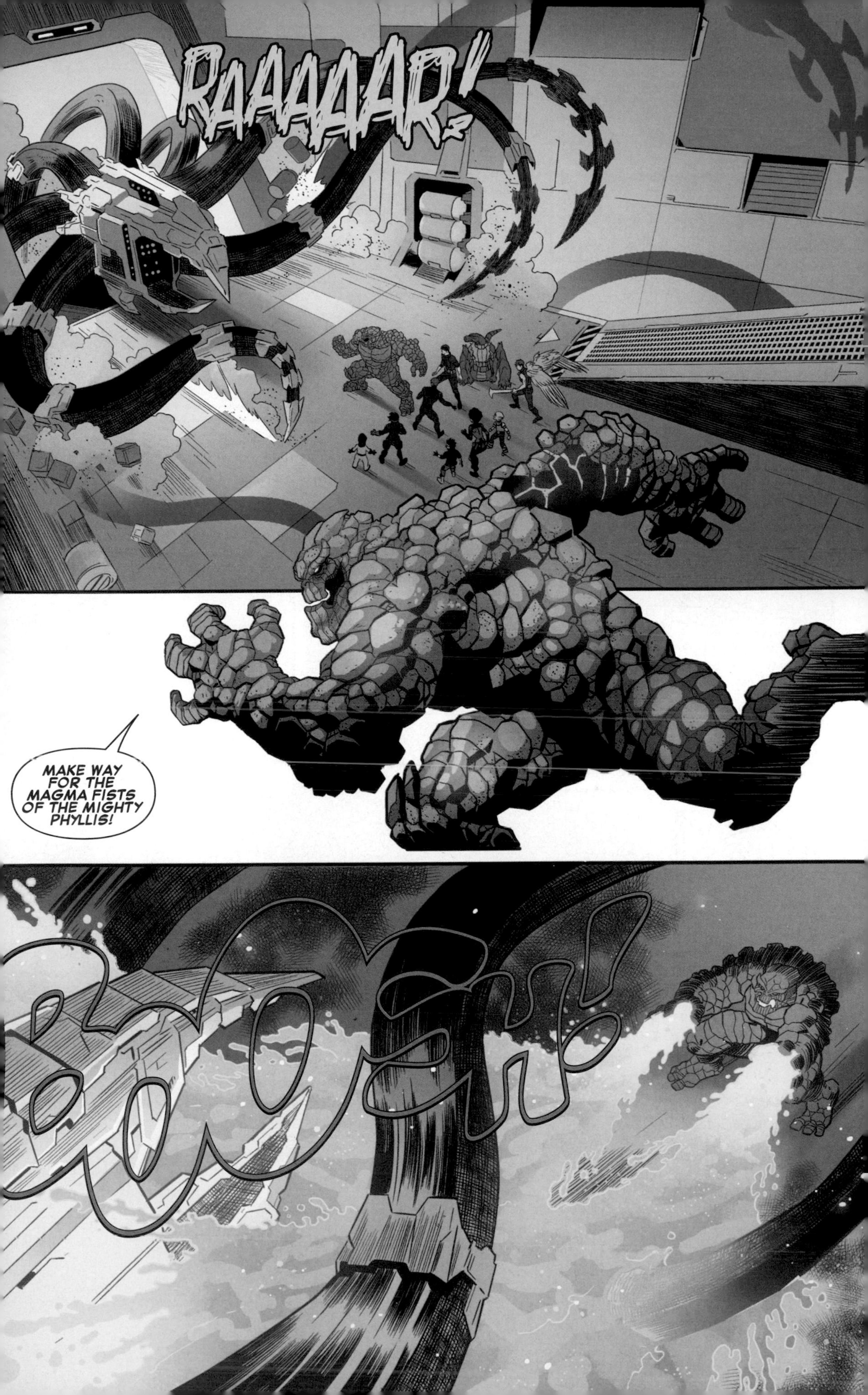
RAAAAAAR!
MAKE WAY FOR THE MAGMA FISTS OF THE MIGHTY PHYLLIS!
BOOOOSH!

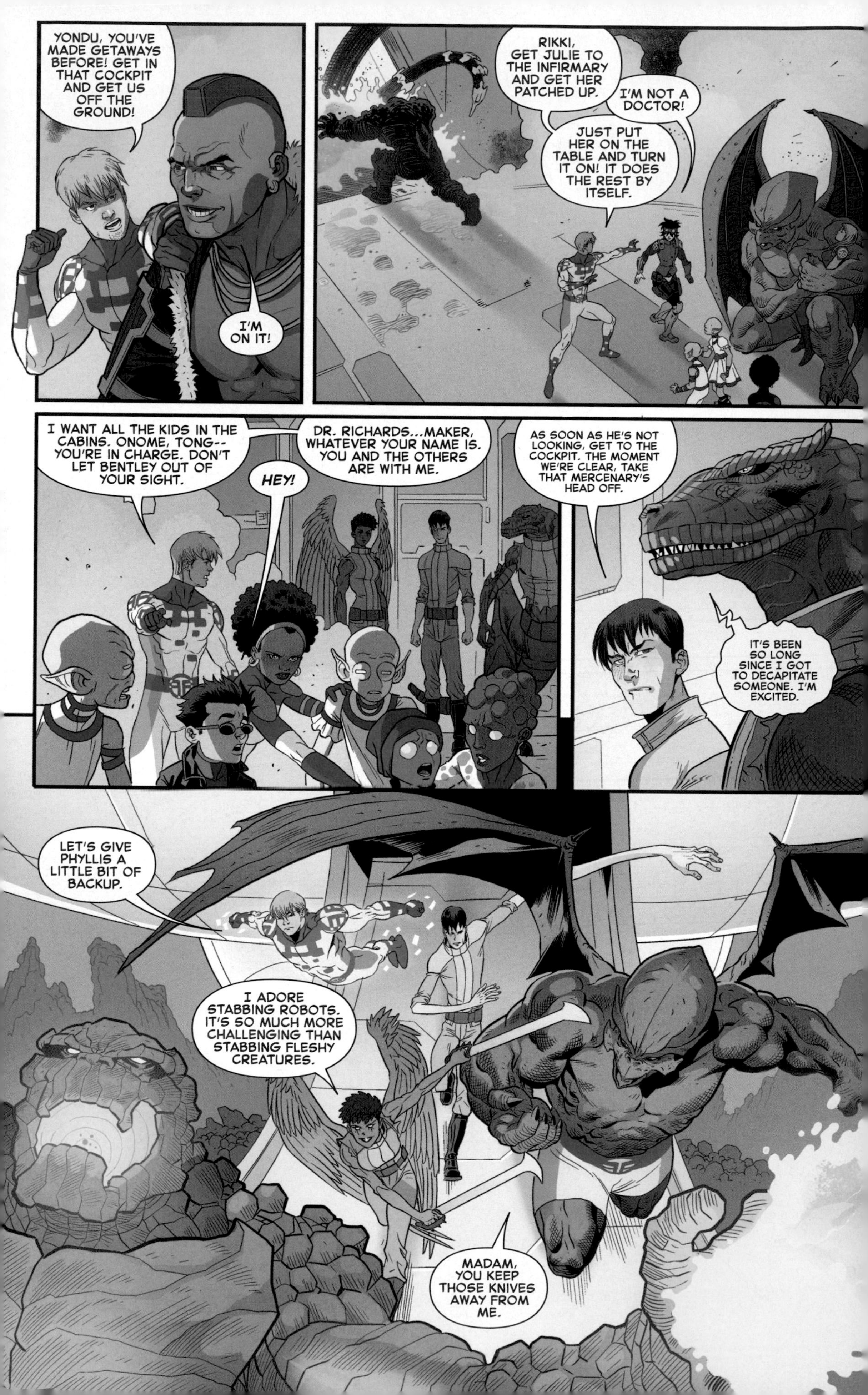

YONDU, YOU'VE MADE GETAWAYS BEFORE! GET IN THAT COCKPIT AND GET US OFF THE GROUND!
I'M ON IT!
RIKKI, GET JULIE TO THE INFIRMARY AND GET HER PATCHED UP.
I'M NOT A DOCTOR!
JUST PUT HER ON THE TABLE AND TURN IT ON! IT DOES THE REST BY ITSELF.
I WANT ALL THE KIDS IN THE CABINS. ONOME, TONG-- YOU'RE IN CHARGE. DON'T LET BENTLEY OUT OF YOUR SIGHT.
HEY!
DR. RICHARDS...MAKER, WHATEVER YOUR NAME IS. YOU AND THE OTHERS ARE WITH ME.
AS SOON AS HE'S NOT LOOKING, GET TO THE COCKPIT. THE MOMENT WE'RE CLEAR, TAKE THAT MERCENARY'S HEAD OFF.
IT'S BEEN SO LONG SINCE I GOT TO DECAPITATE SOMEONE. I'M EXCITED.
LET'S GIVE PHYLLIS A LITTLE BIT OF BACKUP.
I ADORE STABBING ROBOTS. IT'S SO MUCH MORE CHALLENGING THAN STABBING FLESHY CREATURES.
MADAM, YOU KEEP THOSE KNIVES AWAY FROM ME.

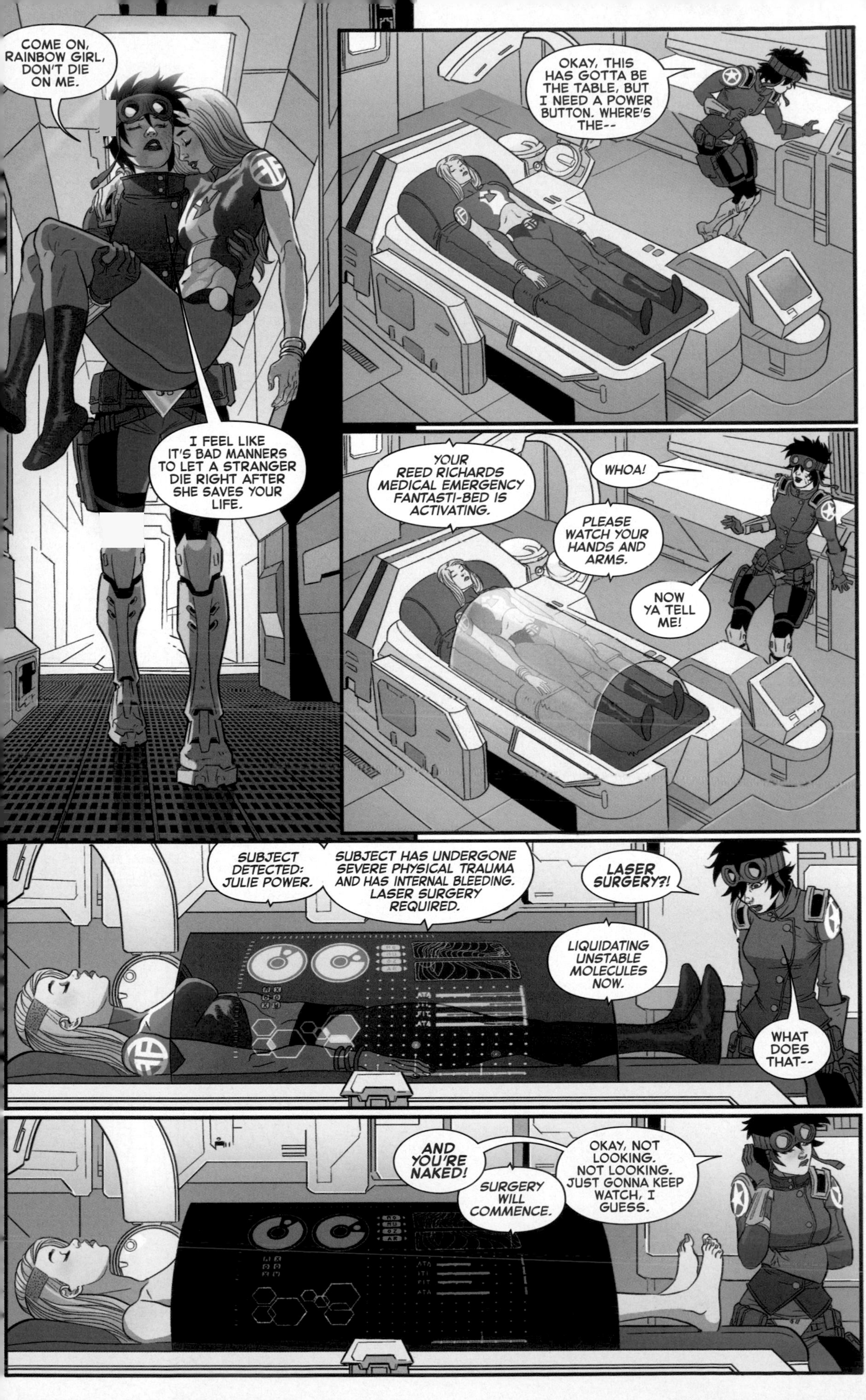
COME ON, RAINBOW GIRL, DON'T DIE ON ME.
I FEEL LIKE IT'S BAD MANNERS TO LET A STRANGER DIE RIGHT AFTER SHE SAVES YOUR LIFE.
OKAY, THIS HAS GOTTA BE THE TABLE, BUT I NEED A POWER BUTTON. WHERE'S THE--
YOUR REED RICHARDS MEDICAL EMERGENCY FANTASTI-BED IS ACTIVATING.
WHOA!
PLEASE WATCH YOUR HANDS AND ARMS.
NOW YA TELL ME!
SUBJECT DETECTED: JULIE POWER.
SUBJECT HAS UNDERGONE SEVERE PHYSICAL TRAUMA AND HAS INTERNAL BLEEDING. LASER SURGERY REQUIRED.
LASER SURGERY?!
LIQUIDATING UNSTABLE MOLECULES NOW.
WHAT DOES THAT--
AND YOU'RE NAKED!
SURGERY WILL COMMENCE.
OKAY, NOT LOOKING. NOT LOOKING. JUST GONNA KEEP WATCH, I GUESS.

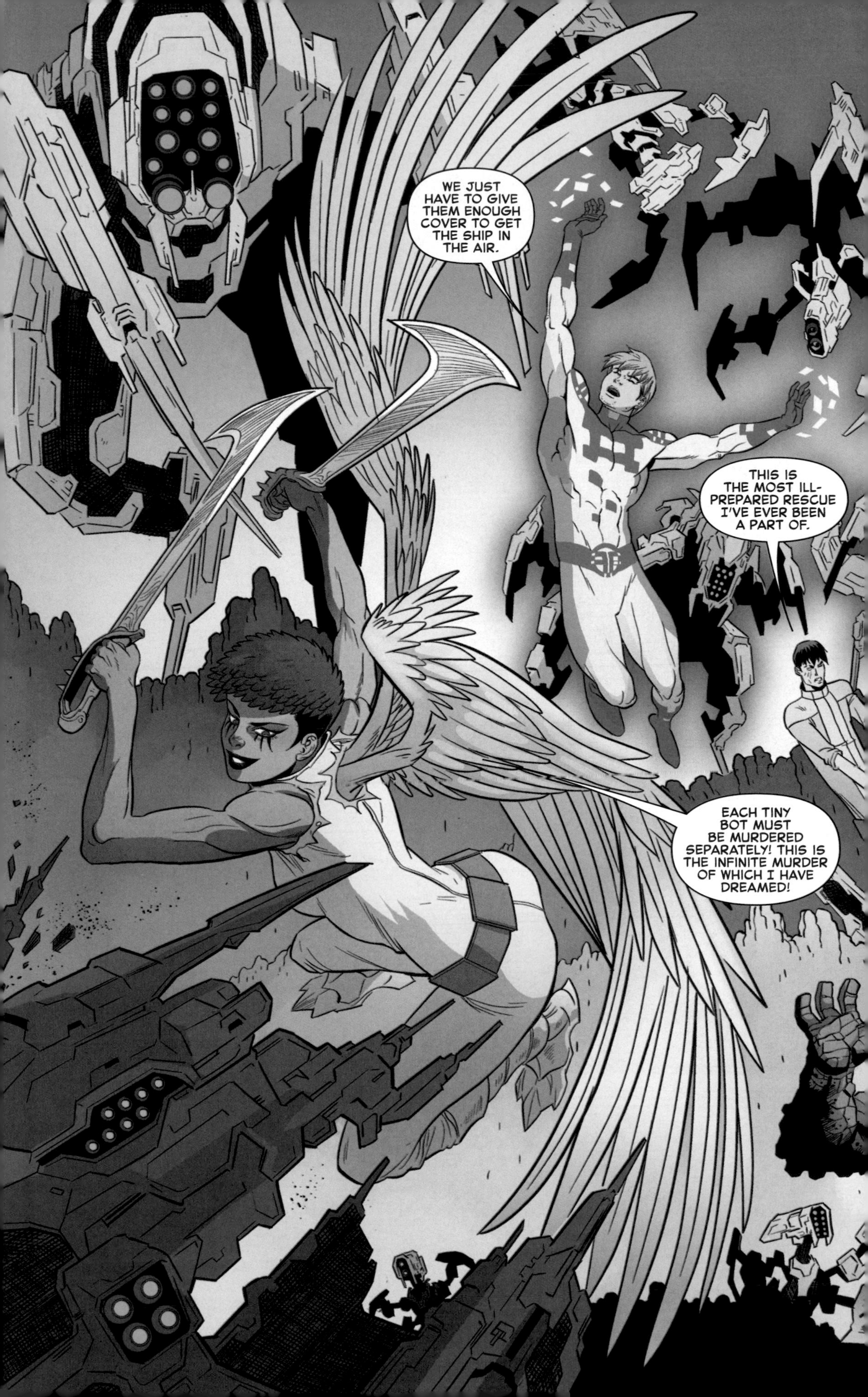
WE JUST HAVE TO GIVE THEM ENOUGH COVER TO GET THE SHIP IN THE AIR.
THIS IS THE MOST ILL-PREPARED RESCUE I'VE EVER BEEN A PART OF.
EACH TINY BOT MUST BE MURDERED SEPARATELY! THIS IS THE INFINITE MURDER OF WHICH I HAVE DREAMED!

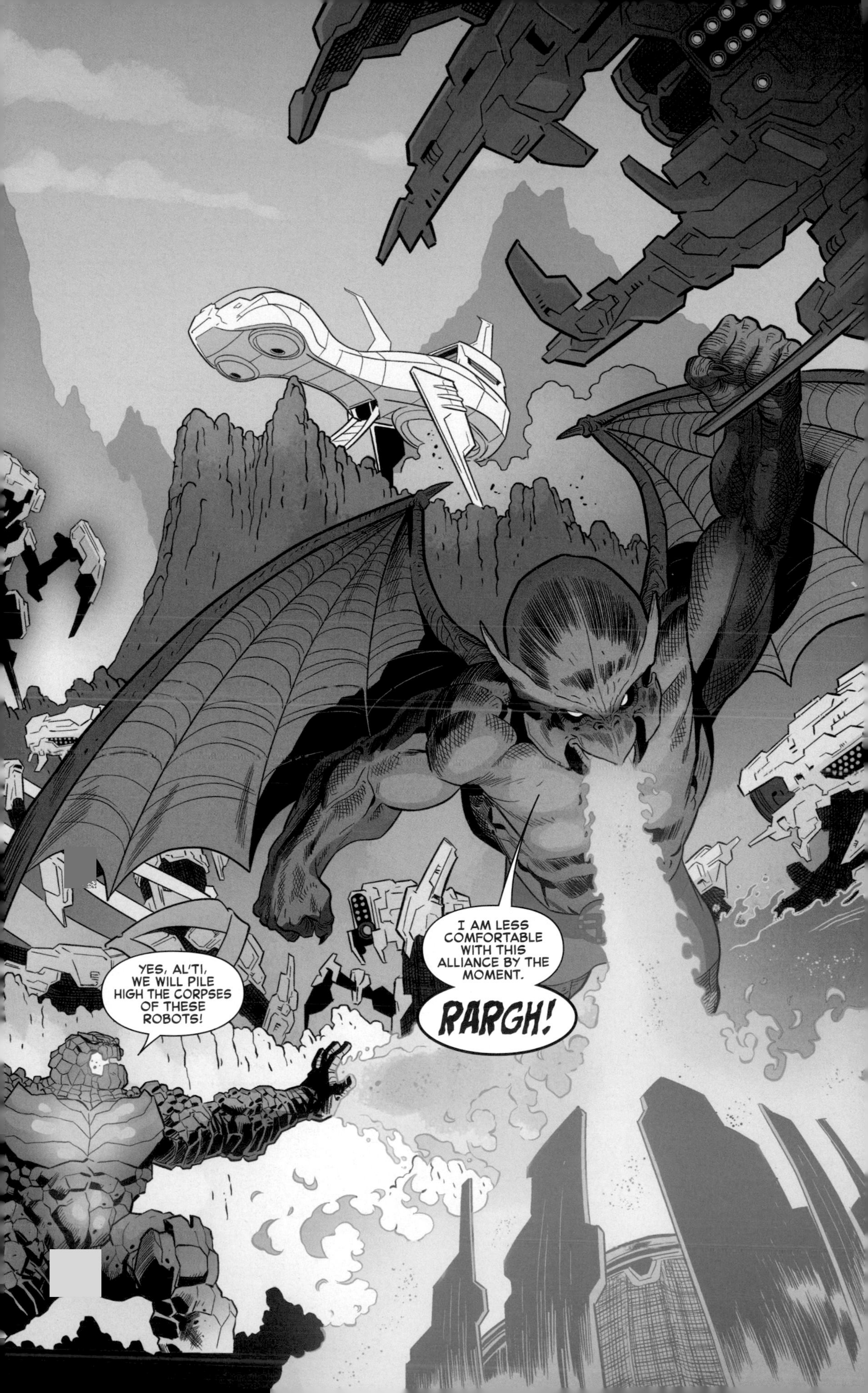
YES, AL'TI, WE WILL PILE HIGH THE CORPSES OF THESE ROBOTS!
I AM LESS COMFORTABLE WITH THIS ALLIANCE BY THE MOMENT.
RARGH!

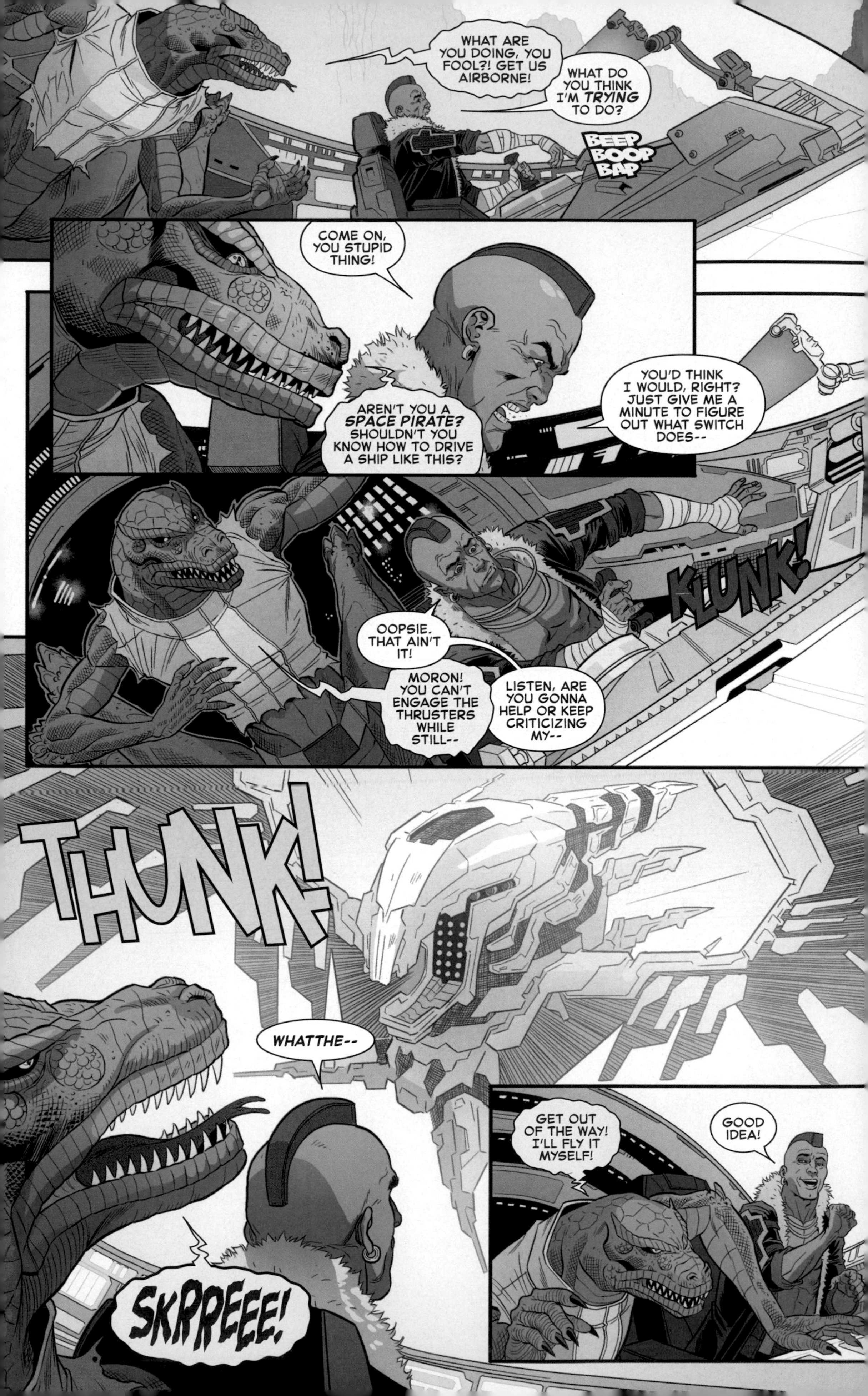
WHAT ARE YOU DOING, YOU FOOL?! GET US AIRBORNE!
WHAT DO YOU THINK I'M *TRYING* TO DO?
BEEP BOOP BAP
COME ON, YOU STUPID THING!
AREN'T YOU A *SPACE PIRATE?* SHOULDN'T YOU KNOW HOW TO DRIVE A SHIP LIKE THIS?
YOU'D THINK I WOULD, RIGHT? JUST GIVE ME A MINUTE TO FIGURE OUT WHAT SWITCH DOES--
KLUNK!
OOPSIE. THAT AIN'T IT!
MORON! YOU CAN'T ENGAGE THE THRUSTERS WHILE STILL--
LISTEN, ARE YOU GONNA HELP OR KEEP CRITICIZING MY--
THUNK!
WHATTHE--
SKREEE!
GET OUT OF THE WAY! I'LL FLY IT MYSELF!
GOOD IDEA!

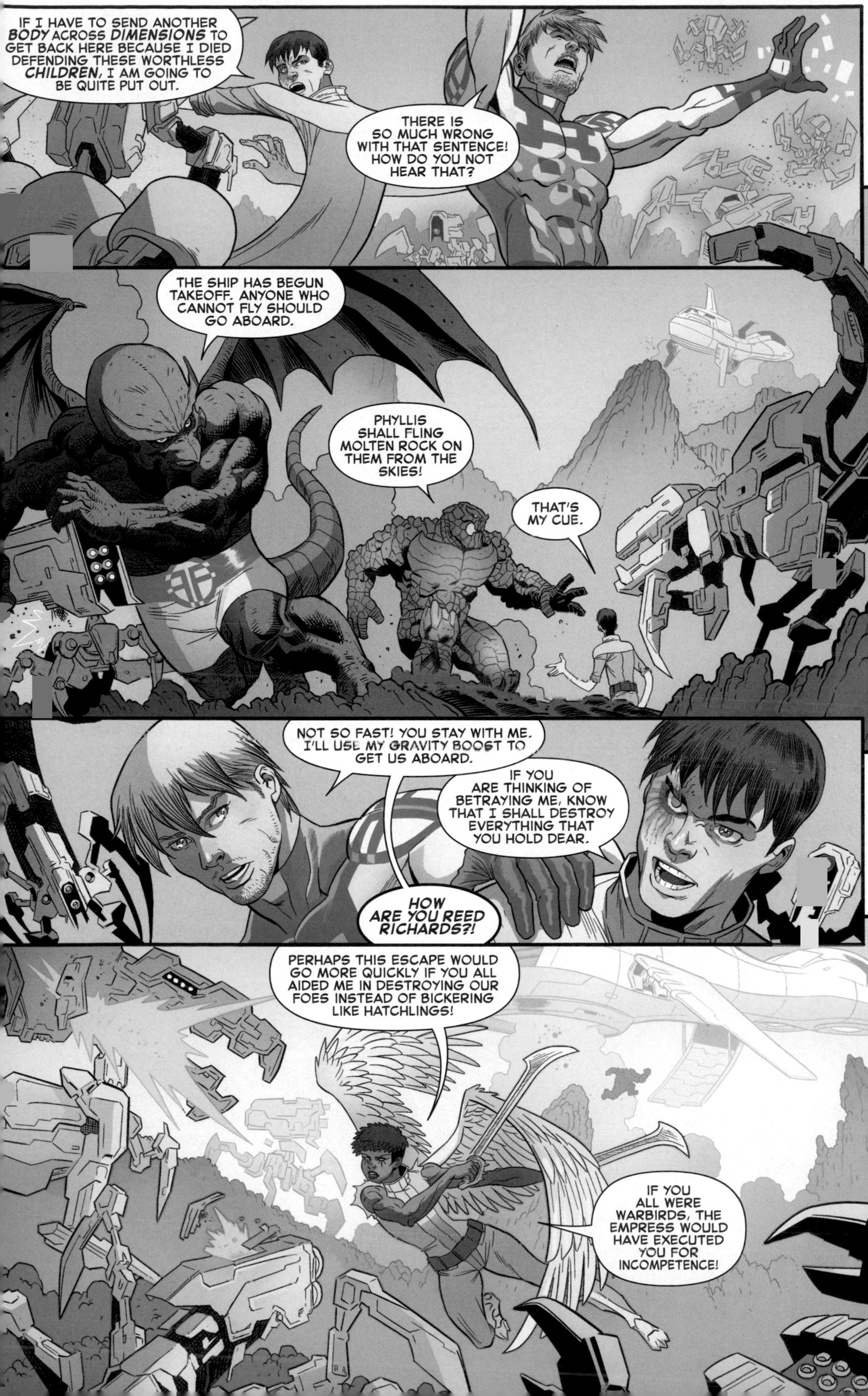
IF I HAVE TO SEND ANOTHER BODY ACROSS DIMENSIONS TO GET BACK HERE BECAUSE I DIED DEFENDING THESE WORTHLESS CHILDREN, I AM GOING TO BE QUITE PUT OUT.
THERE IS SO MUCH WRONG WITH THAT SENTENCE! HOW DO YOU NOT HEAR THAT?
THE SHIP HAS BEGUN TAKEOFF. ANYONE WHO CANNOT FLY SHOULD GO ABOARD.
PHYLLIS SHALL FLING MOLTEN ROCK ON THEM FROM THE SKIES!
THAT'S MY CUE.
NOT SO FAST! YOU STAY WITH ME. I'LL USE MY GRAVITY BOOST TO GET US ABOARD.
IF YOU ARE THINKING OF BETRAYING ME, KNOW THAT I SHALL DESTROY EVERYTHING THAT YOU HOLD DEAR.
HOW ARE YOU REED RICHARDS?!
PERHAPS THIS ESCAPE WOULD GO MORE QUICKLY IF YOU ALL AIDED ME IN DESTROYING OUR FOES INSTEAD OF BICKERING LIKE HATCHLINGS!
IF YOU ALL WERE WARBIRDS, THE EMPRESS WOULD HAVE EXECUTED YOU FOR INCOMPETENCE!

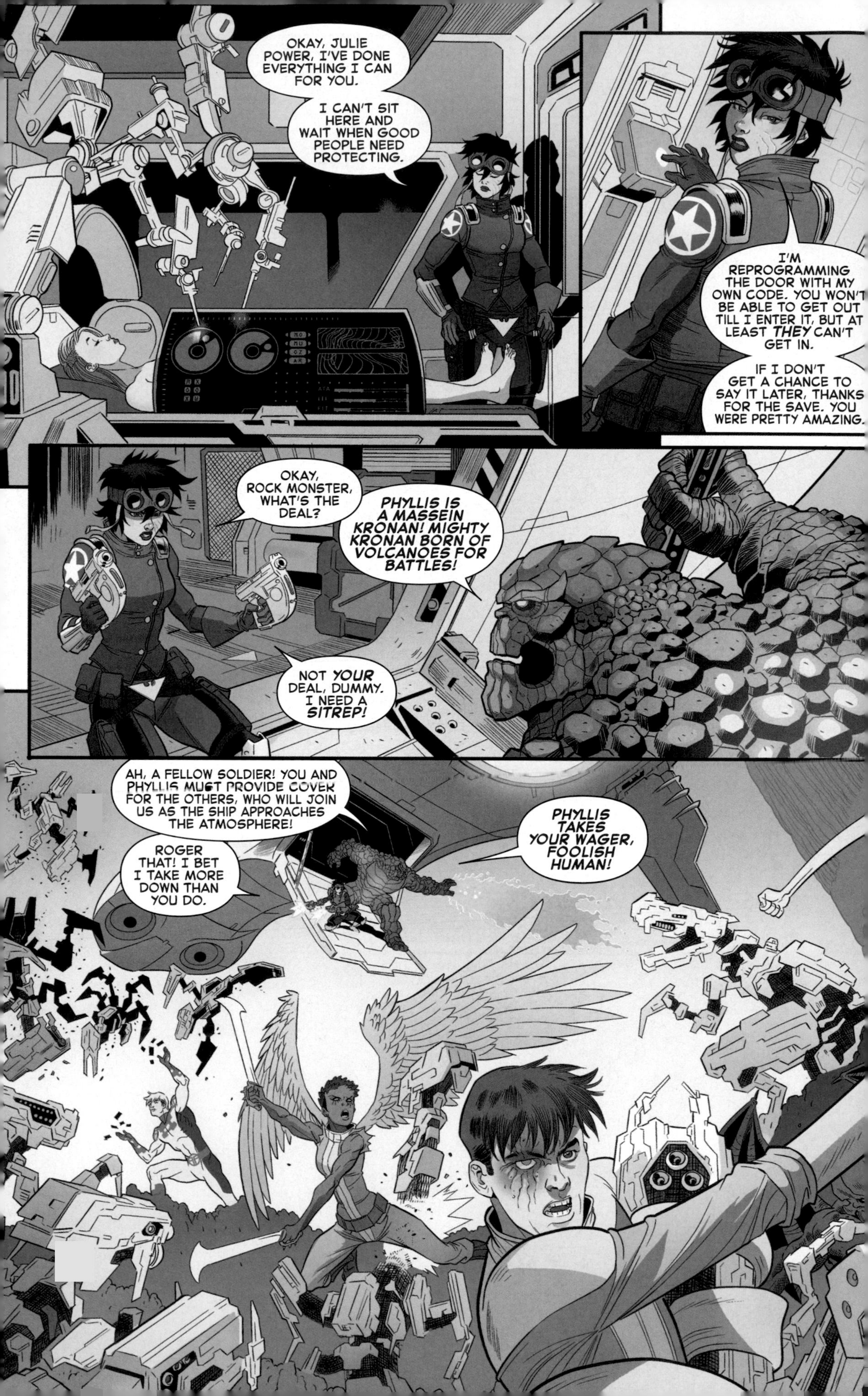
OKAY, JULIE POWER, I'VE DONE EVERYTHING I CAN FOR YOU.
I CAN'T SIT HERE AND WAIT WHEN GOOD PEOPLE NEED PROTECTING.
I'M REPROGRAMMING THE DOOR WITH MY OWN CODE. YOU WON'T BE ABLE TO GET OUT TILL I ENTER IT, BUT AT LEAST THEY CAN'T GET IN.
IF I DON'T GET A CHANCE TO SAY IT LATER, THANKS FOR THE SAVE. YOU WERE PRETTY AMAZING.
OKAY, ROCK MONSTER, WHAT'S THE DEAL?
PHYLLIS IS A MASSEIN KRONAN! MIGHTY KRONAN BORN OF VOLCANOES FOR BATTLES!
NOT YOUR DEAL, DUMMY. I NEED A SITREP!
AH, A FELLOW SOLDIER! YOU AND PHYLLIS MUST PROVIDE COVER FOR THE OTHERS, WHO WILL JOIN US AS THE SHIP APPROACHES THE ATMOSPHERE!
ROGER THAT! I BET I TAKE MORE DOWN THAN YOU DO.
PHYLLIS TAKES YOUR WAGER, FOOLISH HUMAN!

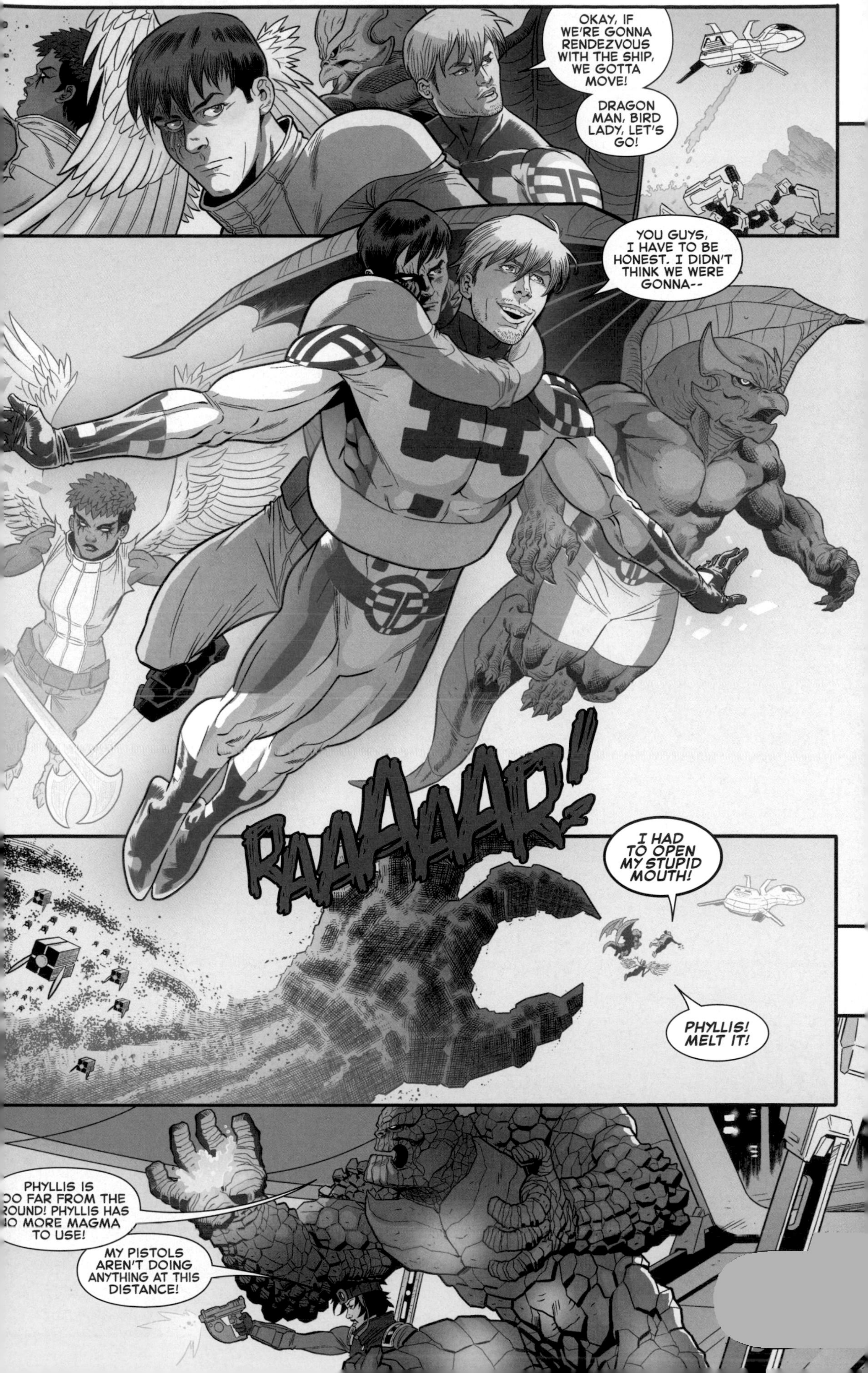
OKAY, IF WE'RE GONNA RENDEZVOUS WITH THE SHIP, WE GOTTA MOVE!
DRAGON MAN, BIRD LADY, LET'S GO!
YOU GUYS, I HAVE TO BE HONEST. I DIDN'T THINK WE WERE GONNA--
RAAAAAR!
I HAD TO OPEN MY STUPID MOUTH!
PHYLLIS! MELT IT!
PHYLLIS IS OO FAR FROM THE ROUND! PHYLLIS HAS NO MORE MAGMA TO USE!
MY PISTOLS AREN'T DOING ANYTHING AT THIS DISTANCE!

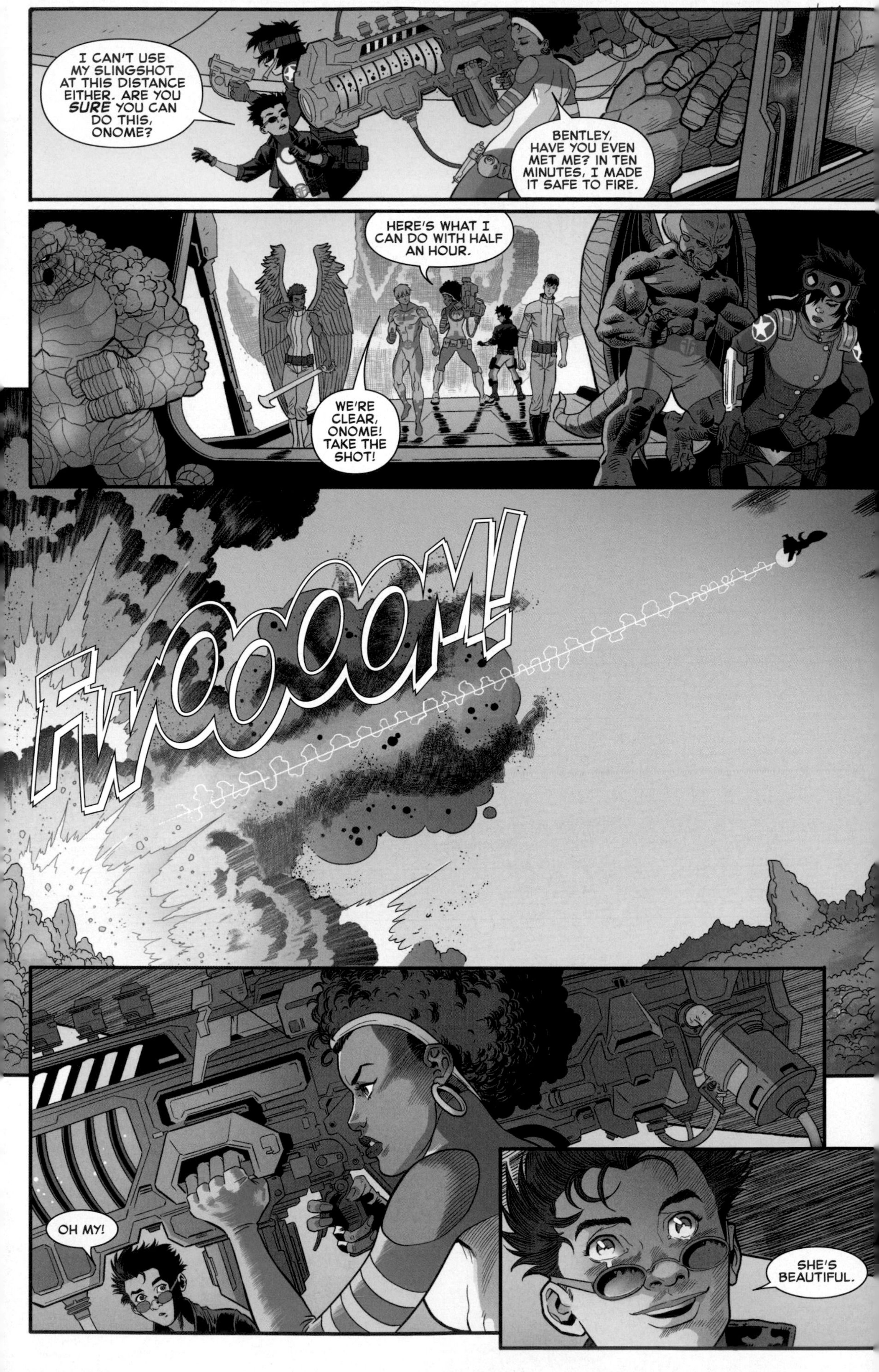
I CAN'T USE MY SLINGSHOT AT THIS DISTANCE EITHER. ARE YOU SURE YOU CAN DO THIS, ONOME?
BENTLEY, HAVE YOU EVEN MET ME? IN TEN MINUTES, I MADE IT SAFE TO FIRE.
HERE'S WHAT I CAN DO WITH HALF AN HOUR.
WE'RE CLEAR, ONOME! TAKE THE SHOT!
FWOOOOM!
OH MY!
SHE'S BEAUTIFUL.

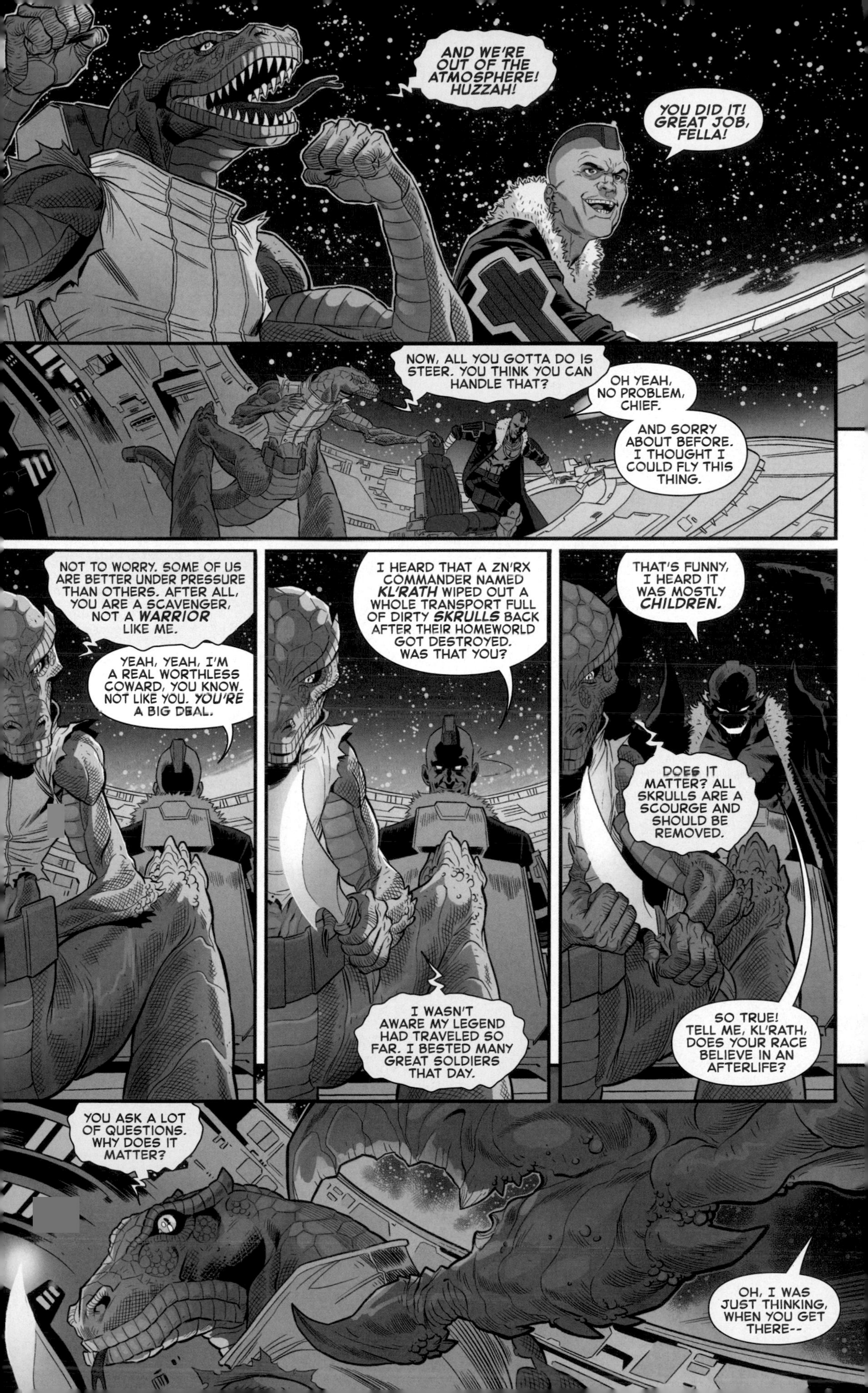
AND WE'RE OUT OF THE ATMOSPHERE! HUZZAH!
YOU DID IT! GREAT JOB, FELLA!
NOW, ALL YOU GOTTA DO IS STEER. YOU THINK YOU CAN HANDLE THAT?
OH YEAH, NO PROBLEM, CHIEF.
AND SORRY ABOUT BEFORE. I THOUGHT I COULD FLY THIS THING.
NOT TO WORRY. SOME OF US ARE BETTER UNDER PRESSURE THAN OTHERS. AFTER ALL, YOU ARE A SCAVENGER, NOT A WARRIOR LIKE ME.
YEAH, YEAH, I'M A REAL WORTHLESS COWARD, YOU KNOW. NOT LIKE YOU. YOU'RE A BIG DEAL.
I HEARD THAT A ZN'RX COMMANDER NAMED KL'RATH WIPED OUT A WHOLE TRANSPORT FULL OF DIRTY SKRULLS BACK AFTER THEIR HOMEWORLD GOT DESTROYED. WAS THAT YOU?
I WASN'T AWARE MY LEGEND HAD TRAVELED SO FAR. I BESTED MANY GREAT SOLDIERS THAT DAY.
THAT'S FUNNY, I HEARD IT WAS MOSTLY CHILDREN.
DOES IT MATTER? ALL SKRULLS ARE A SCOURGE AND SHOULD BE REMOVED.
SO TRUE! TELL ME, KL'RATH, DOES YOUR RACE BELIEVE IN AN AFTERLIFE?
YOU ASK A LOT OF QUESTIONS. WHY DOES IT MATTER?
OH, I WAS JUST THINKING, WHEN YOU GET THERE--

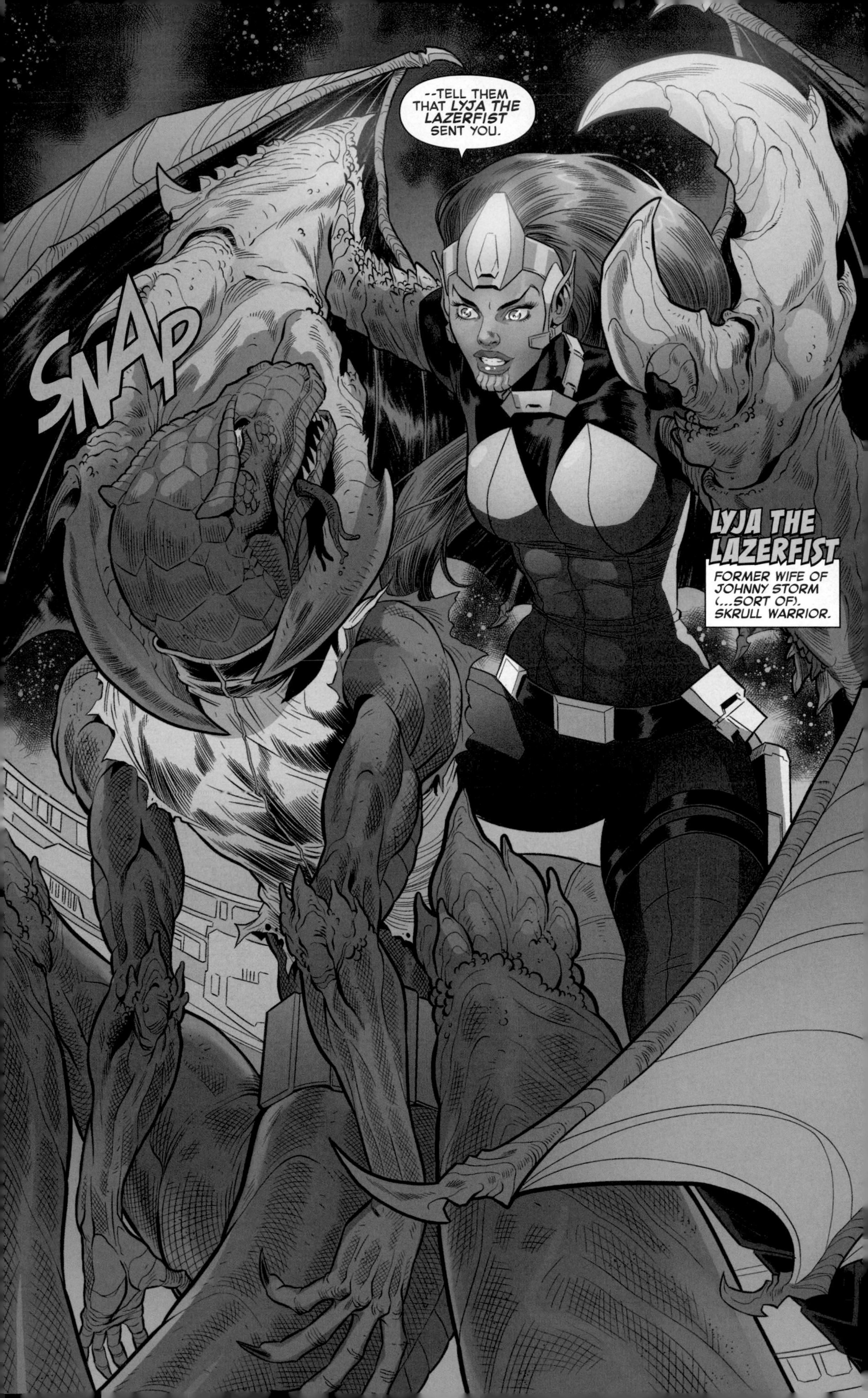

SNAP
--TELL THEM THAT LYJA THE LAZERFIST SENT YOU.
LYJA THE LAZERFIST
FORMER WIFE OF JOHNNY STORM (...SORT OF). SKRULL WARRIOR.

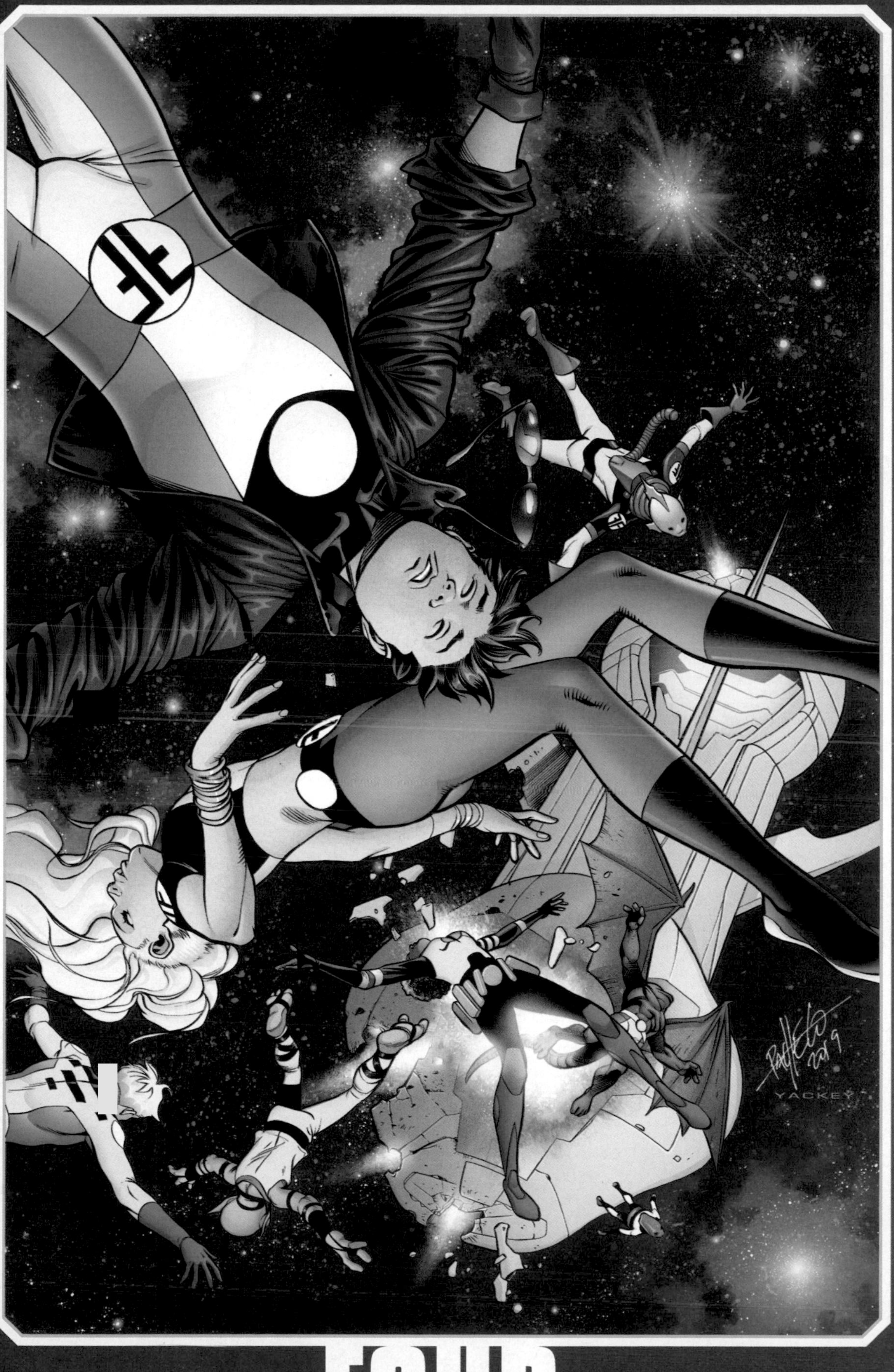
YACKEY

FOUR

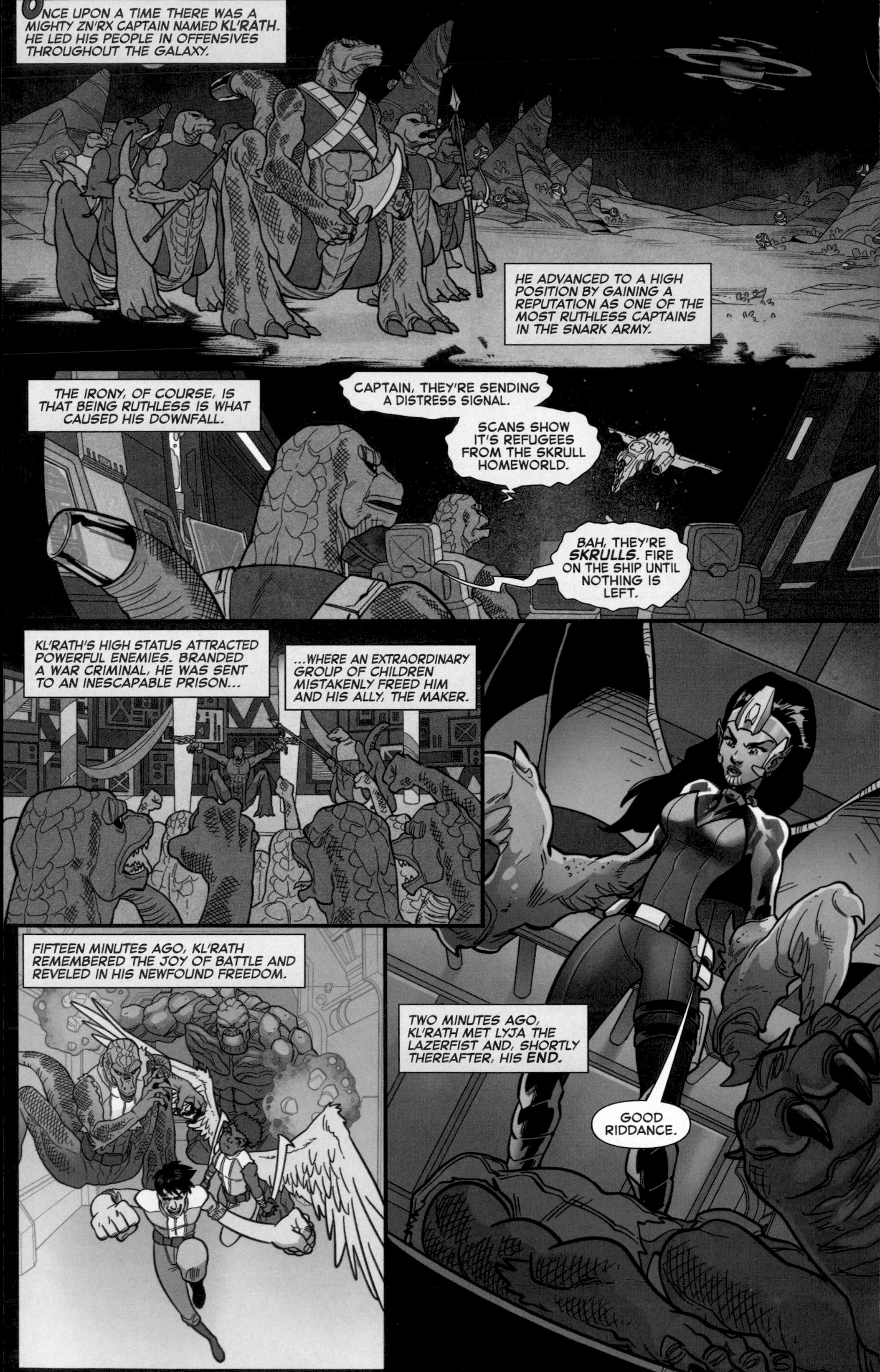
ONCE UPON A TIME THERE WAS A MIGHTY ZN'RX CAPTAIN NAMED KL'RATH. HE LED HIS PEOPLE IN OFFENSIVES THROUGHOUT THE GALAXY.
HE ADVANCED TO A HIGH POSITION BY GAINING A REPUTATION AS ONE OF THE MOST RUTHLESS CAPTAINS IN THE SNARK ARMY.
THE IRONY, OF COURSE, IS THAT BEING RUTHLESS IS WHAT CAUSED HIS DOWNFALL.
CAPTAIN, THEY'RE SENDING A DISTRESS SIGNAL.
SCANS SHOW IT'S REFUGEES FROM THE SKRULL HOMEWORLD.
BAH, THEY'RE SKRULLS. FIRE ON THE SHIP UNTIL NOTHING IS LEFT.
KL'RATH'S HIGH STATUS ATTRACTED POWERFUL ENEMIES. BRANDED A WAR CRIMINAL, HE WAS SENT TO AN INESCAPABLE PRISON...
...WHERE AN EXTRAORDINARY GROUP OF CHILDREN MISTAKENLY FREED HIM AND HIS ALLY, THE MAKER.
FIFTEEN MINUTES AGO, KL'RATH REMEMBERED THE JOY OF BATTLE AND REVELED IN HIS NEWFOUND FREEDOM.
TWO MINUTES AGO, KL'RATH MET LYJA THE LAZERFIST AND, SHORTLY THEREAFTER, HIS END.
GOOD RIDDANCE.

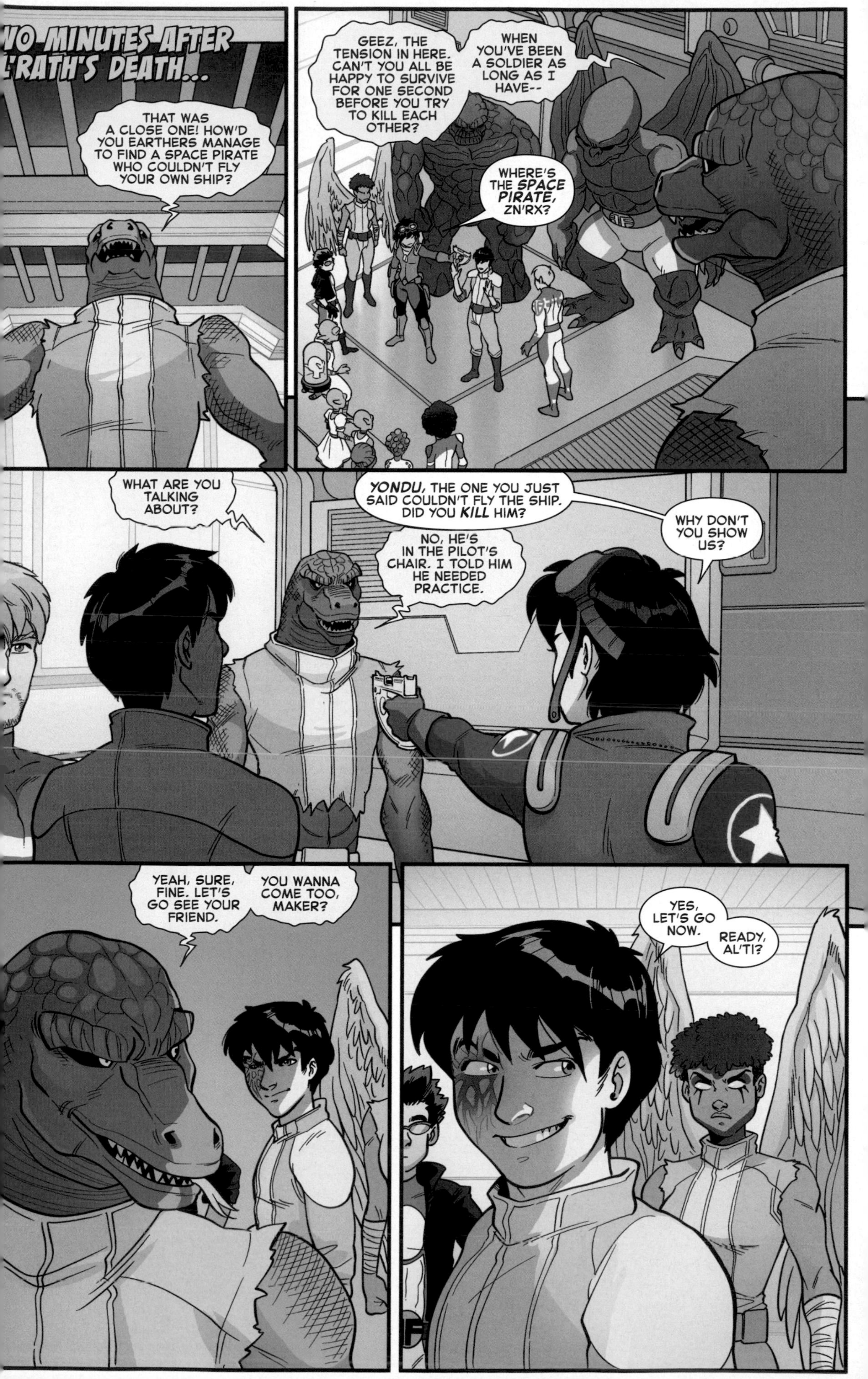
WO MINUTES AFTER
'RATH'S DEATH...
THAT WAS A CLOSE ONE! HOW'D YOU EARTHERS MANAGE TO FIND A SPACE PIRATE WHO COULDN'T FLY YOUR OWN SHIP?
GEEZ, THE TENSION IN HERE. CAN'T YOU ALL BE HAPPY TO SURVIVE FOR ONE SECOND BEFORE YOU TRY TO KILL EACH OTHER?
WHEN YOU'VE BEEN A SOLDIER AS LONG AS I HAVE--
WHERE'S THE SPACE PIRATE, ZN'RX?
WHAT ARE YOU TALKING ABOUT?
YONDU, THE ONE YOU JUST SAID COULDN'T FLY THE SHIP. DID YOU KILL HIM?
NO, HE'S IN THE PILOT'S CHAIR. I TOLD HIM HE NEEDED PRACTICE.
WHY DON'T YOU SHOW US?
YEAH, SURE, FINE. LET'S GO SEE YOUR FRIEND.
YOU WANNA COME TOO, MAKER?
YES, LET'S GO NOW.
READY, AL'TI?

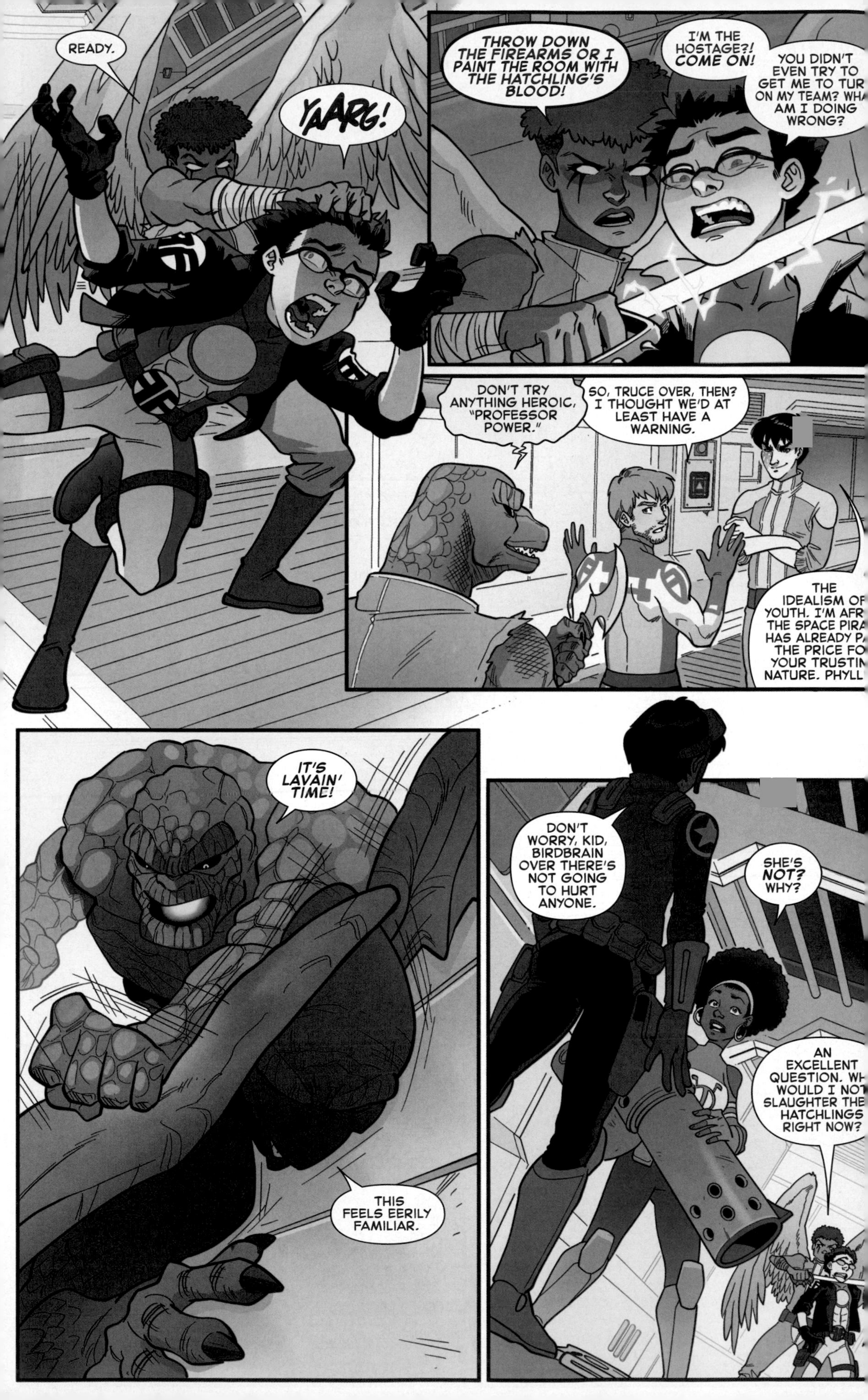
READY.
YAARG!
THROW DOWN THE FIREARMS OR I PAINT THE ROOM WITH THE HATCHLING'S BLOOD!
I'M THE HOSTAGE?! COME ON!
YOU DIDN'T EVEN TRY TO GET ME TO TUR ON MY TEAM? WH AM I DOING WRONG?
DON'T TRY ANYTHING HEROIC, "PROFESSOR POWER."
SO, TRUCE OVER, THEN? I THOUGHT WE'D AT LEAST HAVE A WARNING.
THE IDEALISM OF YOUTH. I'M AFR THE SPACE PIRA HAS ALREADY P THE PRICE FO YOUR TRUSTIN NATURE. PHYLL
IT'S LAVAIN' TIME!
THIS FEELS EERILY FAMILIAR.
DON'T WORRY, KID, BIRDBRAIN OVER THERE'S NOT GOING TO HURT ANYONE.
SHE'S NOT? WHY?
AN EXCELLENT QUESTION. WH WOULD I NOT SLAUGHTER THE HATCHLINGS RIGHT NOW?

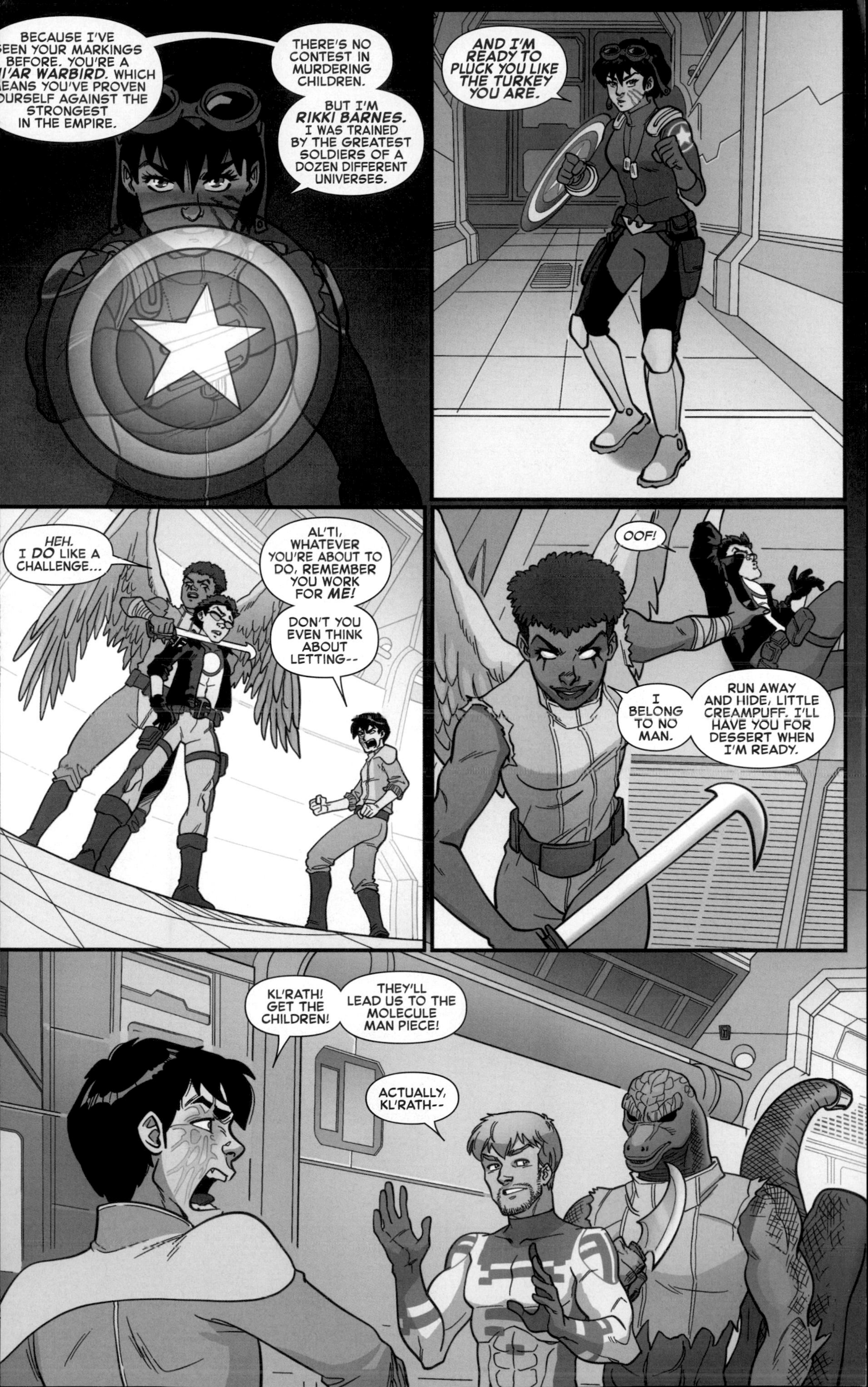
BECAUSE I'VE SEEN YOUR MARKINGS BEFORE. YOU'RE A I'AR WARBIRD. WHICH EANS YOU'VE PROVEN OURSELF AGAINST THE STRONGEST IN THE EMPIRE.
THERE'S NO CONTEST IN MURDERING CHILDREN.
BUT I'M RIKKI BARNES. I WAS TRAINED BY THE GREATEST SOLDIERS OF A DOZEN DIFFERENT UNIVERSES.
AND I'M READY TO PLUCK YOU LIKE THE TURKEY YOU ARE.
HEH. I DO LIKE A CHALLENGE...
AL'TI, WHATEVER YOU'RE ABOUT TO DO, REMEMBER YOU WORK FOR ME!
DON'T YOU EVEN THINK ABOUT LETTING--
OOF!
I BELONG TO NO MAN.
RUN AWAY AND HIDE, LITTLE CREAMPUFF. I'LL HAVE YOU FOR DESSERT WHEN I'M READY.
KL'RATH! GET THE CHILDREN!
THEY'LL LEAD US TO THE MOLECULE MAN PIECE!
ACTUALLY, KL'RATH--

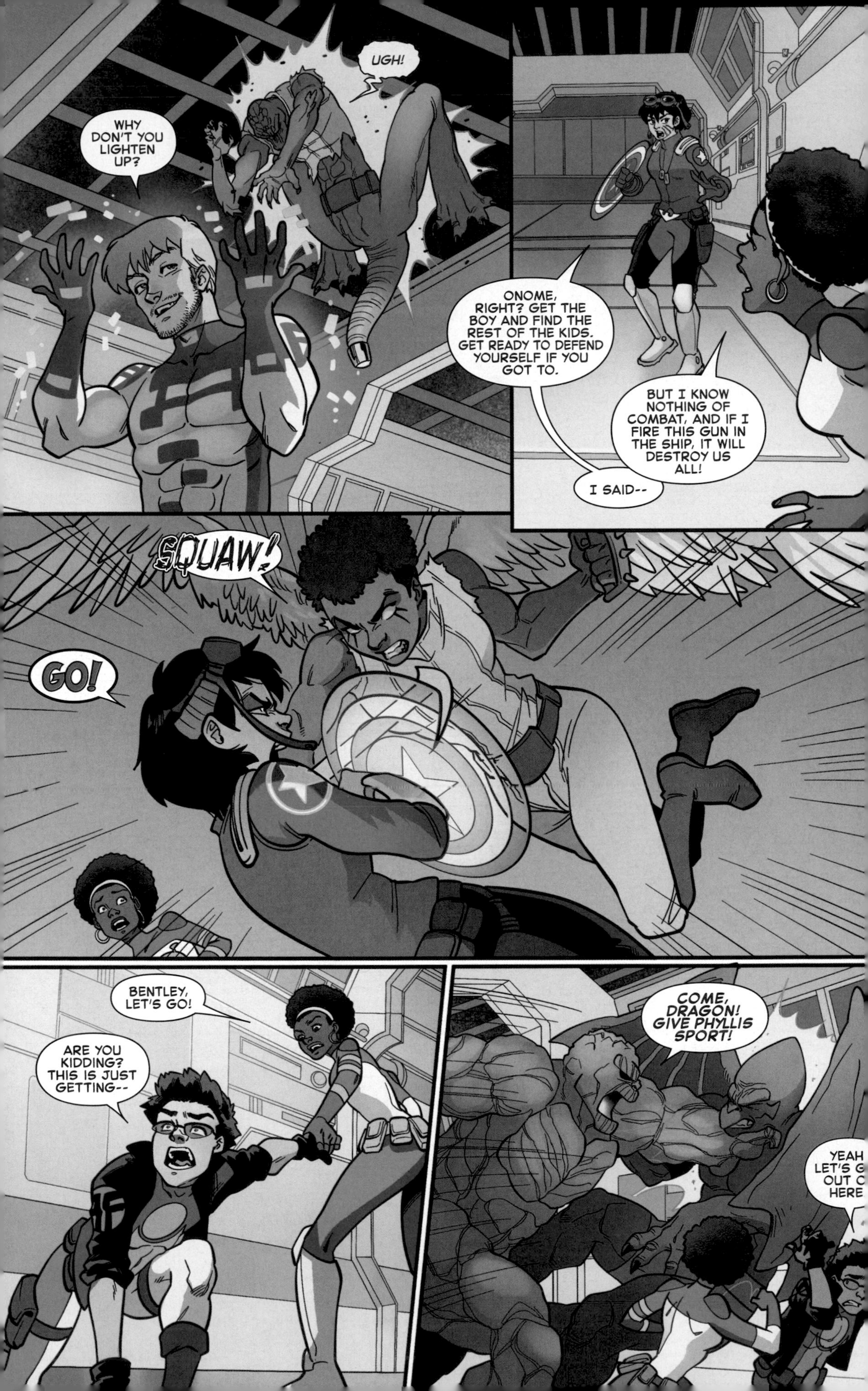
UGH!
WHY DON'T YOU LIGHTEN UP?
ONOME, RIGHT? GET THE BOY AND FIND THE REST OF THE KIDS. GET READY TO DEFEND YOURSELF IF YOU GOT TO.
BUT I KNOW NOTHING OF COMBAT, AND IF I FIRE THIS GUN IN THE SHIP, IT WILL DESTROY US ALL!
I SAID--
SQUAW!
GO!
BENTLEY, LET'S GO!
ARE YOU KIDDING? THIS IS JUST GETTING--
COME, DRAGON! GIVE PHYLLIS SPORT!

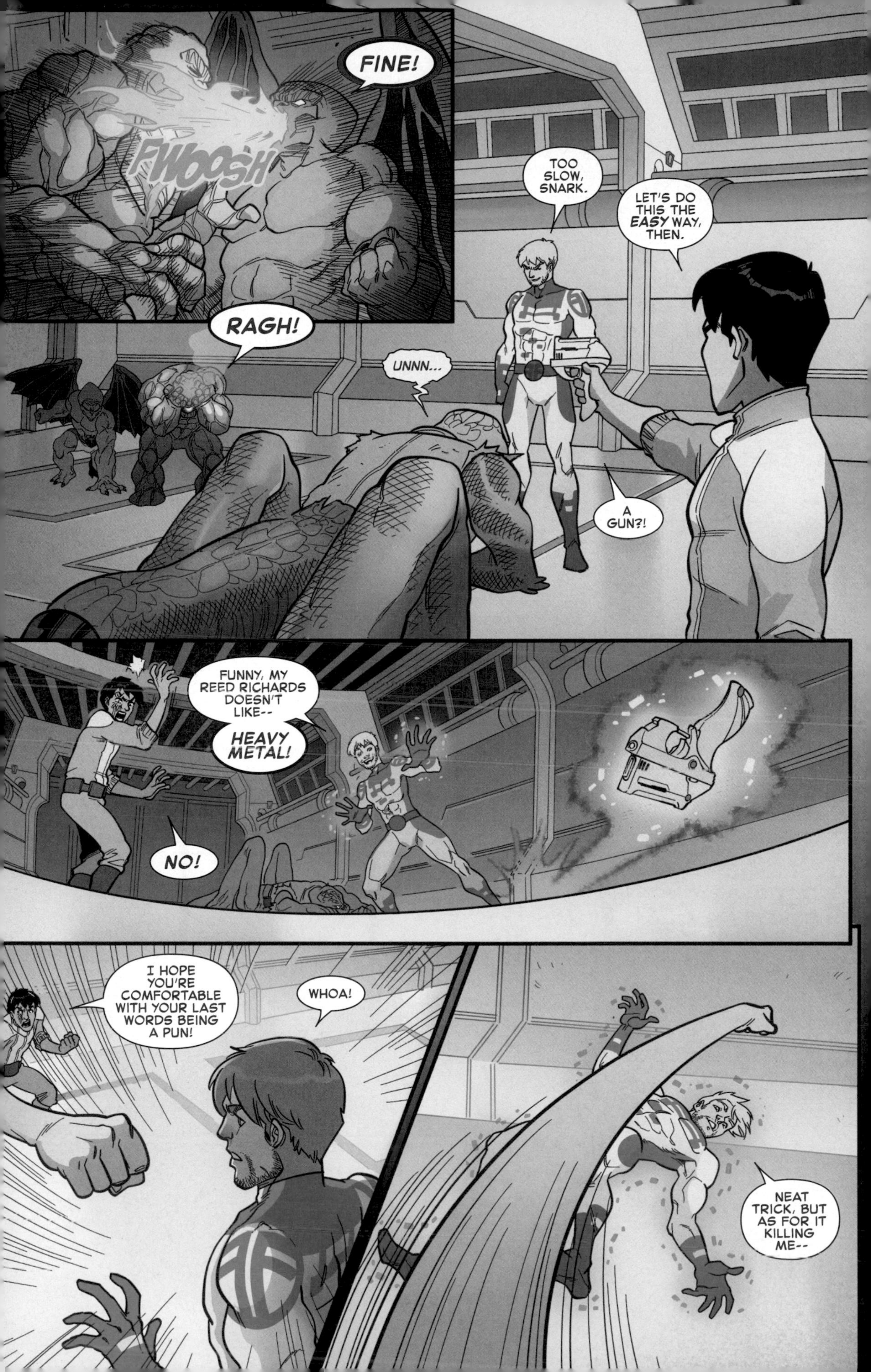
FINE!
FWOOSH
TOO SLOW, SNARK.
LET'S DO THIS THE EASY WAY, THEN.
RAGH!
UNNN...
A GUN?!
FUNNY, MY REED RICHARDS DOESN'T LIKE--
HEAVY METAL!
NO!
I HOPE YOU'RE COMFORTABLE WITH YOUR LAST WORDS BEING A PUN!
WHOA!
NEAT TRICK, BUT AS FOR IT KILLING ME--

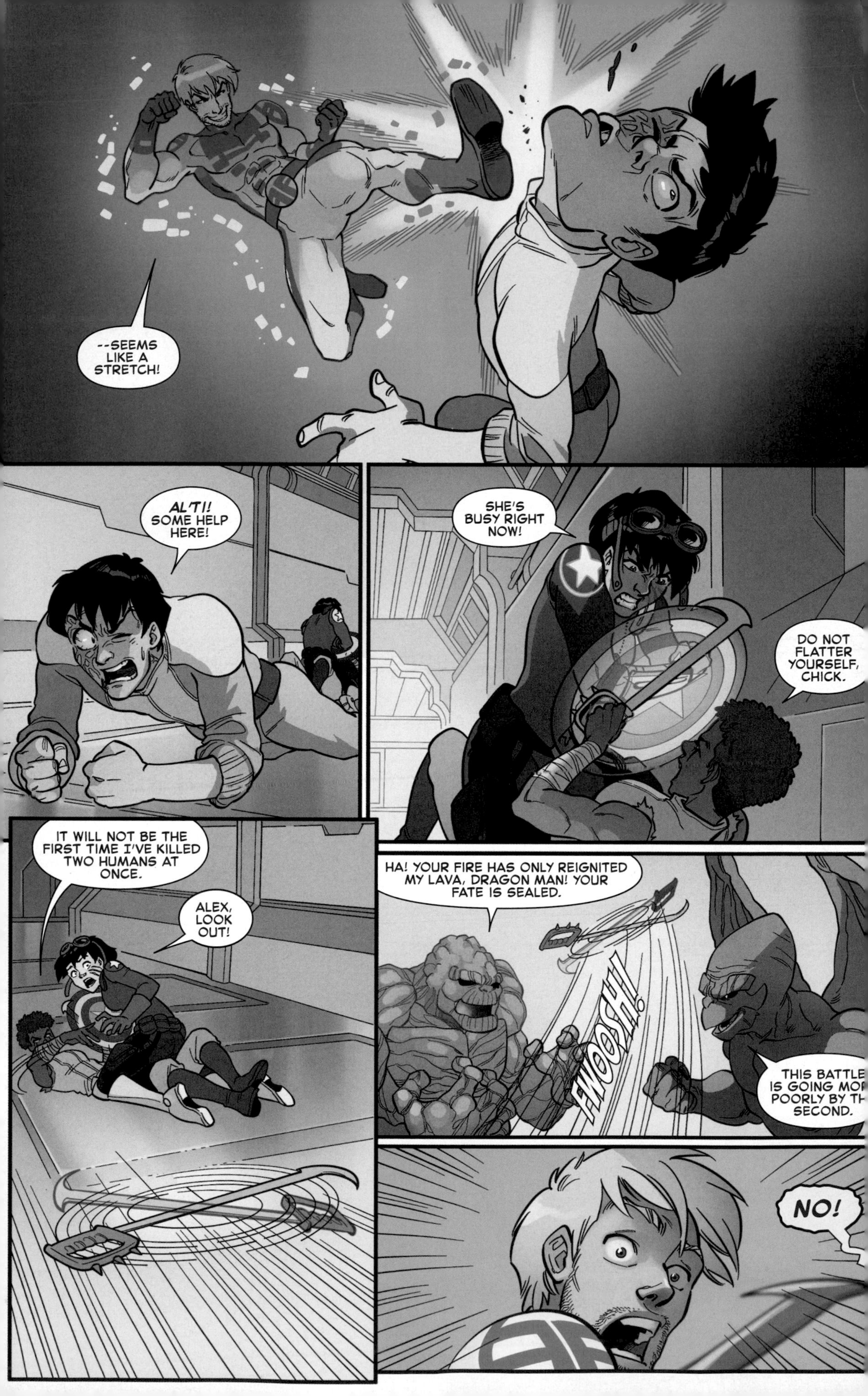
--SEEMS LIKE A STRETCH!
ALTI! SOME HELP HERE!
SHE'S BUSY RIGHT NOW!
DO NOT FLATTER YOURSELF, CHICK.
IT WILL NOT BE THE FIRST TIME I'VE KILLED TWO HUMANS AT ONCE.
ALEX, LOOK OUT!
HA! YOUR FIRE HAS ONLY REIGNITED MY LAVA, DRAGON MAN! YOUR FATE IS SEALED.
FWOOSH!!
NO!

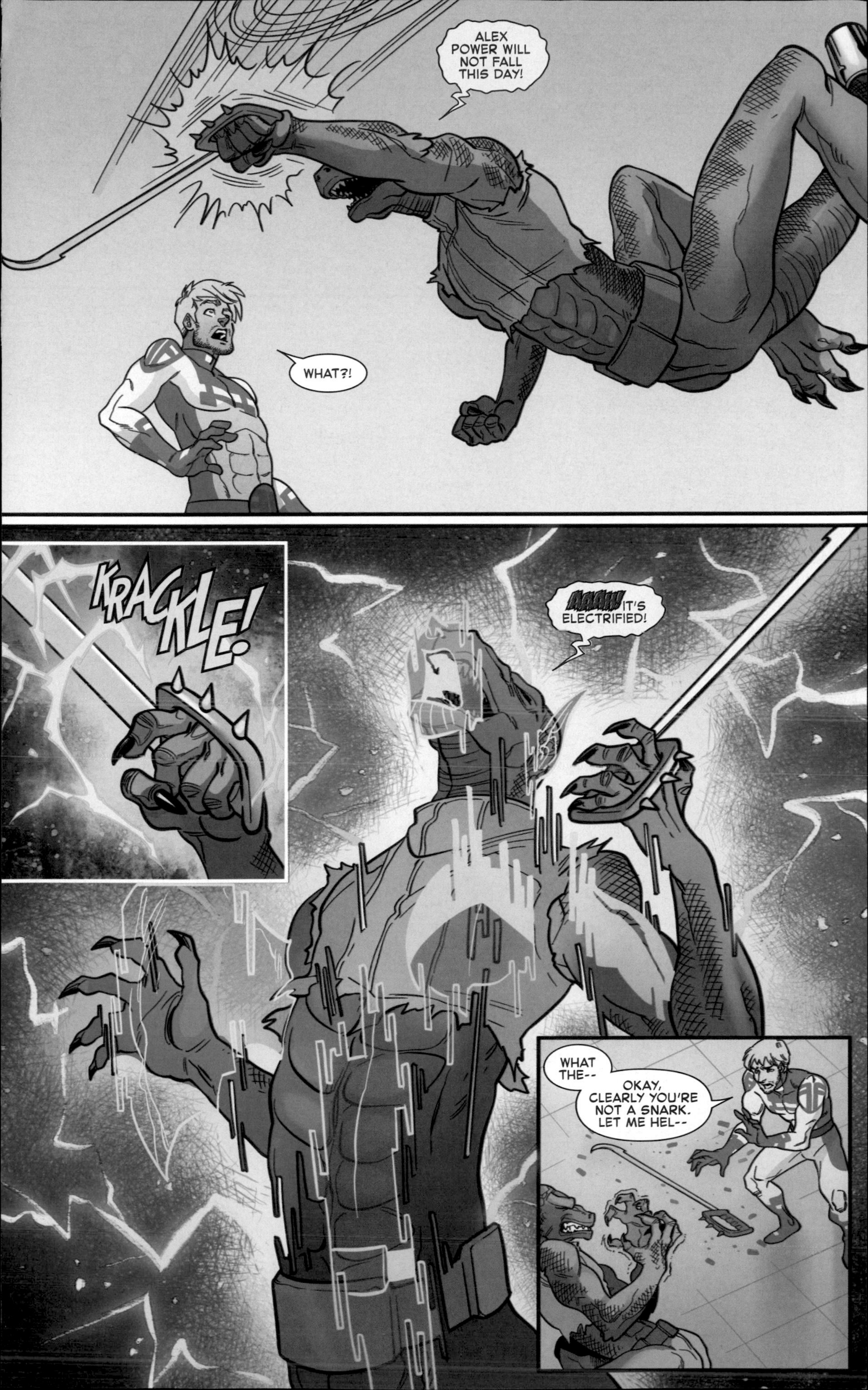
ALEX POWER WILL NOT FALL THIS DAY!
WHAT?!
KRACKLE!
AAAW! IT'S ELECTRIFIED!
WHAT THE--
OKAY, CLEARLY YOU'RE NOT A SNARK. LET ME HEL--

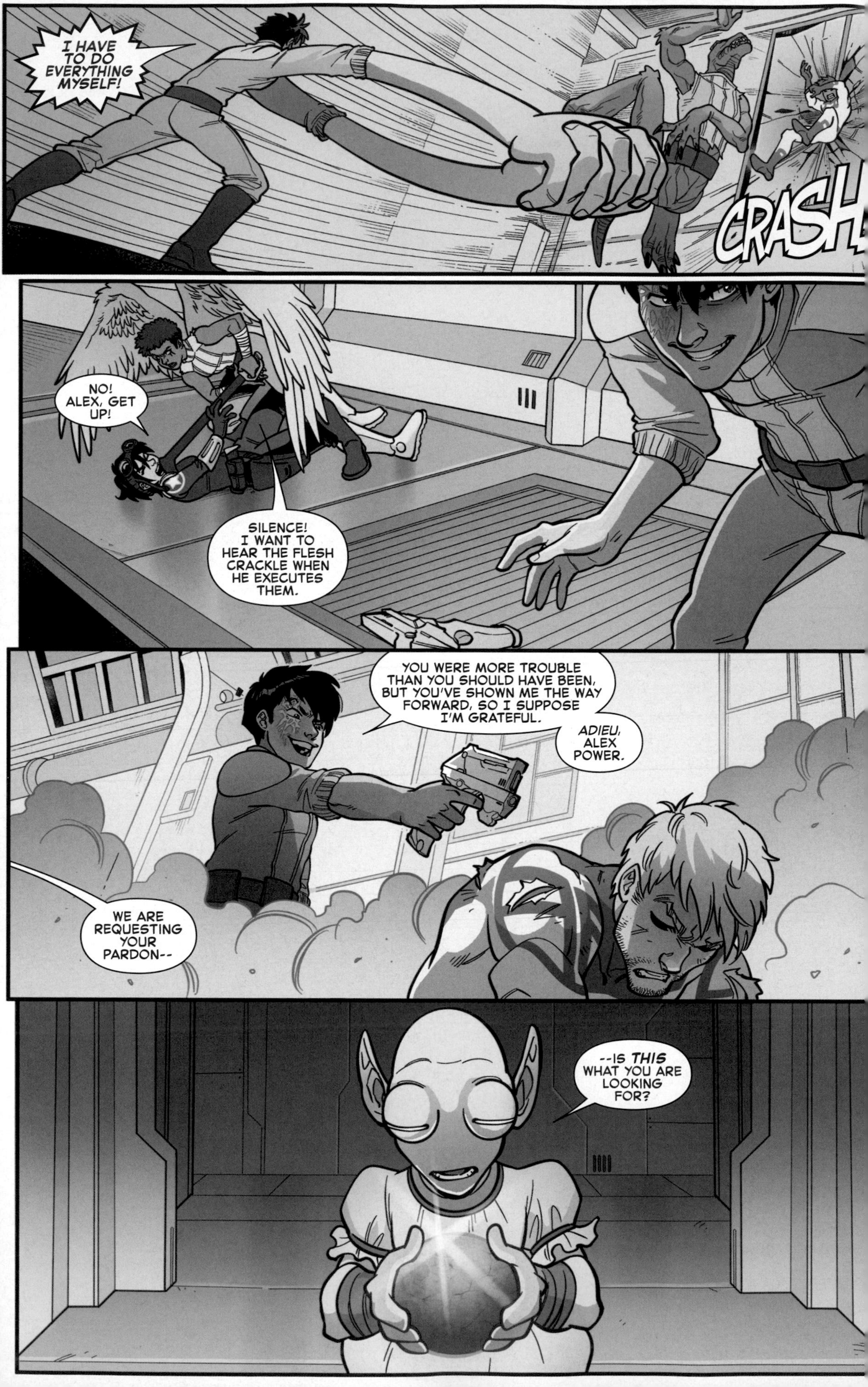
I HAVE TO DO EVERYTHING MYSELF!
CRASH
NO! ALEX, GET UP!
SILENCE! I WANT TO HEAR THE FLESH CRACKLE WHEN HE EXECUTES THEM.
YOU WERE MORE TROUBLE THAN YOU SHOULD HAVE BEEN, BUT YOU'VE SHOWN ME THE WAY FORWARD, SO I SUPPOSE I'M GRATEFUL.
ADIEU, ALEX POWER.
WE ARE REQUESTING YOUR PARDON--
--IS THIS WHAT YOU ARE LOOKING FOR?

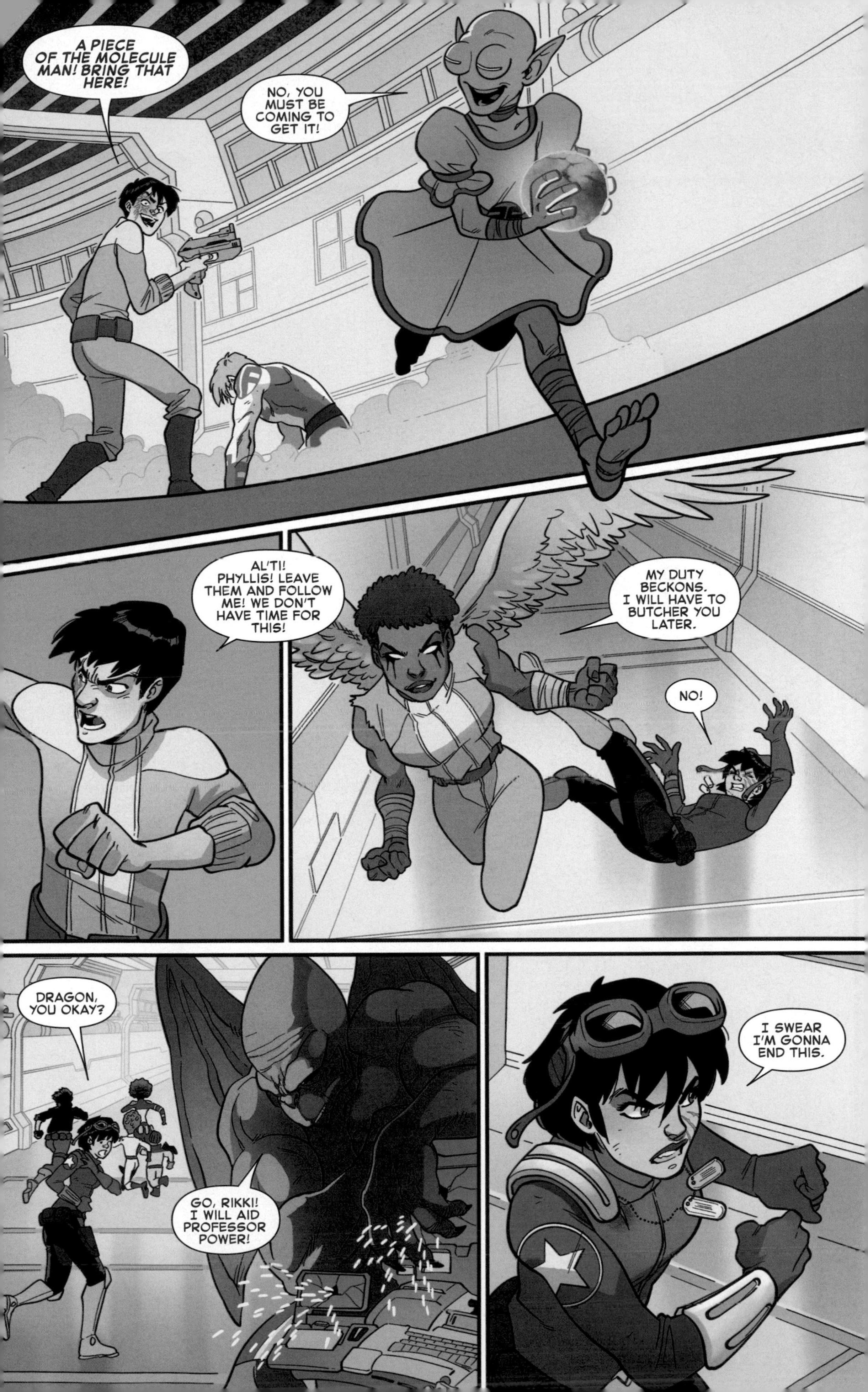
A PIECE OF THE MOLECULE MAN! BRING THAT HERE!
NO, YOU MUST BE COMING TO GET IT!
AL'TI! PHYLLIS! LEAVE THEM AND FOLLOW ME! WE DON'T HAVE TIME FOR THIS!
MY DUTY BECKONS. I WILL HAVE TO BUTCHER YOU LATER.
NO!
DRAGON, YOU OKAY?
GO, RIKKI! I WILL AID PROFESSOR POWER!
I SWEAR I'M GONNA END THIS.

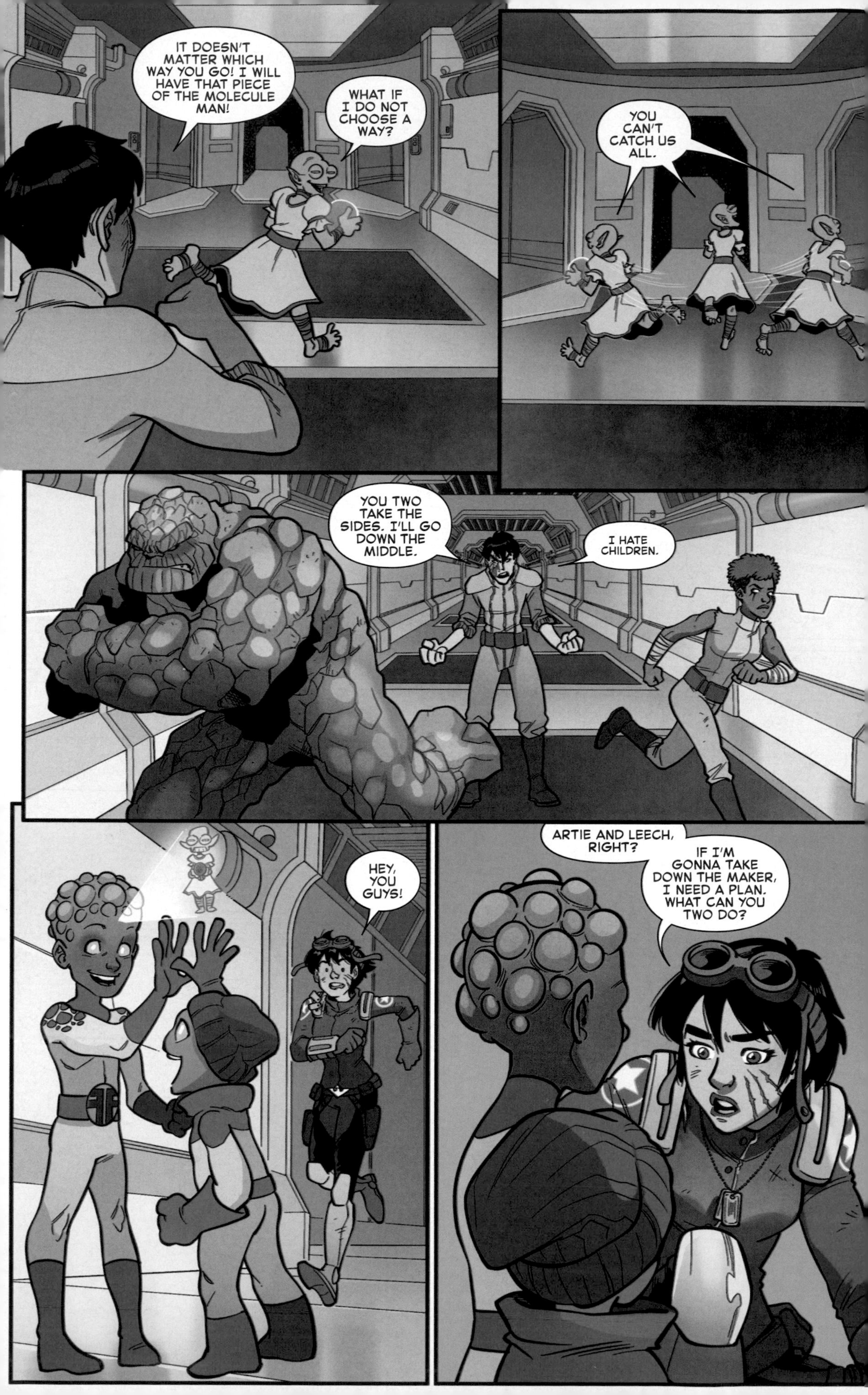
IT DOESN'T MATTER WHICH WAY YOU GO! I WILL HAVE THAT PIECE OF THE MOLECULE MAN!
WHAT IF I DO NOT CHOOSE A WAY?
YOU CAN'T CATCH US ALL.
YOU TWO TAKE THE SIDES. I'LL GO DOWN THE MIDDLE.
I HATE CHILDREN.
HEY, YOU GUYS!
ARTIE AND LEECH, RIGHT?
IF I'M GONNA TAKE DOWN THE MAKER, I NEED A PLAN. WHAT CAN YOU TWO DO?

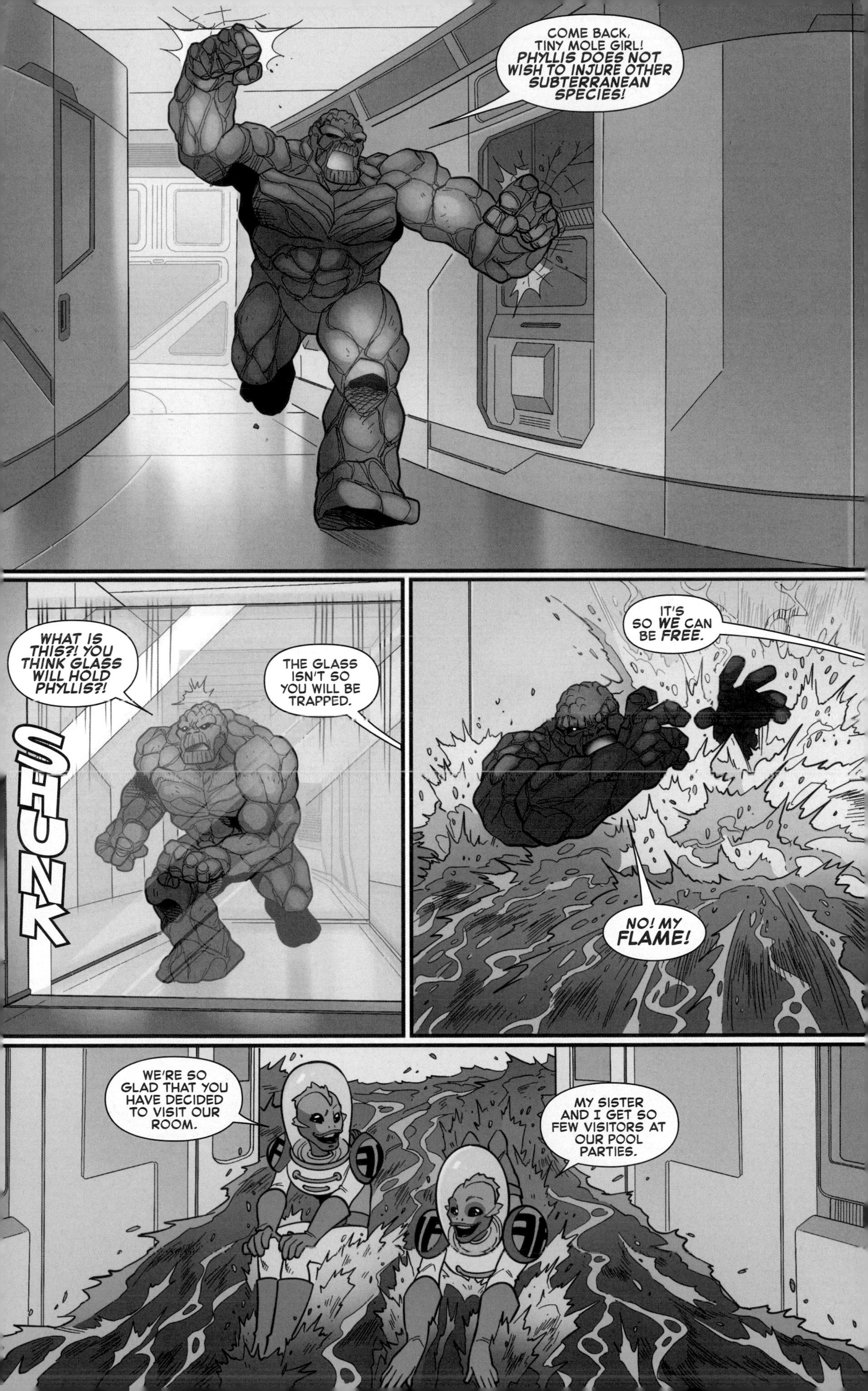
COME BACK, TINY MOLE GIRL! PHYLLIS DOES NOT WISH TO INJURE OTHER SUBTERRANEAN SPECIES!
WHAT IS THIS?! YOU THINK GLASS WILL HOLD PHYLLIS?!
SHUNK
THE GLASS ISN'T SO YOU WILL BE TRAPPED.
IT'S SO WE CAN BE FREE.
NO! MY FLAME!
WE'RE SO GLAD THAT YOU HAVE DECIDED TO VISIT OUR ROOM.
MY SISTER AND I GET SO FEW VISITORS AT OUR POOL PARTIES.

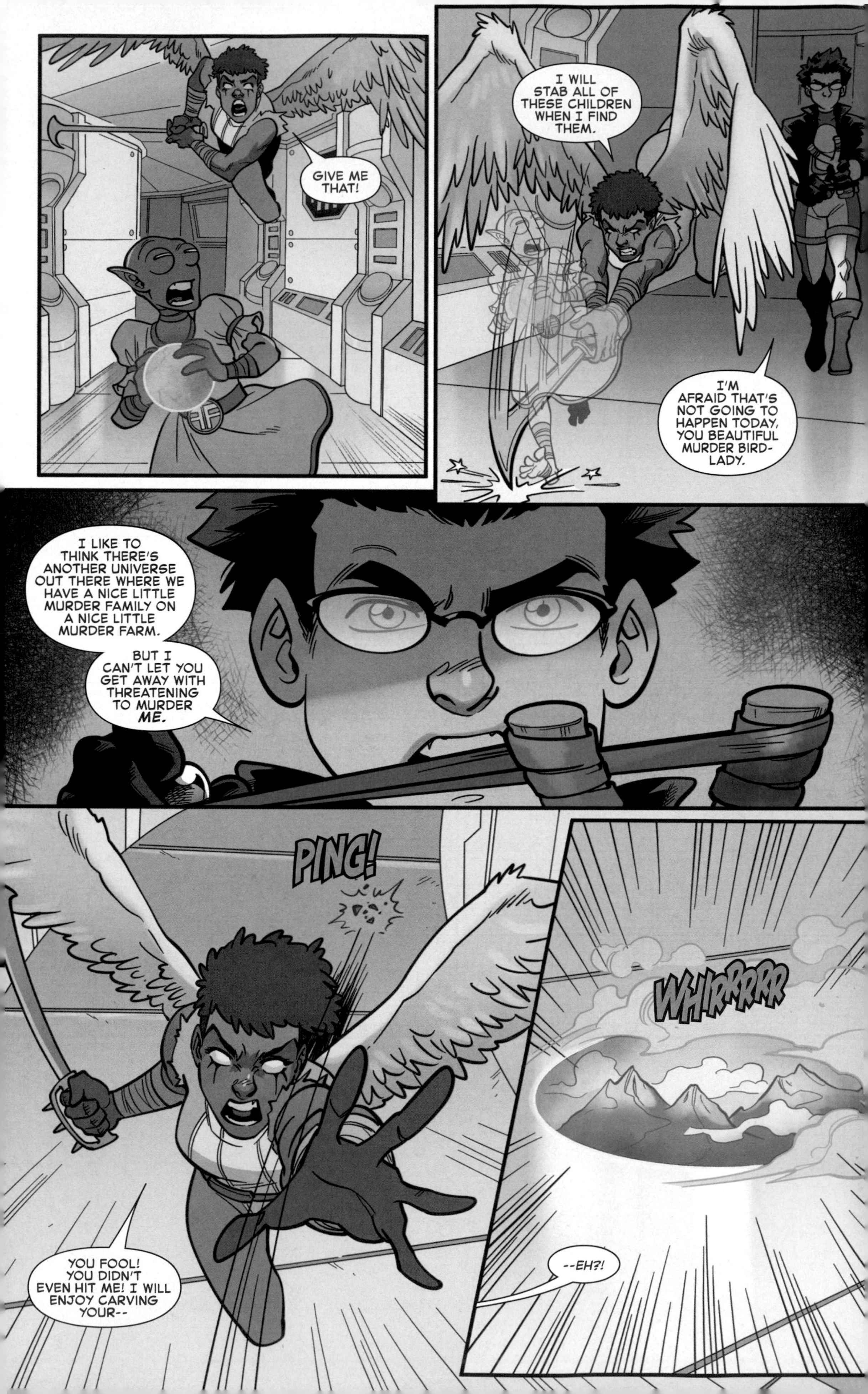
GIVE ME THAT!
I WILL STAB ALL OF THESE CHILDREN WHEN I FIND THEM.
I'M AFRAID THAT'S NOT GOING TO HAPPEN TODAY, YOU BEAUTIFUL MURDER BIRD-LADY.
I LIKE TO THINK THERE'S ANOTHER UNIVERSE OUT THERE WHERE WE HAVE A NICE LITTLE MURDER FAMILY ON A NICE LITTLE MURDER FARM.
BUT I CAN'T LET YOU GET AWAY WITH THREATENING TO MURDER *ME.*
PING!
YOU FOOL! YOU DIDN'T EVEN HIT ME! I WILL ENJOY CARVING YOUR--
WHIRRRR
--EH?!

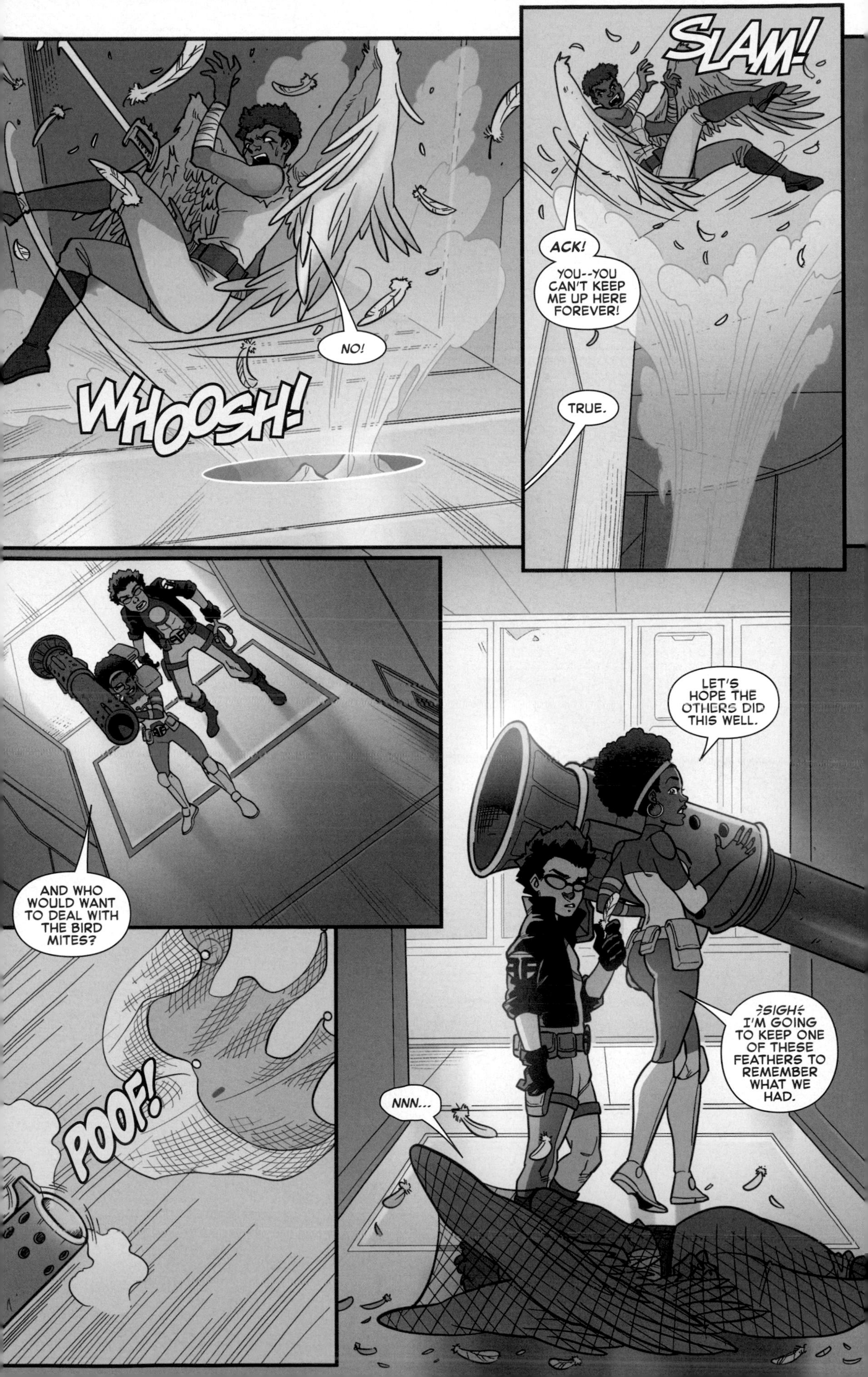
NO!
WHOOSH!
SLAM!
ACK!
YOU--YOU CAN'T KEEP ME UP HERE FOREVER!
TRUE.
AND WHO WOULD WANT TO DEAL WITH THE BIRD MITES?
POOF!
LET'S HOPE THE OTHERS DID THIS WELL.
NNN...
SIGH I'M GOING TO KEEP ONE OF THESE FEATHERS TO REMEMBER WHAT WE HAD.

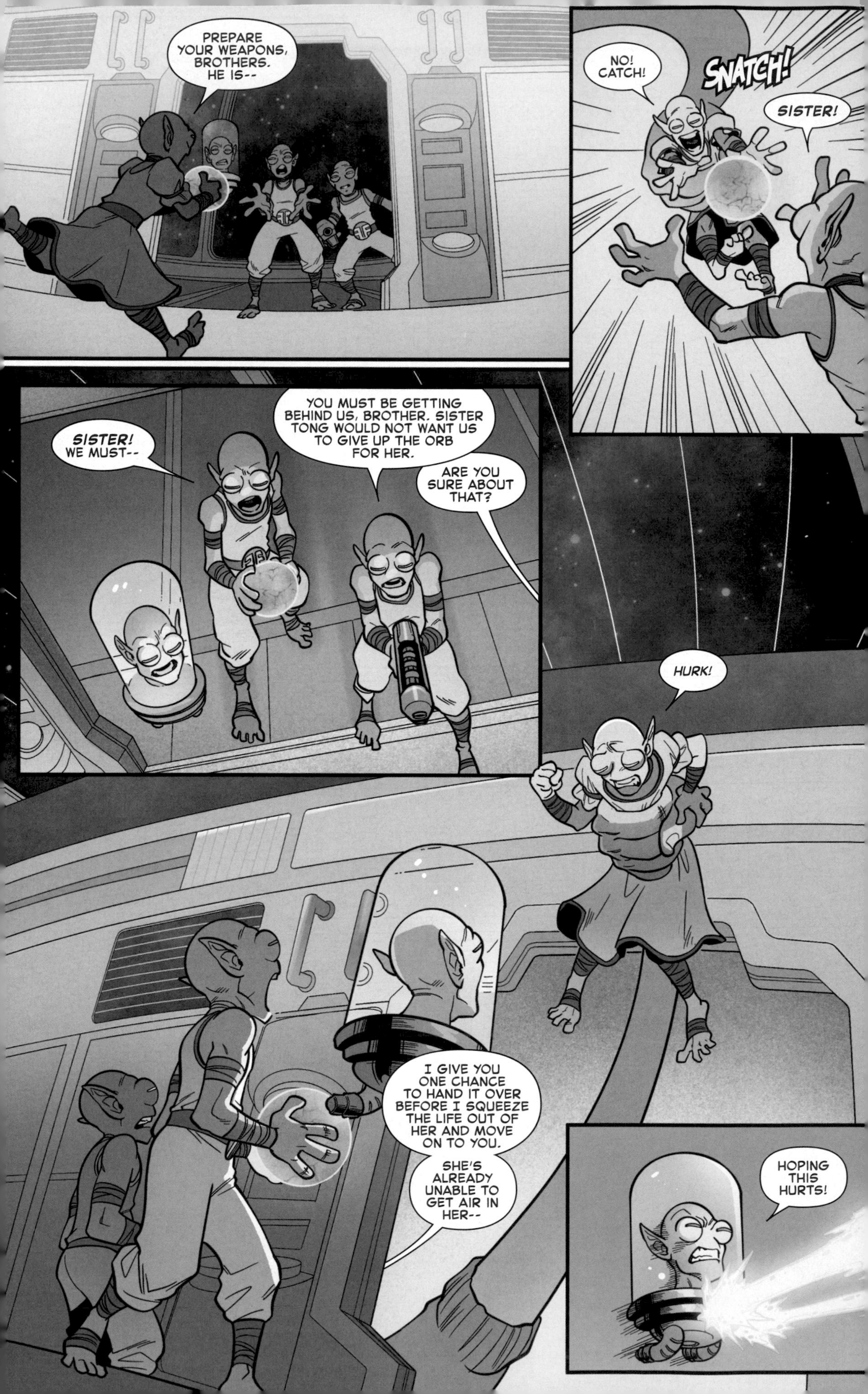
PREPARE YOUR WEAPONS, BROTHERS. HE IS--
NO! CATCH!
SNATCH!
SISTER!
SISTER! WE MUST--
YOU MUST BE GETTING BEHIND US, BROTHER. SISTER TONG WOULD NOT WANT US TO GIVE UP THE ORB FOR HER.
ARE YOU SURE ABOUT THAT?
HURK!
I GIVE YOU ONE CHANCE TO HAND IT OVER BEFORE I SQUEEZE THE LIFE OUT OF HER AND MOVE ON TO YOU.
SHE'S ALREADY UNABLE TO GET AIR IN HER--
HOPING THIS HURTS!

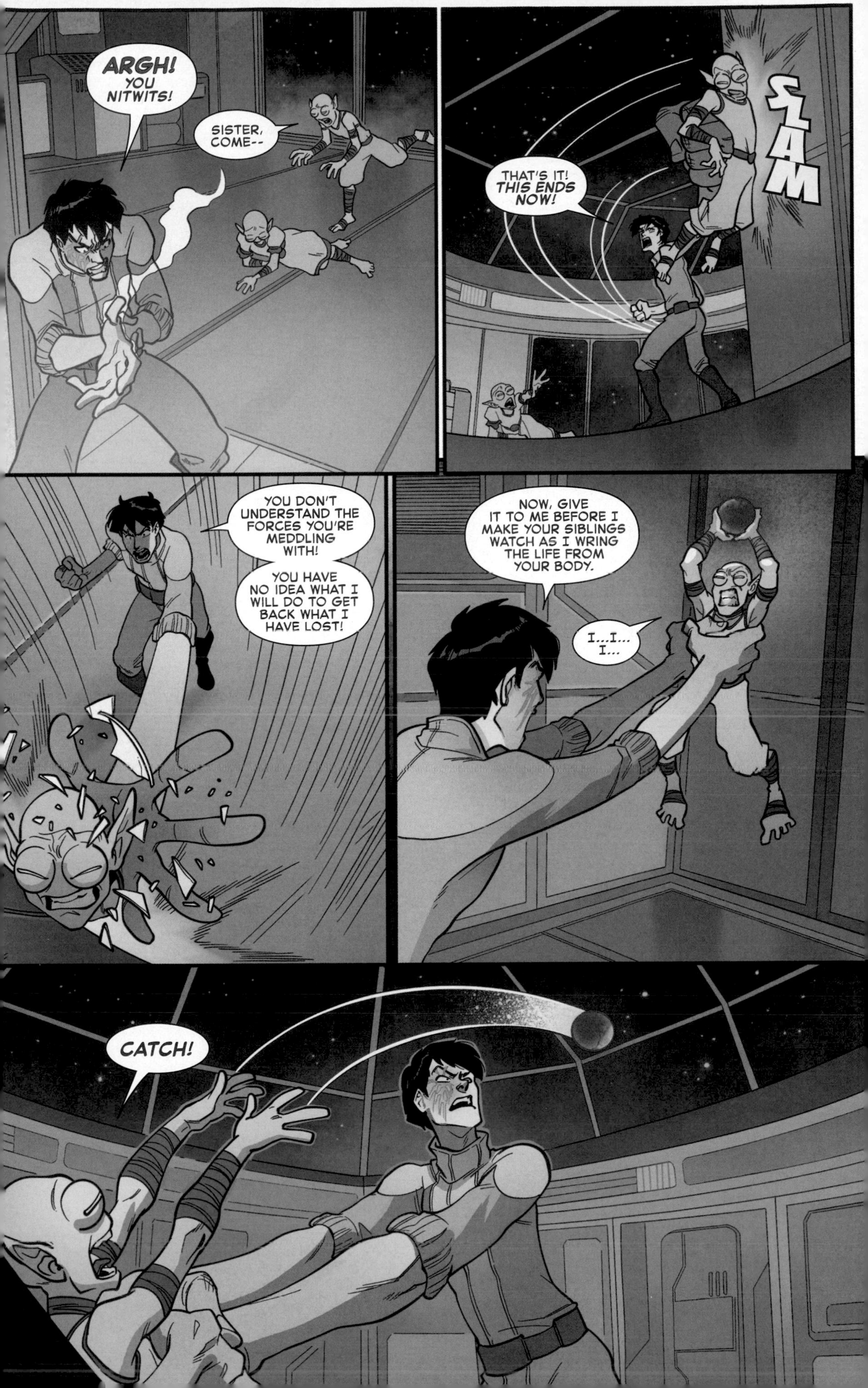
ARGH! YOU NITWITS!
SISTER, COME--
THAT'S IT! THIS ENDS NOW!
SLAM
YOU DON'T UNDERSTAND THE FORCES YOU'RE MEDDLING WITH!
YOU HAVE NO IDEA WHAT I WILL DO TO GET BACK WHAT I HAVE LOST!
NOW, GIVE IT TO ME BEFORE I MAKE YOUR SIBLINGS WATCH AS I WRING THE LIFE FROM YOUR BODY.
I...I... I...
CATCH!

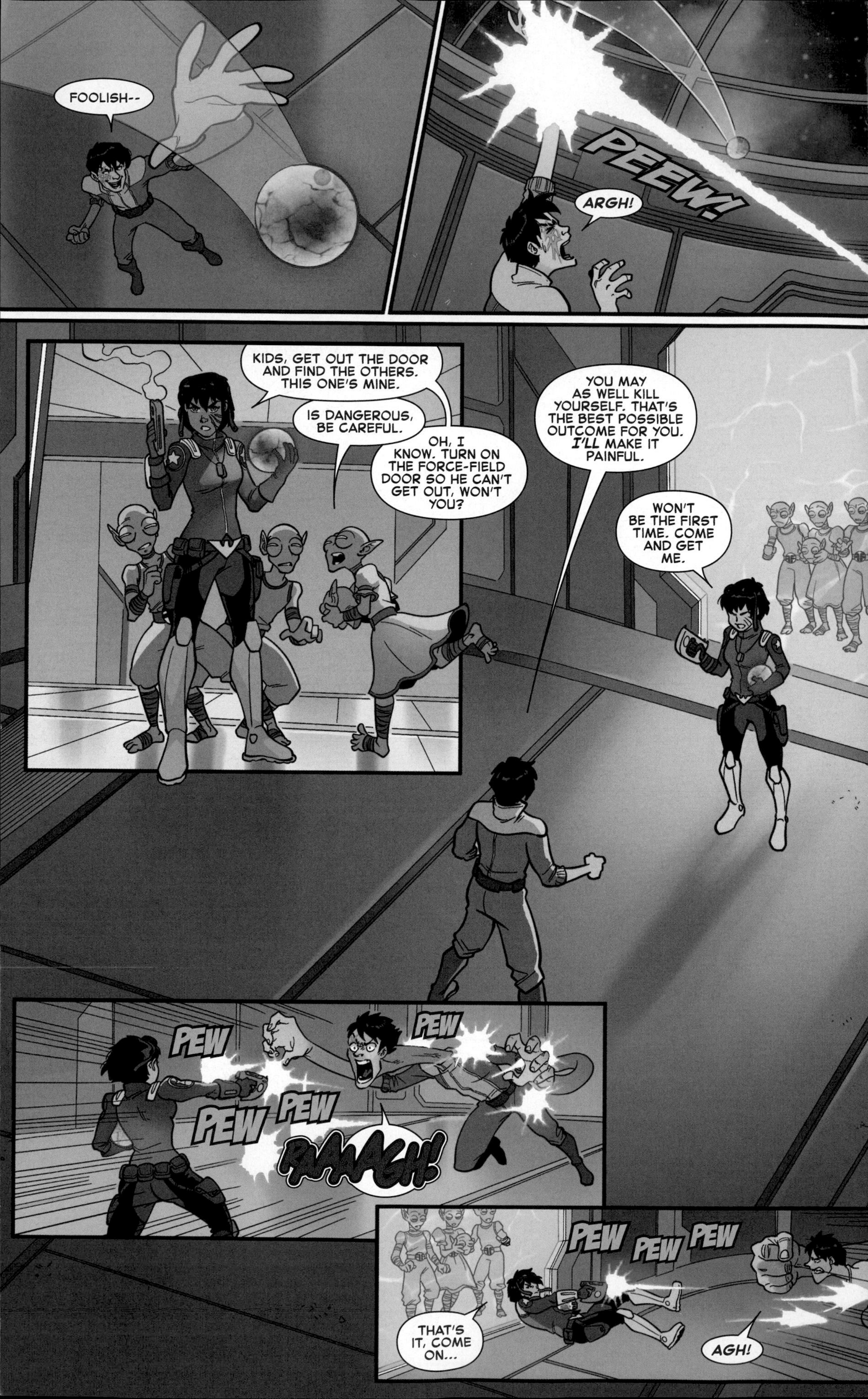
FOOLISH--
PEEW!
ARGH!
KIDS, GET OUT THE DOOR AND FIND THE OTHERS. THIS ONE'S MINE.
IS DANGEROUS, BE CAREFUL.
OH, I KNOW. TURN ON THE FORCE-FIELD DOOR SO HE CAN'T GET OUT, WON'T YOU?
YOU MAY AS WELL KILL YOURSELF. THAT'S THE BEST POSSIBLE OUTCOME FOR YOU. I'LL MAKE IT PAINFUL.
WON'T BE THE FIRST TIME. COME AND GET ME.
PEW
PEW
PEW
PEW
RAAAAGH!
PEW
PEW
PEW
THAT'S IT, COME ON...
AGH!

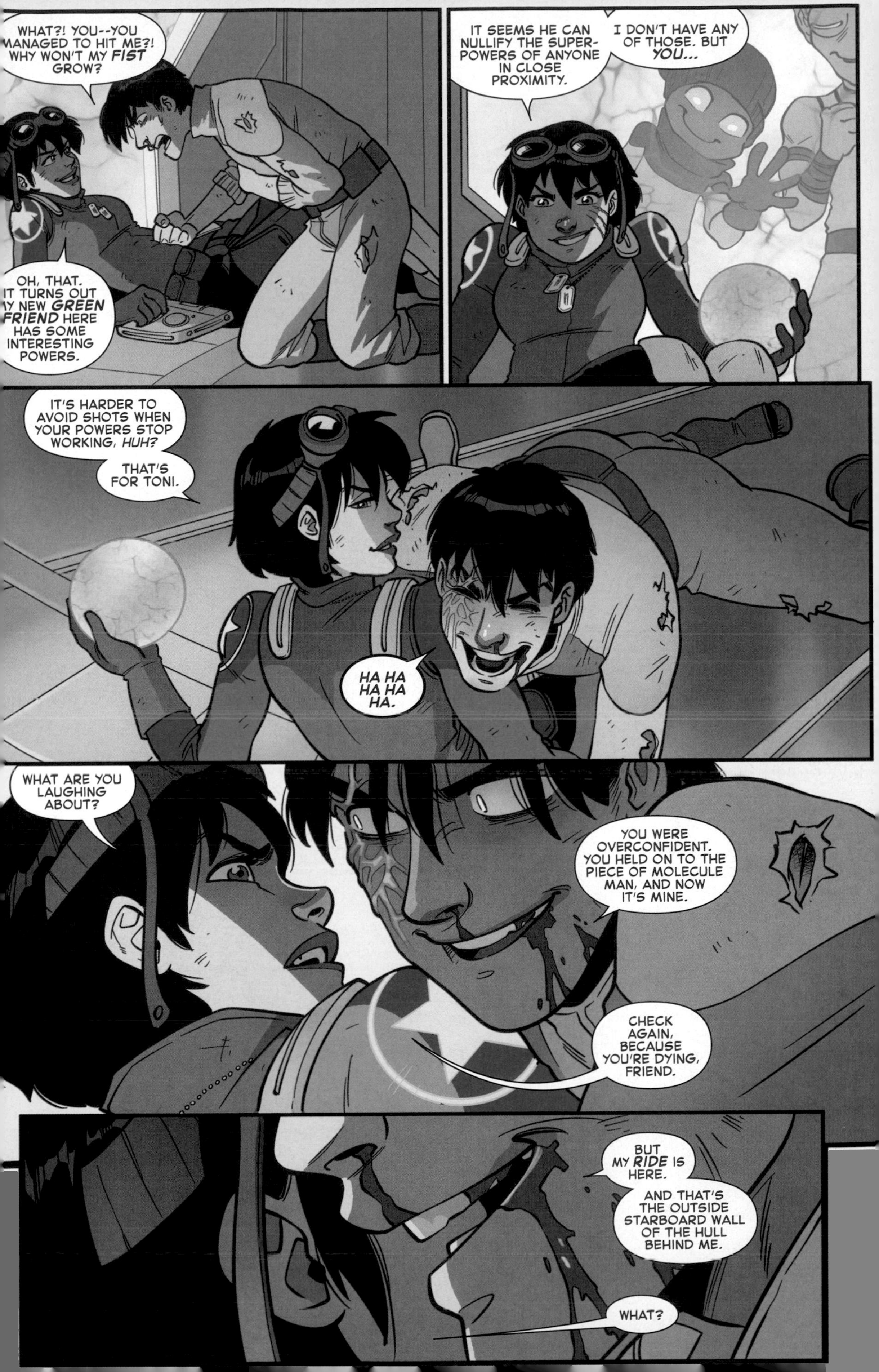
WHAT?! YOU--YOU MANAGED TO HIT ME?! WHY WON'T MY FIST GROW?
OH, THAT. IT TURNS OUT MY NEW GREEN FRIEND HERE HAS SOME INTERESTING POWERS.
IT SEEMS HE CAN NULLIFY THE SUPER-POWERS OF ANYONE IN CLOSE PROXIMITY.
I DON'T HAVE ANY OF THOSE. BUT YOU...
IT'S HARDER TO AVOID SHOTS WHEN YOUR POWERS STOP WORKING, HUH?
THAT'S FOR TONI.
HA HA HA HA HA.
WHAT ARE YOU LAUGHING ABOUT?
YOU WERE OVERCONFIDENT. YOU HELD ON TO THE PIECE OF MOLECULE MAN, AND NOW IT'S MINE.
CHECK AGAIN, BECAUSE YOU'RE DYING, FRIEND.
BUT MY RIDE IS HERE.
AND THAT'S THE OUTSIDE STARBOARD WALL OF THE HULL BEHIND ME.
WHAT?

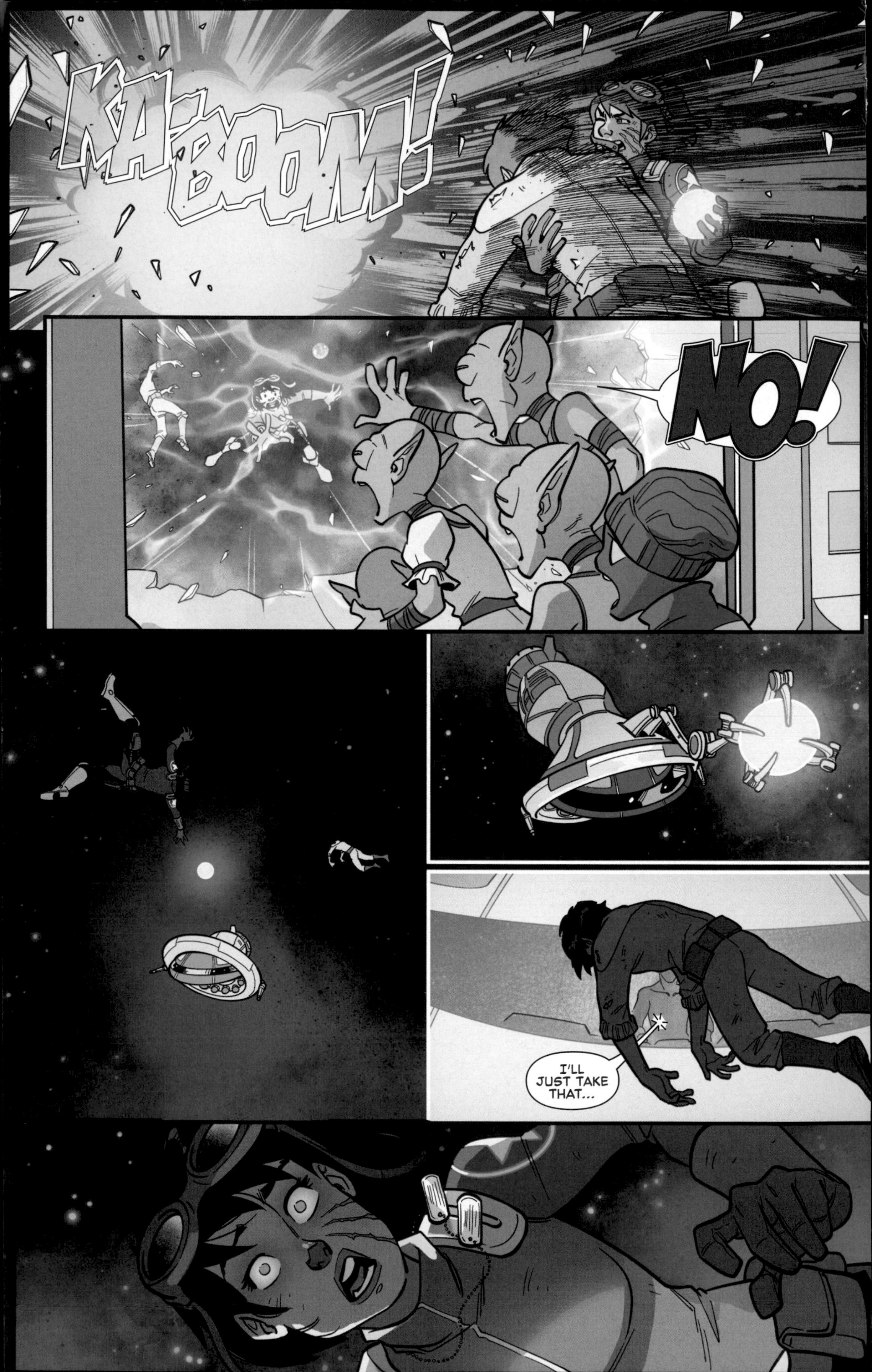
KA-BOOM!
NO!
I'LL JUST TAKE THAT...

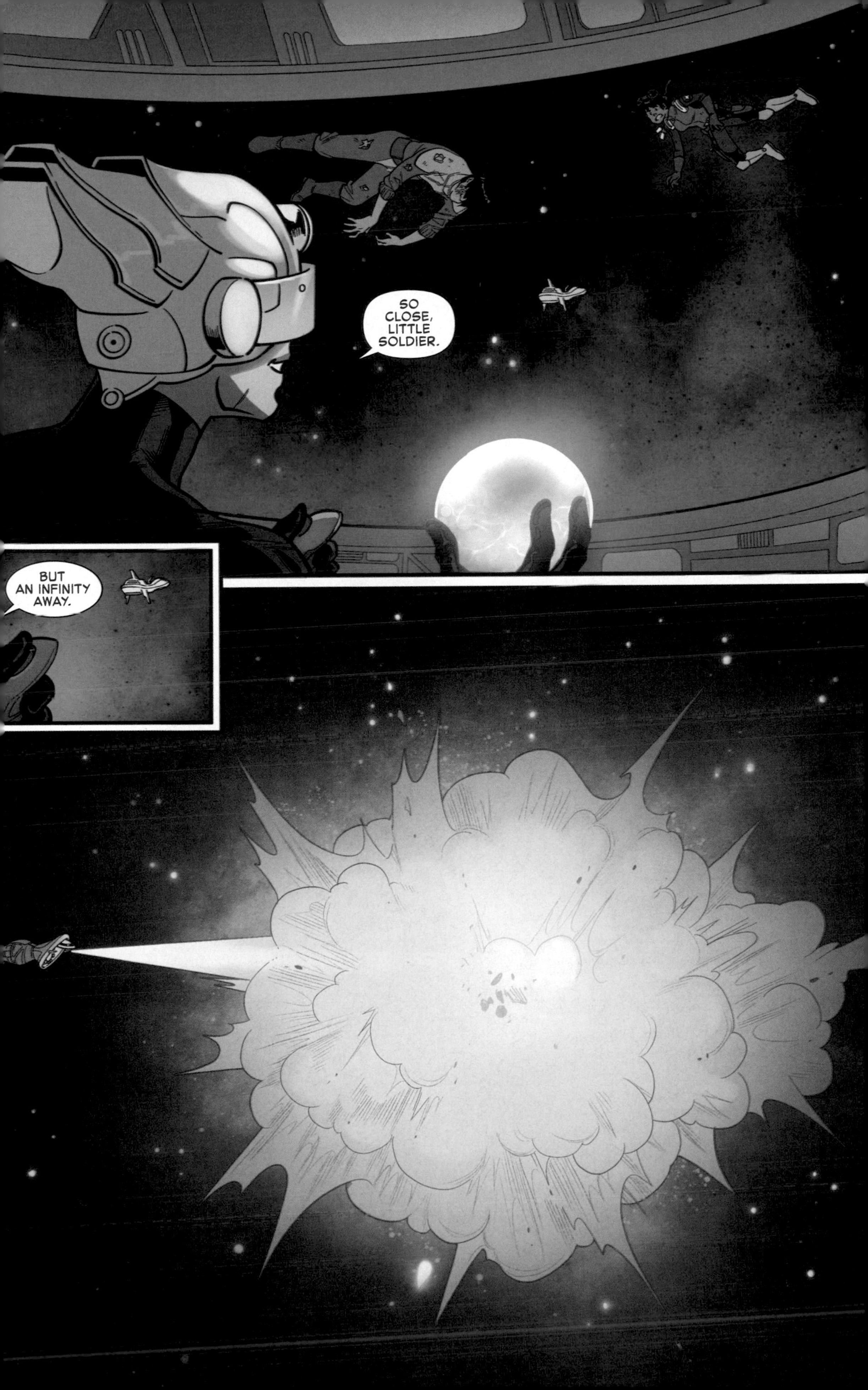
SO CLOSE, LITTLE SOLDIER.
BUT AN INFINITY AWAY.

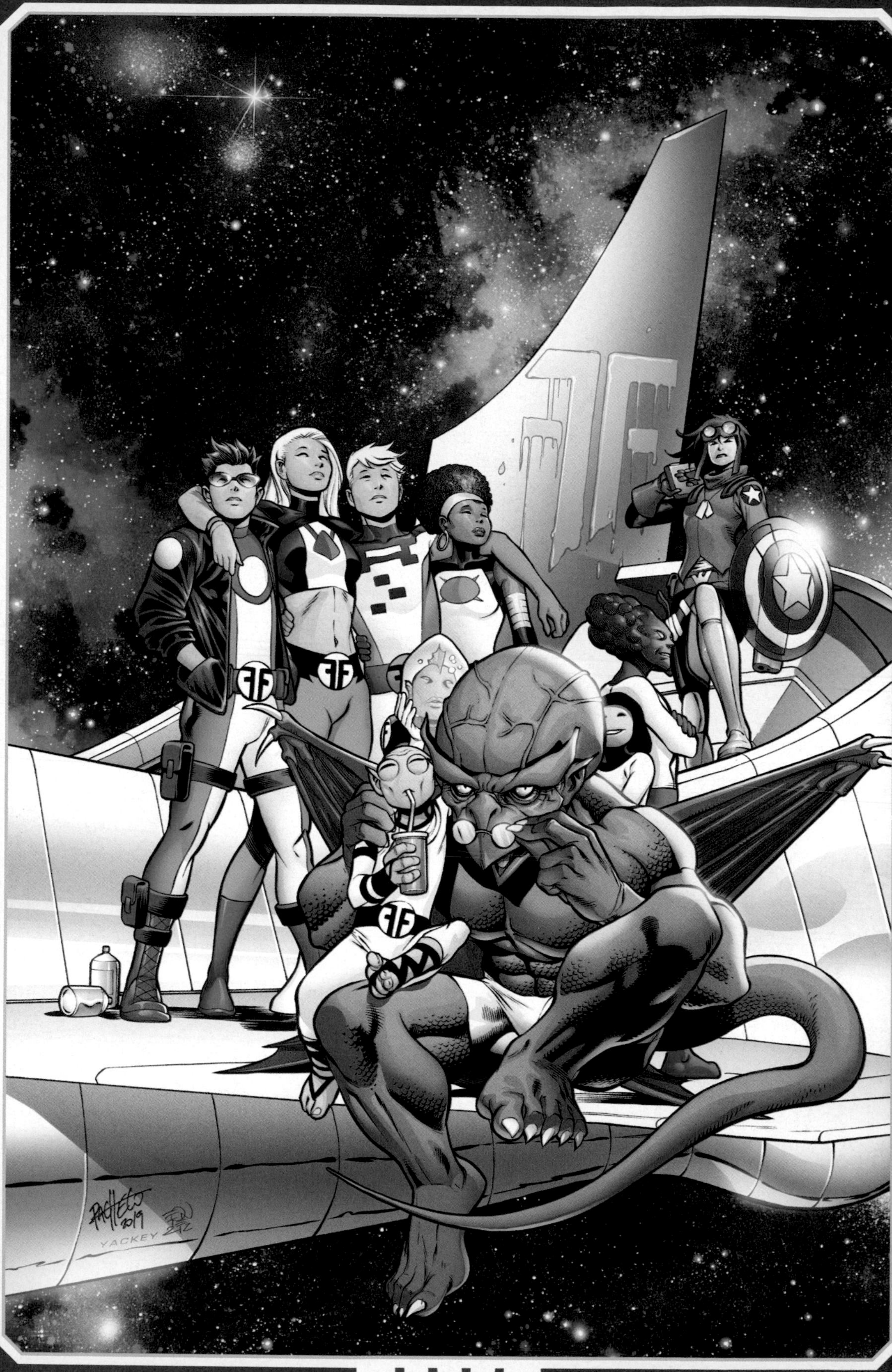
YACKEY

FIVE

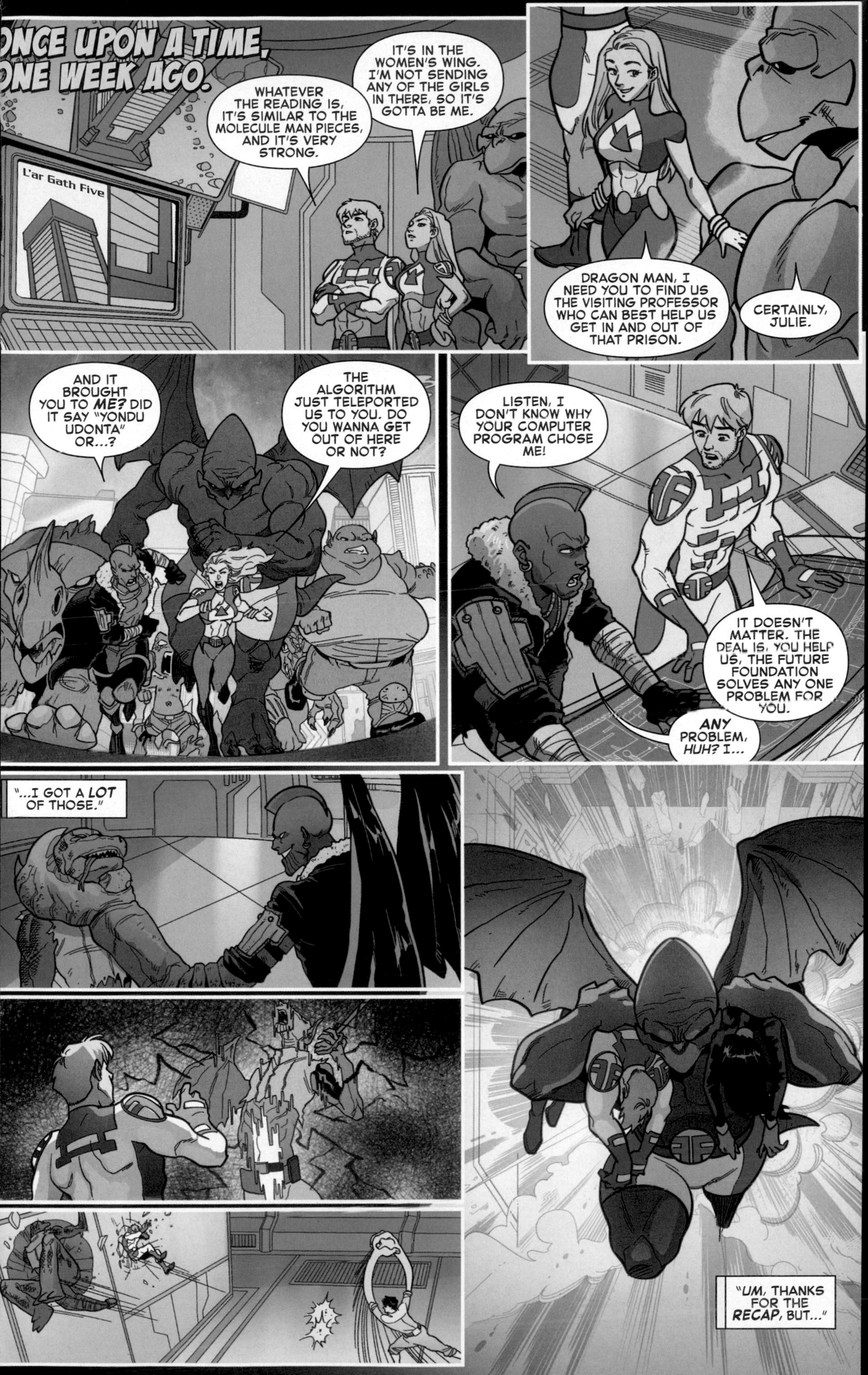
ONCE UPON A TIME, ONE WEEK AGO.
L'ar Gath Five
WHATEVER THE READING IS, IT'S SIMILAR TO THE MOLECULE MAN PIECES, AND IT'S VERY STRONG.
IT'S IN THE WOMEN'S WING. I'M NOT SENDING ANY OF THE GIRLS IN THERE, SO IT'S GOTTA BE ME.
DRAGON MAN, I NEED YOU TO FIND US THE VISITING PROFESSOR WHO CAN BEST HELP US GET IN AND OUT OF THAT PRISON.
CERTAINLY, JULIE.
AND IT BROUGHT YOU TO ME? DID IT SAY "YONDU UDONTA" OR...?
THE ALGORITHM JUST TELEPORTED US TO YOU. DO YOU WANNA GET OUT OF HERE OR NOT?
LISTEN, I DON'T KNOW WHY YOUR COMPUTER PROGRAM CHOSE ME!
IT DOESN'T MATTER. THE DEAL IS, YOU HELP US, THE FUTURE FOUNDATION SOLVES ANY ONE PROBLEM FOR YOU.
ANY PROBLEM, HUH? I...
"...I GOT A LOT OF THOSE."
"UM, THANKS FOR THE RECAP, BUT..."

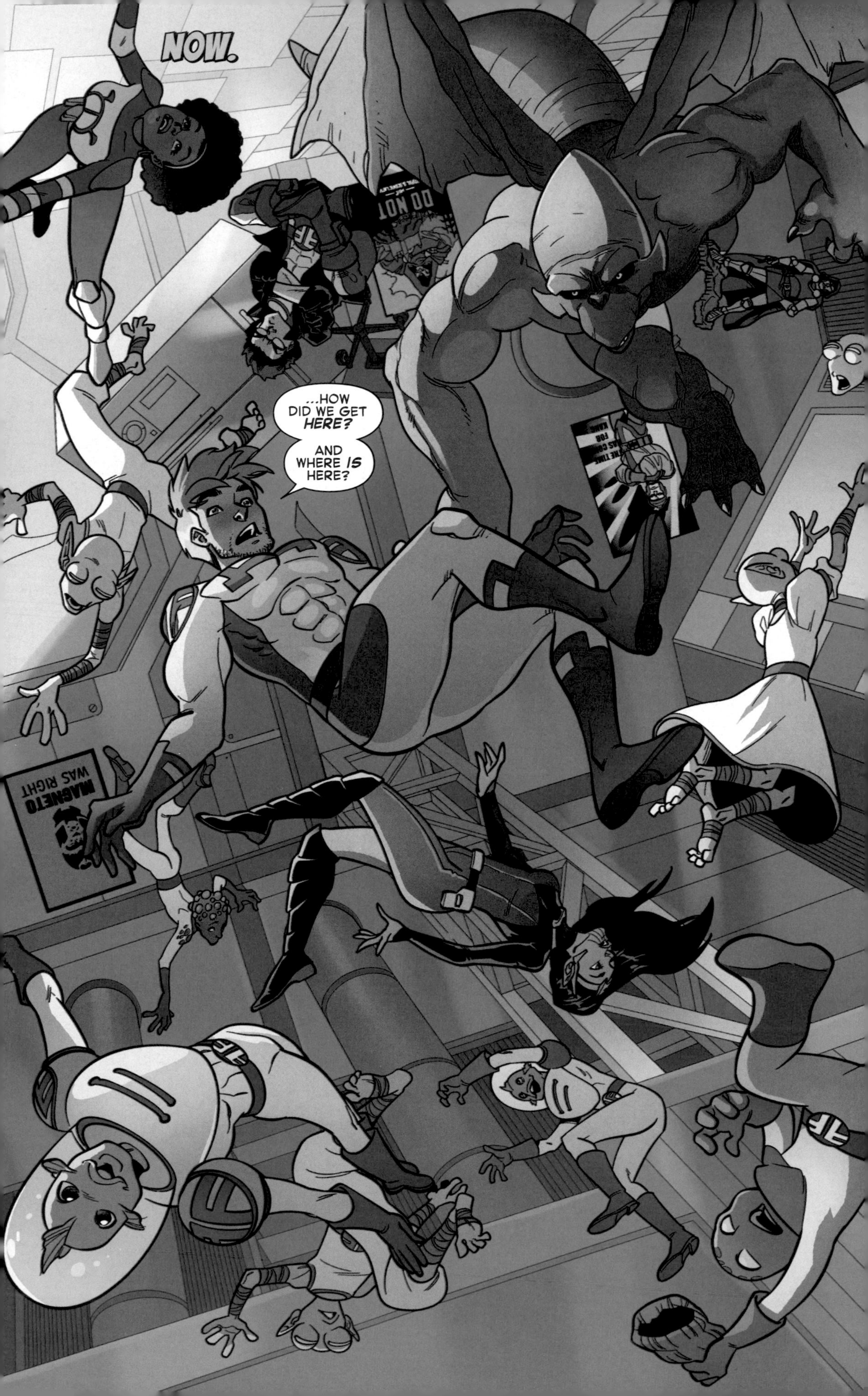
NOW.
...HOW DID WE GET *HERE?*
AND WHERE *IS* HERE?
DO NOT
MAGNETO WAS RIGHT

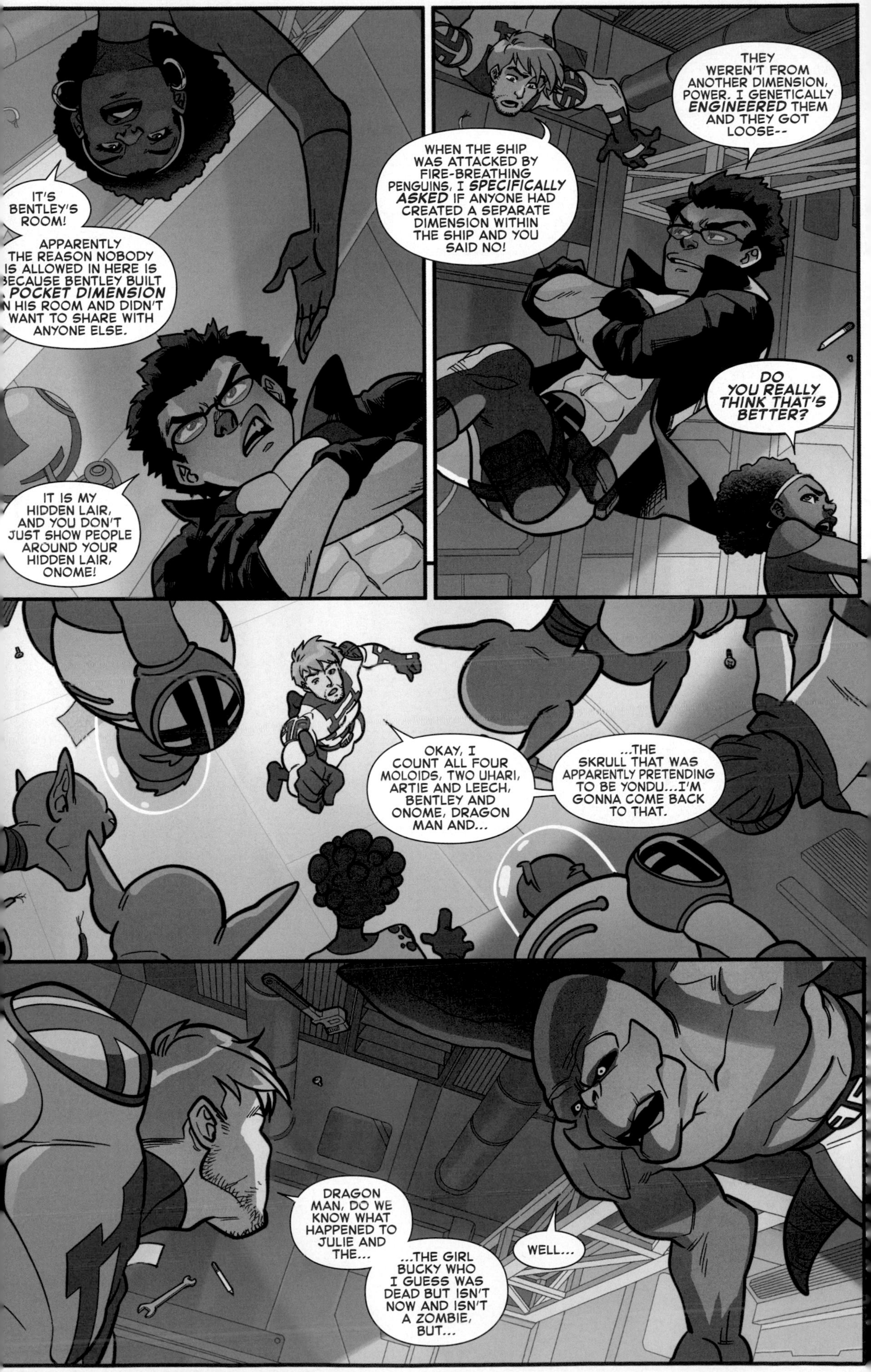
IT'S BENTLEY'S ROOM!
APPARENTLY THE REASON NOBODY IS ALLOWED IN HERE IS BECAUSE BENTLEY BUILT A POCKET DIMENSION IN HIS ROOM AND DIDN'T WANT TO SHARE WITH ANYONE ELSE.
IT IS MY HIDDEN LAIR, AND YOU DON'T JUST SHOW PEOPLE AROUND YOUR HIDDEN LAIR, ONOME!
WHEN THE SHIP WAS ATTACKED BY FIRE-BREATHING PENGUINS, I SPECIFICALLY ASKED IF ANYONE HAD CREATED A SEPARATE DIMENSION WITHIN THE SHIP AND YOU SAID NO!
THEY WEREN'T FROM ANOTHER DIMENSION, POWER. I GENETICALLY ENGINEERED THEM AND THEY GOT LOOSE--
DO YOU REALLY THINK THAT'S BETTER?
OKAY, I COUNT ALL FOUR MOLOIDS, TWO UHARI, ARTIE AND LEECH, BENTLEY AND ONOME, DRAGON MAN AND...
...THE SKRULL THAT WAS APPARENTLY PRETENDING TO BE YONDU...I'M GONNA COME BACK TO THAT.
DRAGON MAN, DO WE KNOW WHAT HAPPENED TO JULIE AND THE...
...THE GIRL BUCKY WHO I GUESS WAS DEAD BUT ISN'T NOW AND ISN'T A ZOMBIE, BUT...
WELL...

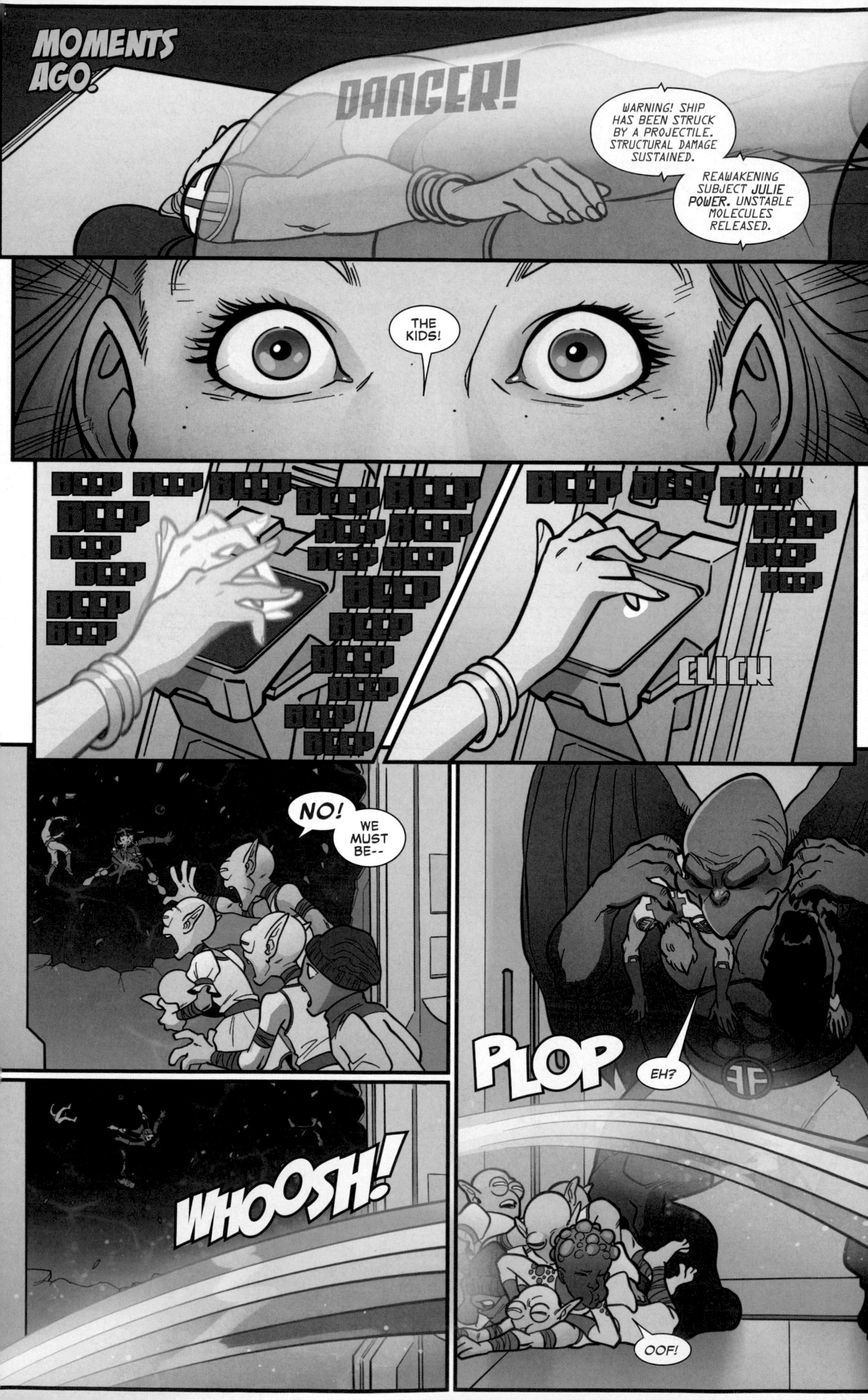
MOMENTS AGO.
DANGER!
WARNING! SHIP HAS BEEN STRUCK BY A PROJECTILE. STRUCTURAL DAMAGE SUSTAINED.
REAWAKENING SUBJECT JULIE POWER. UNSTABLE MOLECULES RELEASED.
THE KIDS!
BEEP BEEP BEEP BEEP BEEP BEEP BEEP BEEP BEEP BEEP BEEP BEEP BEEP BEEP BEEP BEEP BEEP BEEP BEEP
BEEP BEEP BEEP BEEP BEEP BEEP
CLICK
NO!
WE MUST BE--
WHOOSH!
PLOP
EH?
OOF!

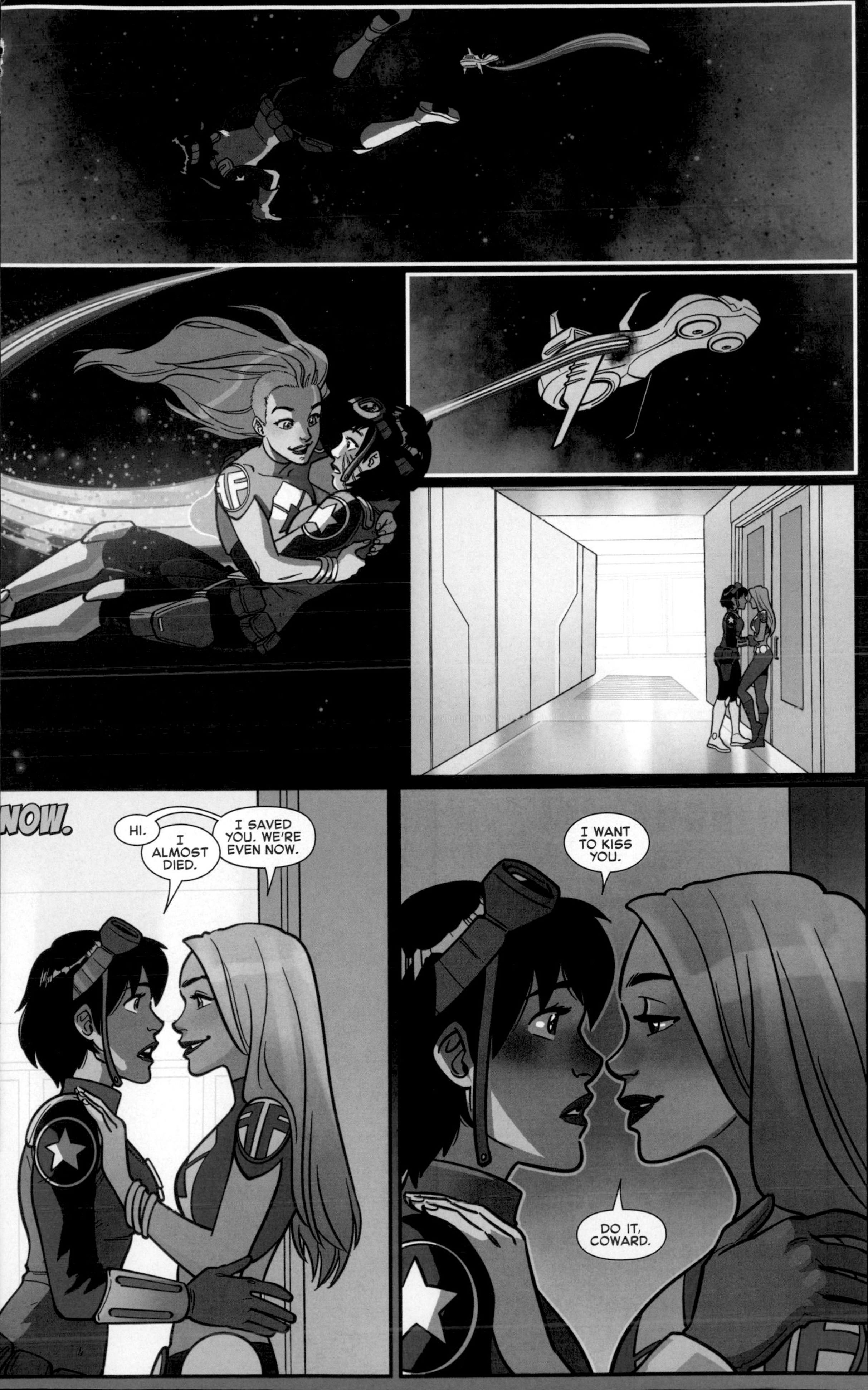

NOW.
HI.
I ALMOST DIED.
I SAVED YOU. WE'RE EVEN NOW.
I WANT TO KISS YOU.
DO IT, COWARD.

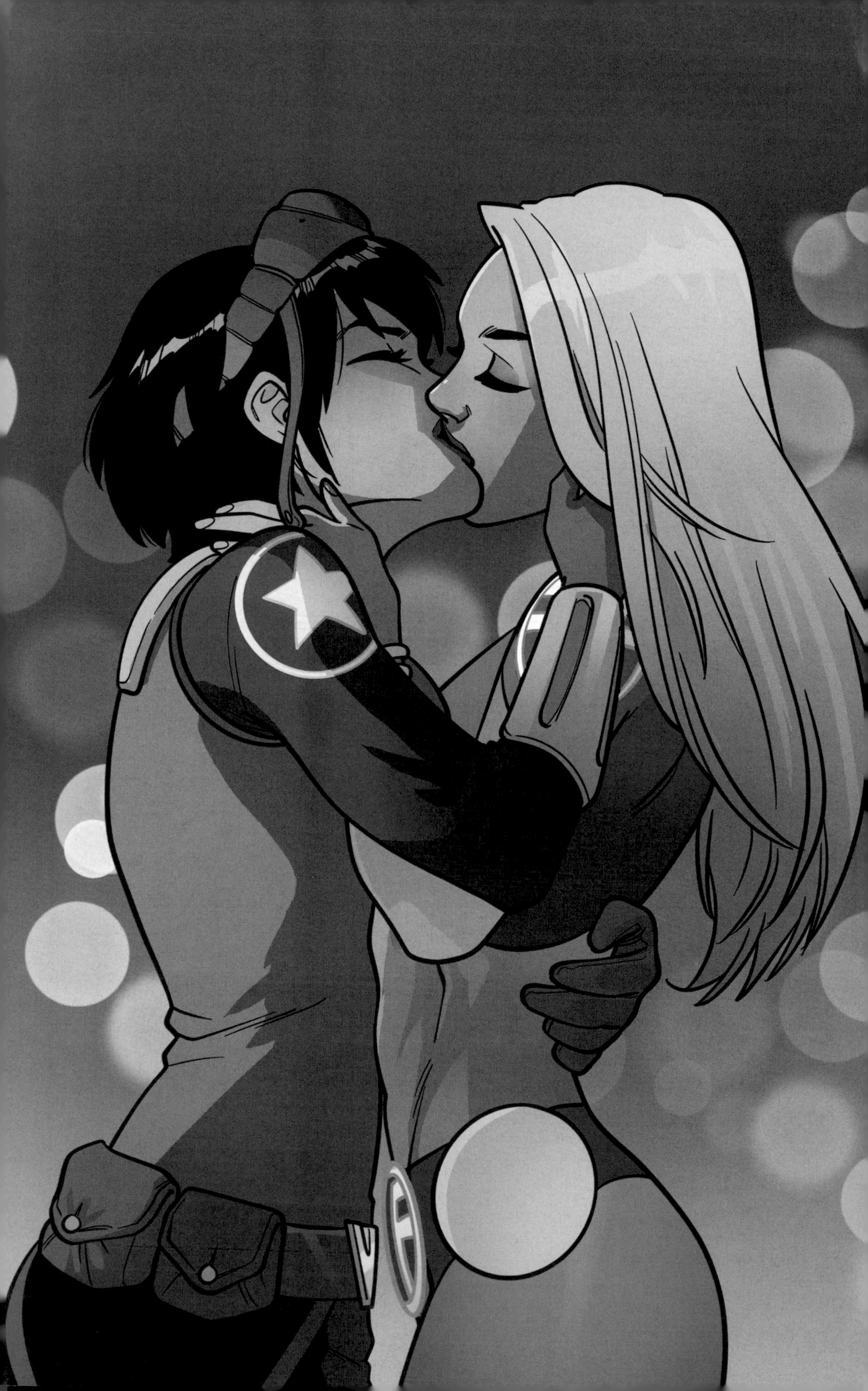

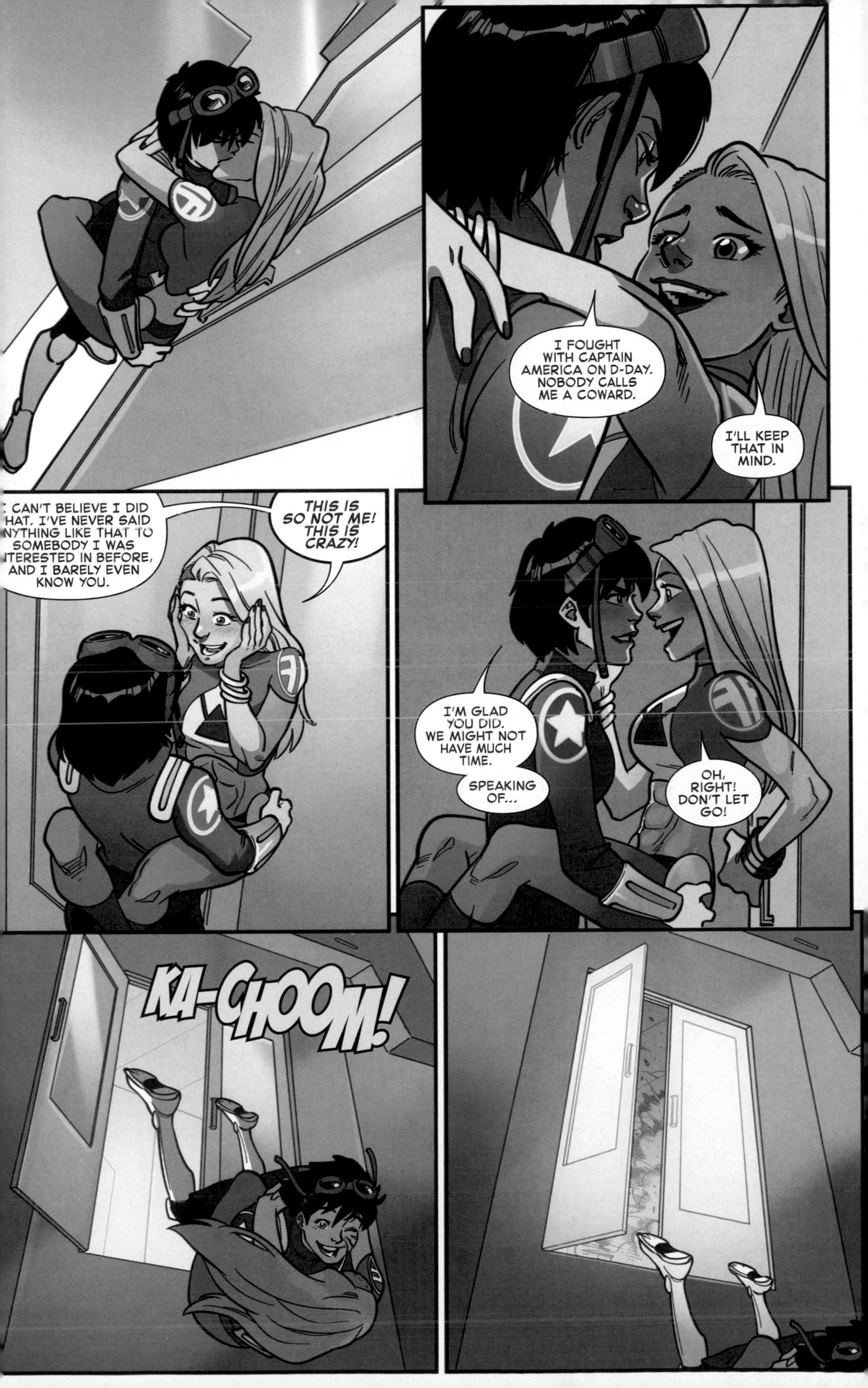
I FOUGHT WITH CAPTAIN AMERICA ON D-DAY. NOBODY CALLS ME A COWARD.
I'LL KEEP THAT IN MIND.
I CAN'T BELIEVE I DID THAT. I'VE NEVER SAID ANYTHING LIKE THAT TO SOMEBODY I WAS INTERESTED IN BEFORE, AND I BARELY EVEN KNOW YOU.
THIS IS SO NOT ME! THIS IS CRAZY!
I'M GLAD YOU DID. WE MIGHT NOT HAVE MUCH TIME.
SPEAKING OF...
OH, RIGHT! DON'T LET GO!
KA-CHOOM!

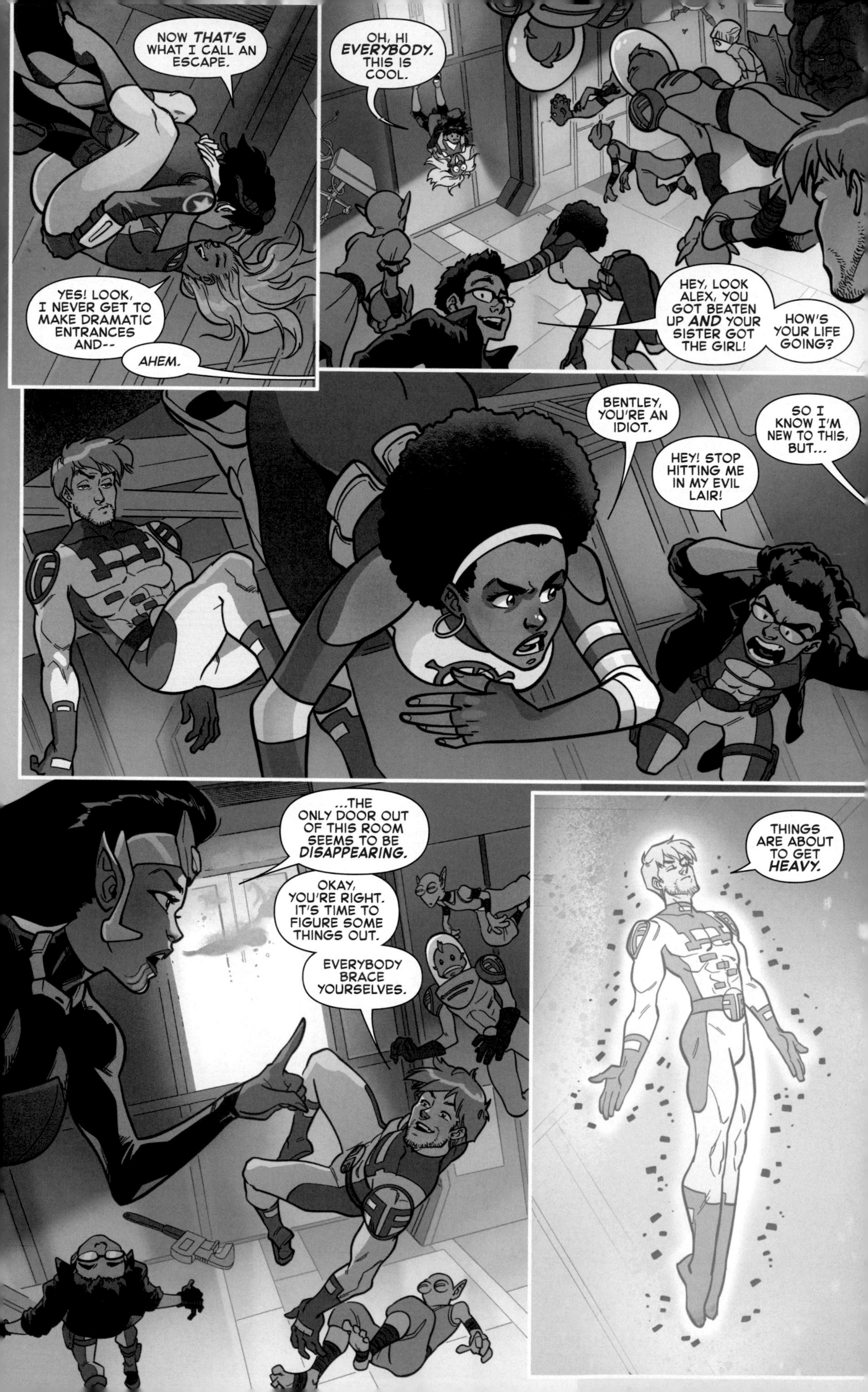
NOW THAT'S WHAT I CALL AN ESCAPE.
YES! LOOK, I NEVER GET TO MAKE DRAMATIC ENTRANCES AND--
AHEM.
OH, HI EVERYBODY. THIS IS COOL.
HEY, LOOK ALEX, YOU GOT BEATEN UP AND YOUR SISTER GOT THE GIRL!
HOW'S YOUR LIFE GOING?
BENTLEY, YOU'RE AN IDIOT.
HEY! STOP HITTING ME IN MY EVIL LAIR!
SO I KNOW I'M NEW TO THIS, BUT...
...THE ONLY DOOR OUT OF THIS ROOM SEEMS TO BE DISAPPEARING.
OKAY, YOU'RE RIGHT. IT'S TIME TO FIGURE SOME THINGS OUT.
EVERYBODY BRACE YOURSELVES.
THINGS ARE ABOUT TO GET HEAVY.

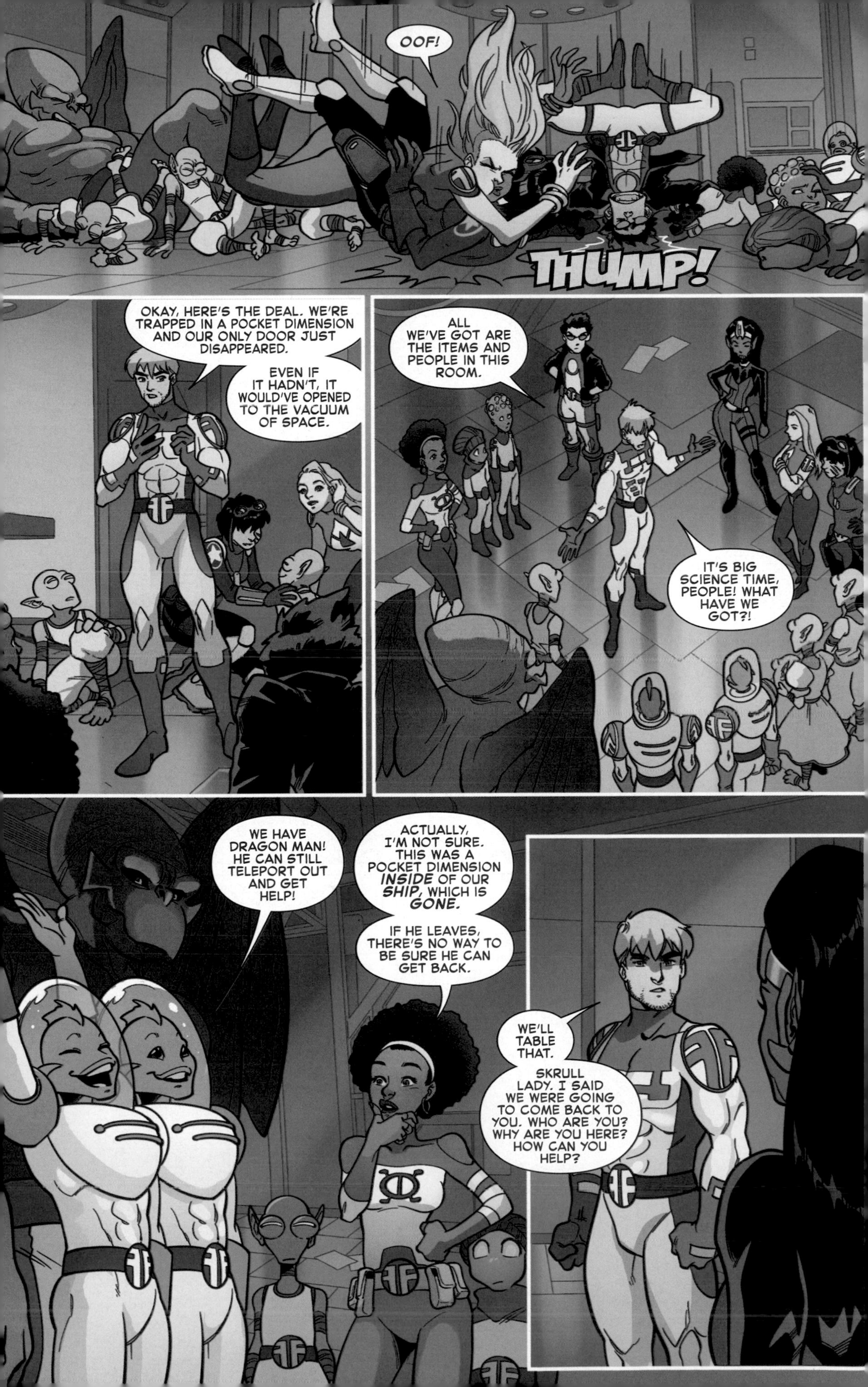
OOF!
THUMP!
OKAY, HERE'S THE DEAL. WE'RE TRAPPED IN A POCKET DIMENSION AND OUR ONLY DOOR JUST DISAPPEARED.
EVEN IF IT HADN'T, IT WOULD'VE OPENED TO THE VACUUM OF SPACE.
ALL WE'VE GOT ARE THE ITEMS AND PEOPLE IN THIS ROOM.
IT'S BIG SCIENCE TIME, PEOPLE! WHAT HAVE WE GOT?!
WE HAVE DRAGON MAN! HE CAN STILL TELEPORT OUT AND GET HELP!
ACTUALLY, I'M NOT SURE. THIS WAS A POCKET DIMENSION *INSIDE* OF OUR *SHIP*, WHICH IS *GONE.*
IF HE LEAVES, THERE'S NO WAY TO BE SURE HE CAN GET BACK.
WE'LL TABLE THAT.
SKRULL LADY. I SAID WE WERE GOING TO COME BACK TO YOU. WHO ARE YOU? WHY ARE YOU HERE? HOW CAN YOU HELP?

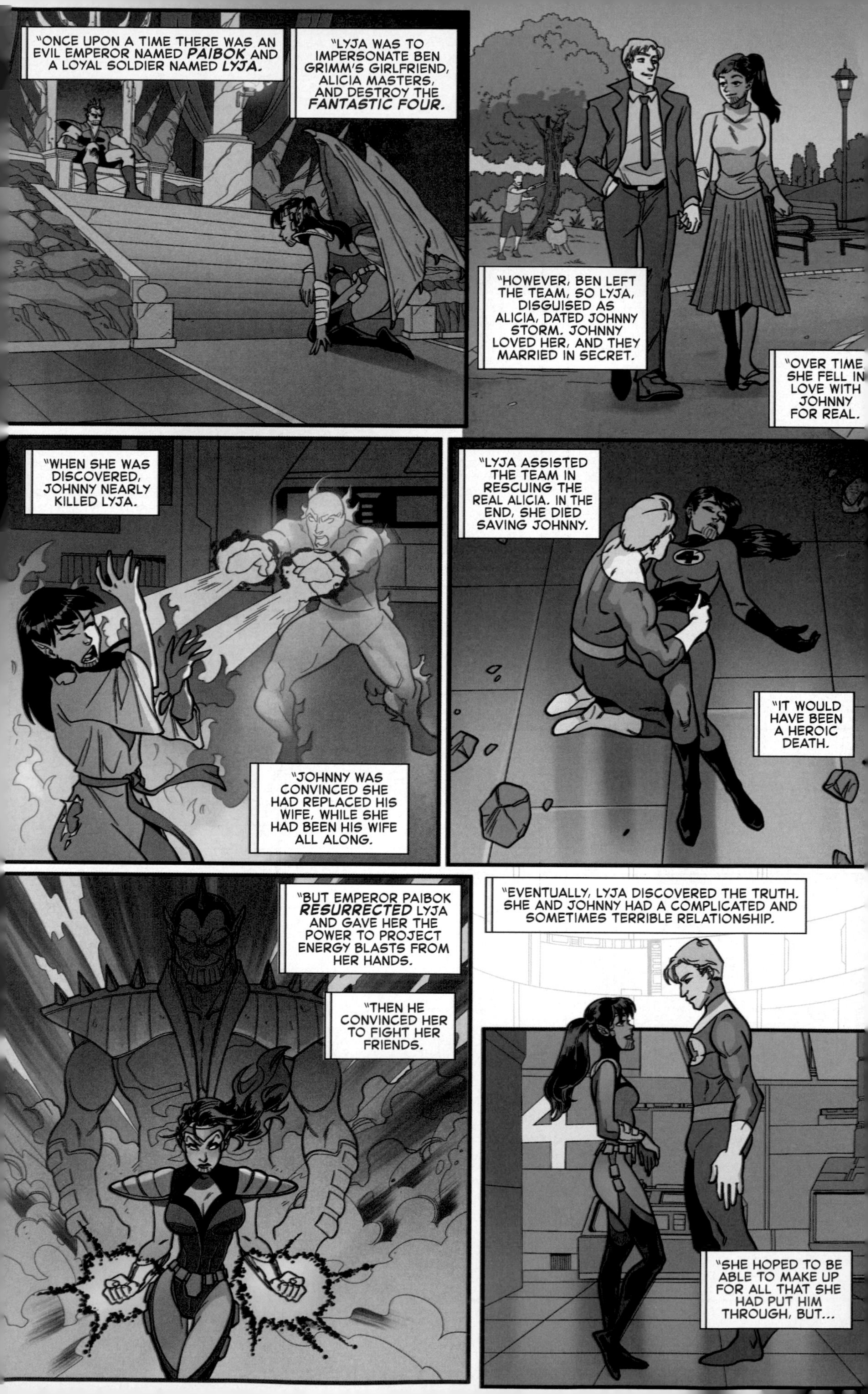
"ONCE UPON A TIME THERE WAS AN EVIL EMPEROR NAMED PAIBOK AND A LOYAL SOLDIER NAMED LYJA.
"LYJA WAS TO IMPERSONATE BEN GRIMM'S GIRLFRIEND, ALICIA MASTERS, AND DESTROY THE FANTASTIC FOUR.
"HOWEVER, BEN LEFT THE TEAM, SO LYJA, DISGUISED AS ALICIA, DATED JOHNNY STORM. JOHNNY LOVED HER, AND THEY MARRIED IN SECRET.
"OVER TIME SHE FELL IN LOVE WITH JOHNNY FOR REAL.
"WHEN SHE WAS DISCOVERED, JOHNNY NEARLY KILLED LYJA.
"JOHNNY WAS CONVINCED SHE HAD REPLACED HIS WIFE, WHILE SHE HAD BEEN HIS WIFE ALL ALONG.
"LYJA ASSISTED THE TEAM IN RESCUING THE REAL ALICIA. IN THE END, SHE DIED SAVING JOHNNY.
"IT WOULD HAVE BEEN A HEROIC DEATH.
"BUT EMPEROR PAIBOK RESURRECTED LYJA AND GAVE HER THE POWER TO PROJECT ENERGY BLASTS FROM HER HANDS.
"THEN HE CONVINCED HER TO FIGHT HER FRIENDS.
"EVENTUALLY, LYJA DISCOVERED THE TRUTH. SHE AND JOHNNY HAD A COMPLICATED AND SOMETIMES TERRIBLE RELATIONSHIP.
"SHE HOPED TO BE ABLE TO MAKE UP FOR ALL THAT SHE HAD PUT HIM THROUGH, BUT...

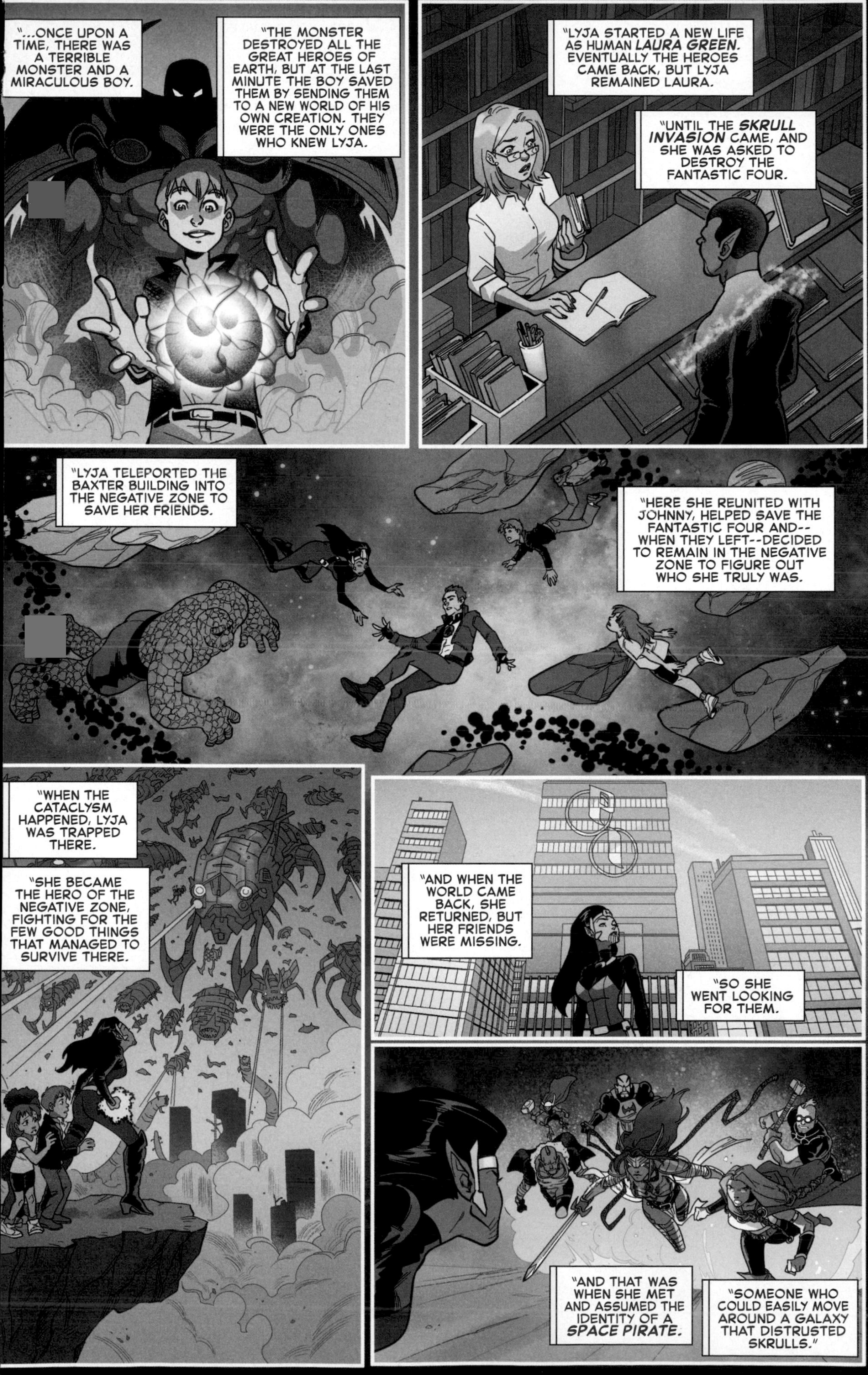
"...ONCE UPON A TIME, THERE WAS A TERRIBLE MONSTER AND A MIRACULOUS BOY.
"THE MONSTER DESTROYED ALL THE GREAT HEROES OF EARTH, BUT AT THE LAST MINUTE THE BOY SAVED THEM BY SENDING THEM TO A NEW WORLD OF HIS OWN CREATION. THEY WERE THE ONLY ONES WHO KNEW LYJA.
"LYJA STARTED A NEW LIFE AS HUMAN LAURA GREEN. EVENTUALLY THE HEROES CAME BACK, BUT LYJA REMAINED LAURA.
"UNTIL THE SKRULL INVASION CAME, AND SHE WAS ASKED TO DESTROY THE FANTASTIC FOUR.
"LYJA TELEPORTED THE BAXTER BUILDING INTO THE NEGATIVE ZONE TO SAVE HER FRIENDS.
"HERE SHE REUNITED WITH JOHNNY, HELPED SAVE THE FANTASTIC FOUR AND--WHEN THEY LEFT--DECIDED TO REMAIN IN THE NEGATIVE ZONE TO FIGURE OUT WHO SHE TRULY WAS.
"WHEN THE CATACLYSM HAPPENED, LYJA WAS TRAPPED THERE.
"SHE BECAME THE HERO OF THE NEGATIVE ZONE, FIGHTING FOR THE FEW GOOD THINGS THAT MANAGED TO SURVIVE THERE.
"AND WHEN THE WORLD CAME BACK, SHE RETURNED, BUT HER FRIENDS WERE MISSING.
"SO SHE WENT LOOKING FOR THEM.
"AND THAT WAS WHEN SHE MET AND ASSUMED THE IDENTITY OF A SPACE PIRATE.
"SOMEONE WHO COULD EASILY MOVE AROUND A GALAXY THAT DISTRUSTED SKRULLS."

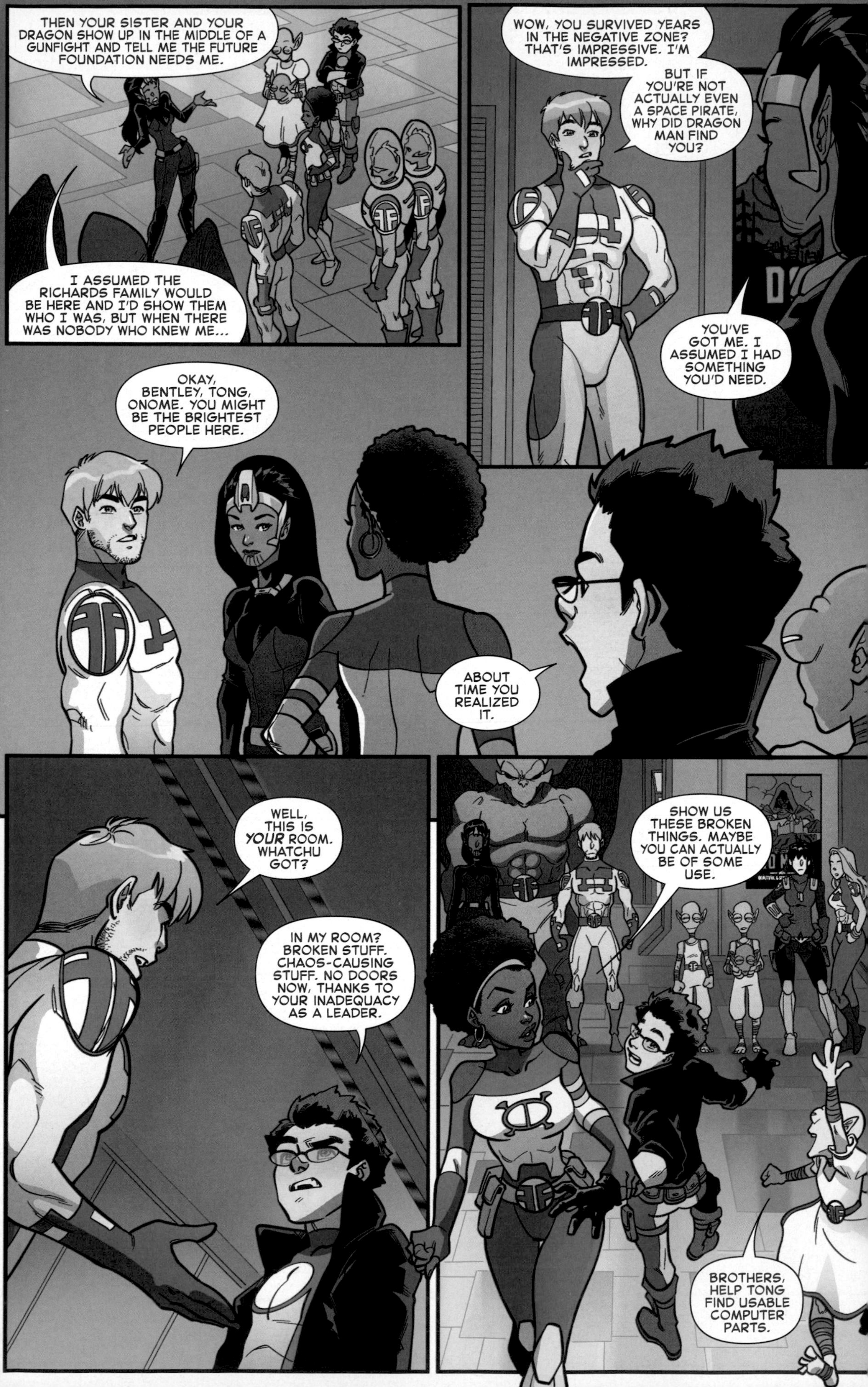
THEN YOUR SISTER AND YOUR DRAGON SHOW UP IN THE MIDDLE OF A GUNFIGHT AND TELL ME THE FUTURE FOUNDATION NEEDS ME.
I ASSUMED THE RICHARDS FAMILY WOULD BE HERE AND I'D SHOW THEM WHO I WAS, BUT WHEN THERE WAS NOBODY WHO KNEW ME...
WOW, YOU SURVIVED YEARS IN THE NEGATIVE ZONE? THAT'S IMPRESSIVE. I'M IMPRESSED.
BUT IF YOU'RE NOT ACTUALLY EVEN A SPACE PIRATE, WHY DID DRAGON MAN FIND YOU?
YOU'VE GOT ME. I ASSUMED I HAD SOMETHING YOU'D NEED.
OKAY, BENTLEY, TONG, ONOME. YOU MIGHT BE THE BRIGHTEST PEOPLE HERE.
ABOUT TIME YOU REALIZED IT.
WELL, THIS IS *YOUR* ROOM. WHATCHU GOT?
IN MY ROOM? BROKEN STUFF. CHAOS-CAUSING STUFF. NO DOORS NOW, THANKS TO YOUR INADEQUACY AS A LEADER.
SHOW US THESE BROKEN THINGS. MAYBE YOU CAN ACTUALLY BE OF SOME USE.
BROTHERS, HELP TONG FIND USABLE COMPUTER PARTS.

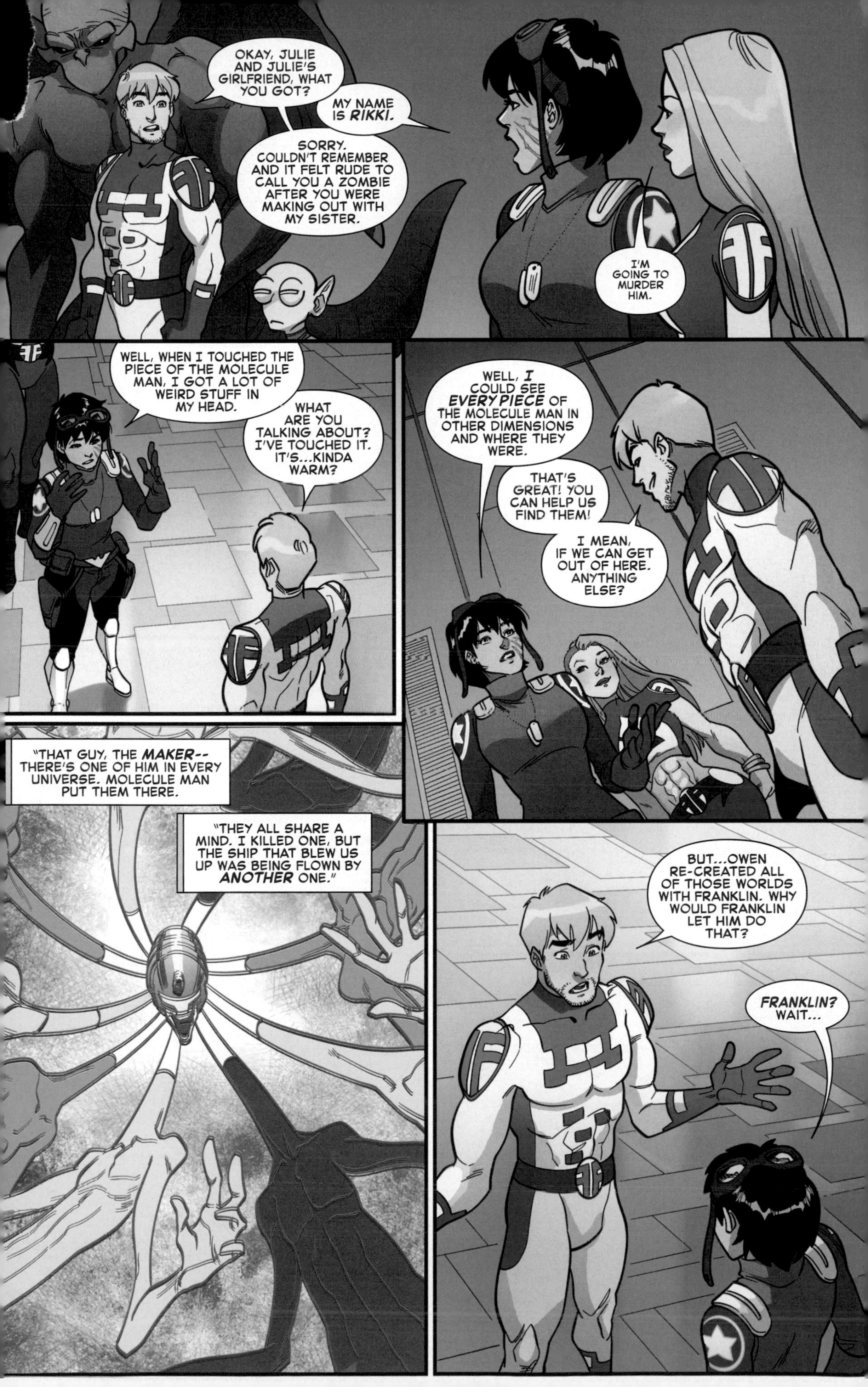
OKAY, JULIE AND JULIE'S GIRLFRIEND, WHAT YOU GOT?
MY NAME IS RIKKI.
SORRY. COULDN'T REMEMBER AND IT FELT RUDE TO CALL YOU A ZOMBIE AFTER YOU WERE MAKING OUT WITH MY SISTER.
I'M GOING TO MURDER HIM.
WELL, WHEN I TOUCHED THE PIECE OF THE MOLECULE MAN, I GOT A LOT OF WEIRD STUFF IN MY HEAD.
WHAT ARE YOU TALKING ABOUT? I'VE TOUCHED IT. IT'S...KINDA WARM?
WELL, I COULD SEE EVERY PIECE OF THE MOLECULE MAN IN OTHER DIMENSIONS AND WHERE THEY WERE.
THAT'S GREAT! YOU CAN HELP US FIND THEM!
I MEAN, IF WE CAN GET OUT OF HERE. ANYTHING ELSE?
"THAT GUY, THE MAKER-- THERE'S ONE OF HIM IN EVERY UNIVERSE. MOLECULE MAN PUT THEM THERE.
"THEY ALL SHARE A MIND. I KILLED ONE, BUT THE SHIP THAT BLEW US UP WAS BEING FLOWN BY ANOTHER ONE."
BUT...OWEN RE-CREATED ALL OF THOSE WORLDS WITH FRANKLIN. WHY WOULD FRANKLIN LET HIM DO THAT?
FRANKLIN? WAIT...

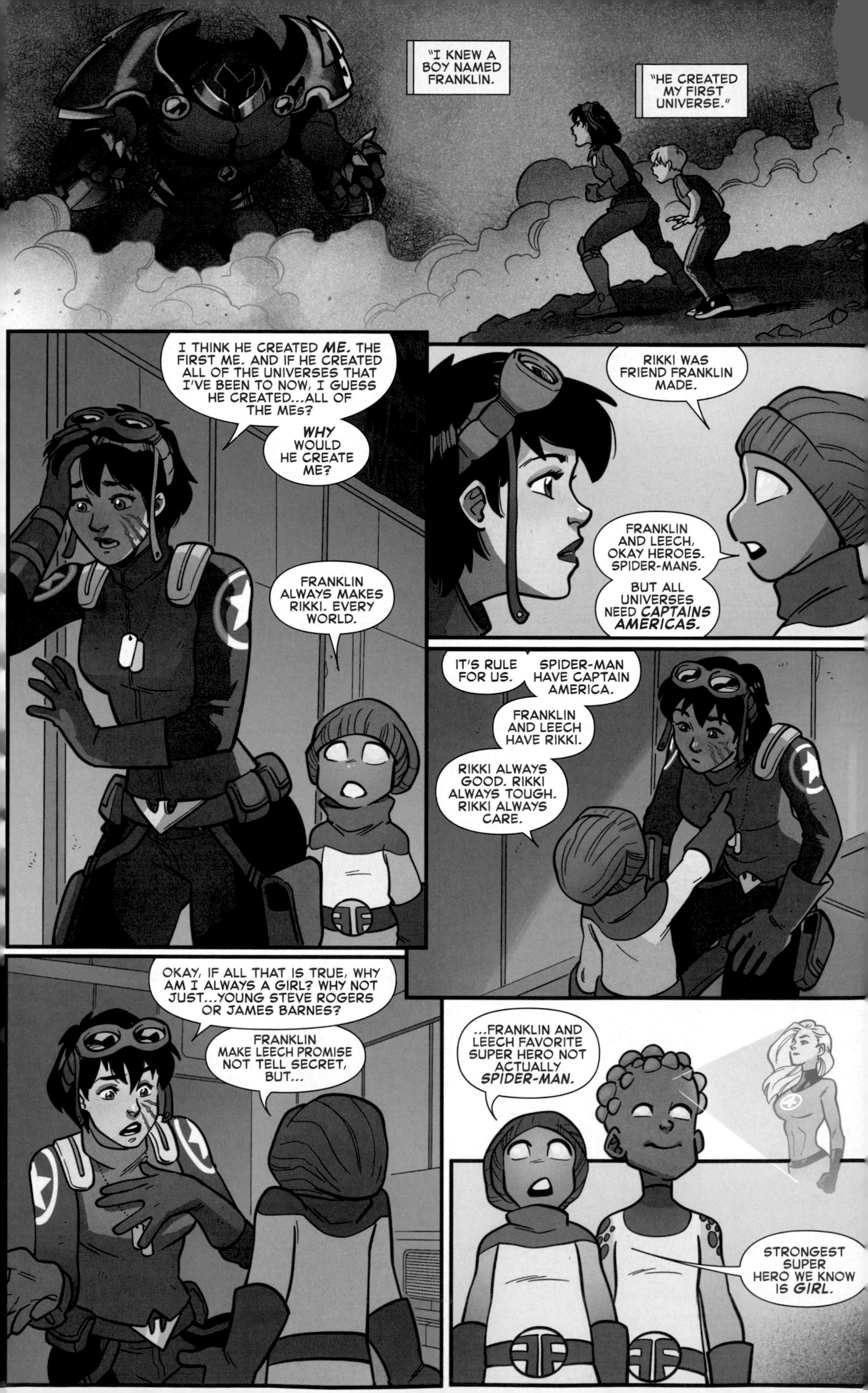

"I KNEW A BOY NAMED FRANKLIN.
"HE CREATED MY FIRST UNIVERSE."
I THINK HE CREATED ME. THE FIRST ME. AND IF HE CREATED ALL OF THE UNIVERSES THAT I'VE BEEN TO NOW, I GUESS HE CREATED...ALL OF THE MEs?
WHY WOULD HE CREATE ME?
FRANKLIN ALWAYS MAKES RIKKI. EVERY WORLD.
RIKKI WAS FRIEND FRANKLIN MADE.
FRANKLIN AND LEECH, OKAY HEROES. SPIDER-MANS.
BUT ALL UNIVERSES NEED CAPTAINS AMERICAS.
IT'S RULE FOR US.
SPIDER-MAN HAVE CAPTAIN AMERICA.
FRANKLIN AND LEECH HAVE RIKKI.
RIKKI ALWAYS GOOD. RIKKI ALWAYS TOUGH. RIKKI ALWAYS CARE.
OKAY, IF ALL THAT IS TRUE, WHY AM I ALWAYS A GIRL? WHY NOT JUST...YOUNG STEVE ROGERS OR JAMES BARNES?
FRANKLIN MAKE LEECH PROMISE NOT TELL SECRET, BUT...
...FRANKLIN AND LEECH FAVORITE SUPER HERO NOT ACTUALLY SPIDER-MAN.
STRONGEST SUPER HERO WE KNOW IS GIRL.

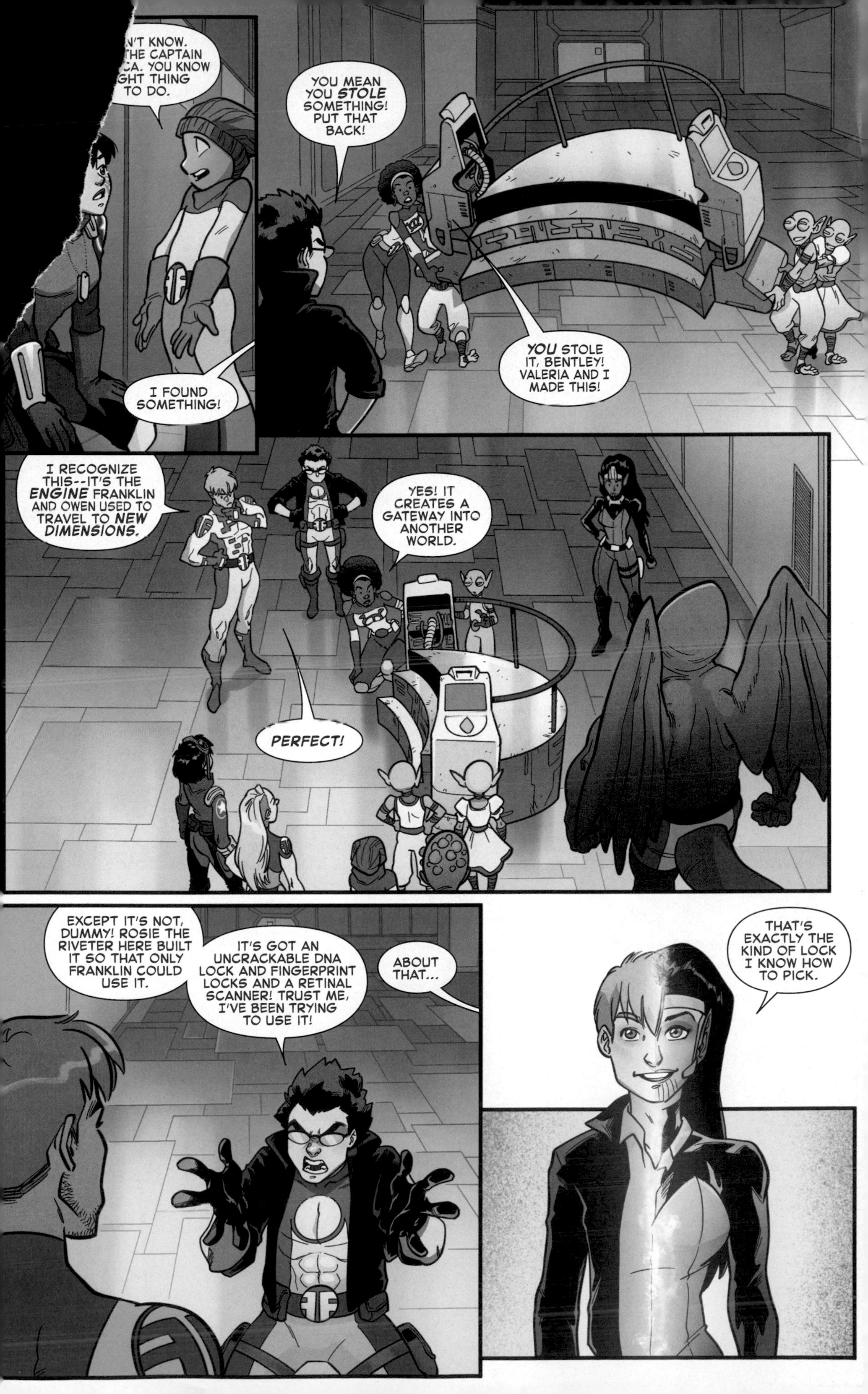
N'T KNOW. THE CAPTAIN CA. YOU KNOW GHT THING TO DO.
I FOUND SOMETHING!
YOU MEAN YOU STOLE SOMETHING! PUT THAT BACK!
YOU STOLE IT, BENTLEY! VALERIA AND I MADE THIS!
I RECOGNIZE THIS--IT'S THE ENGINE FRANKLIN AND OWEN USED TO TRAVEL TO NEW DIMENSIONS.
YES! IT CREATES A GATEWAY INTO ANOTHER WORLD.
PERFECT!
EXCEPT IT'S NOT, DUMMY! ROSIE THE RIVETER HERE BUILT IT SO THAT ONLY FRANKLIN COULD USE IT.
IT'S GOT AN UNCRACKABLE DNA LOCK AND FINGERPRINT LOCKS AND A RETINAL SCANNER! TRUST ME, I'VE BEEN TRYING TO USE IT!
ABOUT THAT...
THAT'S EXACTLY THE KIND OF LOCK I KNOW HOW TO PICK.

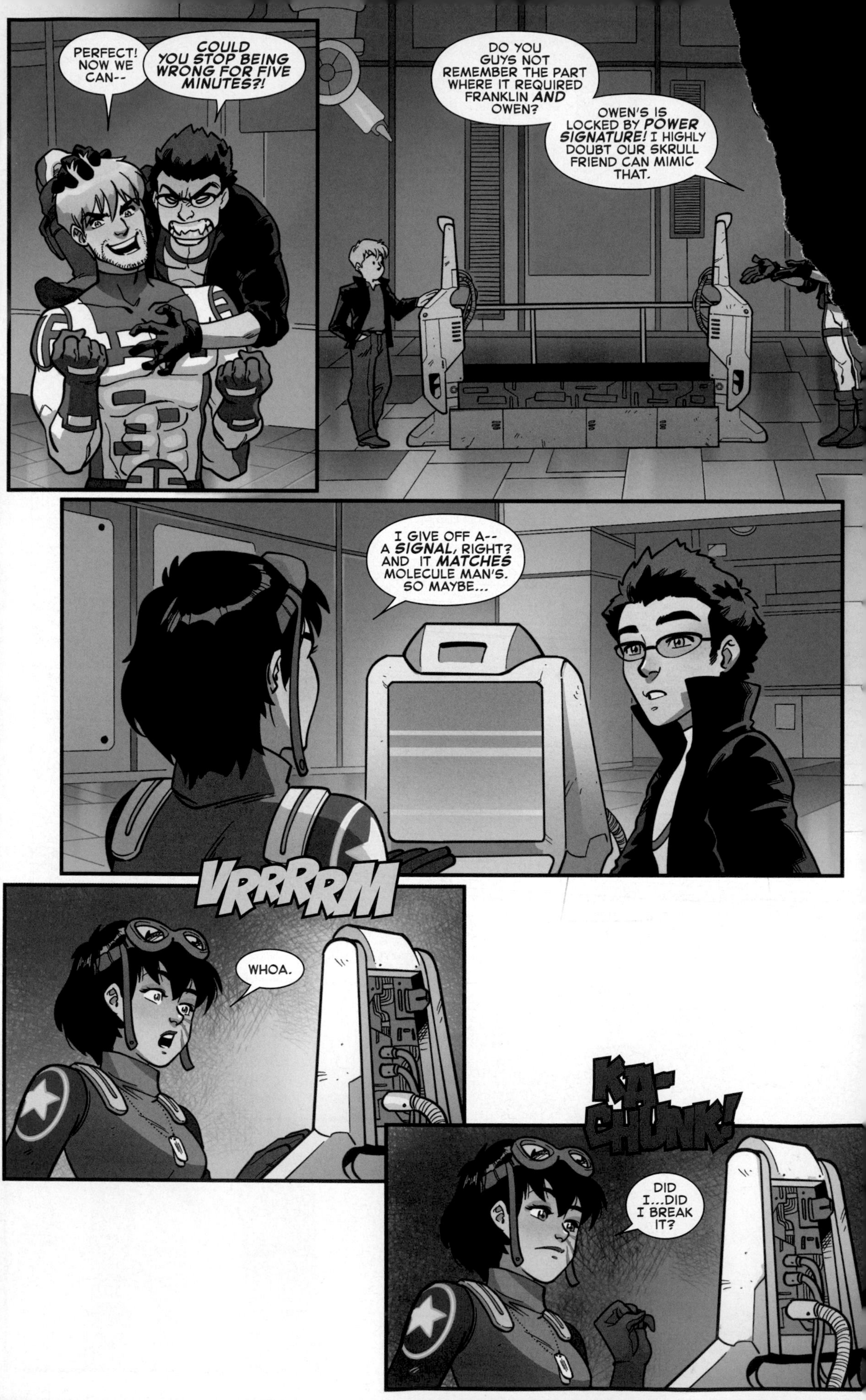
PERFECT! NOW WE CAN--
COULD YOU STOP BEING WRONG FOR FIVE MINUTES?!
DO YOU GUYS NOT REMEMBER THE PART WHERE IT REQUIRED FRANKLIN AND OWEN?
OWEN'S IS LOCKED BY POWER SIGNATURE! I HIGHLY DOUBT OUR SKRULL FRIEND CAN MIMIC THAT.
I GIVE OFF A-- A SIGNAL, RIGHT? AND IT MATCHES MOLECULE MAN'S. SO MAYBE...
VRRRRM
WHOA.
KA-CHUNK!
DID I...DID I BREAK IT?